Barbara Marx Hubbard.

The Hunger of Eve

*ONE WOMAN'S ODYSSEY
TOWARD THE FUTURE*

BY

BARBARA MARX HUBBARD

ISLAND PACIFIC NW
Eastsound, Washington

Cover Artwork : Rob Schouten
Cover Concept: Greag Daly
Cover Design: Carol Wright
Editors: D.K. Shumway and John Clancy
Assoc. Editors: Claude Golden, Kate Clark and
Sue Ann Fazio

Production: Sweet Forever
P.O. Box 1000
Eastsound, WA 98245

Manufactured in the United States of America

Published by: Island Pacific NW
P. O. Box 999
Eastsound, Washington 98245
(206) 376-5005

Library of Congress Cataloging-in-Publication Data

Hubbard, Barbara Marx, 1929-
   The Hunger of Eve: One Woman's Odyssey Toward the Future /
   by Barbara Marx Hubbard.
      p.   cm.
Reprint. Originally Published:Harrisburg, PA
        Stackpole Books, (c) 1976
Bibliography page
1. Hubbard, Barbara Marx, 1929-
2. Politicians -- United States -- Biography
3. Prophets -- United States -- Biography
4. United States -- Biography.
I. Title
CT275.H662A3   1989
973.92'092 -- dc20
[B]   89-32317
ISBN 0-942133-00-5

For information on visionary art and cards by Rob Schouten, please write:
Great Path Publishing
P. O. Box 882
Freeland, Washington 98249 (206) 221-7099

Dedication

I dedicate *The Hunger of Eve* to the vast community of humanity, from the dawn of home sapiens to us, at the threshold of a global age, who have the courage to hold the vision of our collective potential.

Acknowledgements

I acknowledge my parents, my family, my children, and my colleagues throughout the world who have inspired my life. I am particularly grateful for the encouragement of Tovi Daly and the whole team at Island Pacific NW and Sweet Forever, who have made the publication of *The Hunger of Eve* a joy; Greag Daly, D.K. and Michael Shumway, Claude Golden, John Clancy, Carol Wright, Kate Clark, Linda Jones, Becca Hosford and Denise Shaefer.

Knowing Barbara Marx Hubbard is like having your finger on the pulse of humanity. And capturing her life on paper could be compared to filming an explosion. You need a very fast shutter. When I learned I was to be involved in this project I was excited about the possibilities of working with such a brilliant, dynamic woman. Yet my fellow editors and I faced with an interesting dilemma. The original manuscript was finished in 1975. While the manuscript may have been suspended in time, Barbara definitely was not. Her life had continued in typical whirlwind fashion, giving us a wealth of new information that needed to be shared.

After attempting a sequel, for which Barbara literally wrote hundreds of pages in a few short weeks, we realized we could publish ten books on Barbara's life and still not tell you all there is to share about her work. So we opted to revised and lengthen *The Hunger of Eve* manuscript, freeing Barbara's time for another of her many projects.

Chapters one through six are composed of the original manuscript, edited and rewritten for continuity. Chapters seven through ten are the high points of Barbara's life from 1975 to 1988. I stress the words "high points" because they are only a small part of what she has accomplished during the last fifteen years.

I feel privileged to know and work with Barbara Marx Hubbard as well as all the wonderful, creative people who were involved in this project. I especially want to acknowledge Tovi Daly, whose foresight and creative talents brought this project together.

D.K. Shumway

Editor

May, 1989

Contents

Prologue

I always have identified with Eve. Somewhere deep in my memory, I remember the garden. I can recall the peace, the unself-conscious joy of it. And I can remember the attraction to the forbidden tree, the Tree of Knowledge. I wanted to know more, do more, be more. I felt unfinished, that there was more to come than this existence.

When I first read Genesis as a child, this God we called Jehovah seemed unfair. I was amazed that He would put the tree there, then forbid us to eat its fruit. Didn't He want us to grow? Weren't we created in the image of God and designed to be co-creators with God? I felt Eve behaved naturally.

I have a memory of the collective choice we made, to reach for greater knowledge, no matter what the consequences. When I read of Eve, I shared her sense of fear, separation and blame. Had she done something wrong? What was it? Her anxiety was mine, a knot that lay within my solar plexus. I felt innocent. I had no mal-intent. Surely I was good. Surely we were all good.

I remember the second tree also, the Tree of Life. This was the tree of regeneration, of immortality, a healing tree, the tree of the gods. Eve had moved beyond the Tree of Knowledge, toward the Tree of Life, motivated by the desire for God-like being, for union with all creation. There she was stopped. Jehovah, fearing humanity would eat of this tree also and, "Become as us," drove us from the garden and guarded the Tree of Life with cherubim and sword.

Throughout all of human history we have been reaching for this mystical tree. Though religion, art, language, science and technology, we have attempted to transcend the human condition of alienation, pain, scarcity and mortality. Now, we collectively stand at this fateful tree, driven here by our hunger. We have gained the power to destroy this world... or to restore our environment, free ourselves from want, and explore the further reaches of the human spirit and the universe beyond. We can deny our hunger, turn our back on the Tree of Life, and destroy the world. Or, together we can create new worlds of undreamt possibilities for all people. We stand at that point in history where the hunger can be fulfilled, or again denied.

I know Eve's hunger well. It is the same hunger that drove me through a comfortable childhood, beyond a life as a wife and mother of five children, and toward participation in this magnificent collective step into life. I stand on center stage with all the rest of humankind, at the very threshold of destruction or the fulfillment of the dreams of the ages.

One

The Hunger Awakens

I was born in 1929. My earliest memory is of standing in a crib, angry, clutching the bars to keep from falling. I had been put to bed early. The late afternoon sun was shining brightly in my eyes, and I could hear adult voices talking and laughing somewhere else in the house. I rattled the bars of my crib and cried for them to come get me and take me out. I was missing something. I did not know what it was, but I wanted to be part of it.

My father, a toy manufacturer, was a strong, vital, successful, self-made man. I was secure in his love. I still can remember the aroma of his cigar, the excitement of being taken to opening nights at the theatre, the lights of Broadway glimmering on the rainy streets, sledding with my brothers and sisters in Central Park, and the fun we had summers on Lazy Day Farm in Connecticut. Life in New York City felt natural. I was not introspective or self-conscious. I did not even know I was "happy." Each day I walked home from Dalton School to our Fifth Avenue apartment with a contingent of boys. We played the piano, ate chocolate eclairs, had hose fights on the penthouse, and talked endlessly about our friends.

However, there were little incidents that caused fear. Once, when I was six, riding with my father in his gleaming Rolls-Royce through the streets of Harlem, we stopped at a red light on Second Avenue. It was a cold, ugly, rainy twilight in the midst of the depression. Faces of young men pressed against the window and glared at us. I reached for my father's hand and held it tightly under the fur rug. I felt the injustice of being in while they were shut out, but, I thought, 'They don't know what it feels like to be me, inside, scared; it doesn't feel as good as they think. It feels empty.'

My mother was an exquisitely beautiful woman: gentle, loving, submissive. I remember the deep comfort and security I felt when she kissed me goodnight. Yet I also recall the pain and sense of injustice upon seeing her sitting alone in her bed night after night, waiting for my father, who was out entertaining the toy buyers. He would come home late, shouting raucously, dragging my brother, two sisters and me out of bed, telling us 'mean man' stories that frightened us, while she sat quietly. I wondered what she thought, for she never said anything.

When I was twelve years old, she became ill with cancer. I prayed constantly for her to survive this dreadful monster that was devouring her alive. Once, after her first breast was removed, I caught a glimpse of the scar on her chest. I had opened her bathroom door accidentally. I remember catching her eye and sensing her terror, like a deer caught in the flashlight of a hunter, doomed. I was horrified and humiliated, shocked at its ugliness in contrast to her beauty. At night I prayed to God, begging Him to save her, offering my entire being in return for her life.

But one evening my father came back from the hospital, and it was over. She was only thirty-three years old when she died.

"Little mother is dead," he explained as gently as possible. It was the first time I had ever seen him helpless. He always was able to fix the problem. I thought he was all-powerful. He wept, holding the four of us on his lap at once as we all sobbed together. I was more concerned about him than myself. "It's all right to cry," he said, "there is nothing else to do."

Suddenly a fierce anger awoke in me, rising up out of the despair. A powerful, driving force within me said silently, 'No! I will not cry! I do not accept death! There is something more.... I've got to find out. I can't tolerate this.' My mother was innocent. God was unfair. A deep knot of pain lodged itself in my solar plexus. I felt abandoned. I was only thirteen, but the real hunger for meaning had begun. My childhood was over.

I was the oldest of the four children. My mother's death deepened my love for my brother, Louis, and my two sisters, Jacqueline and Patricia. My father was always comparing us with one another and encouraging us to compete against each other. He would say, "Barbara is the best," or "Louis is smarter than all the others," his favor moving arbitrarily from one child to the other. But somehow we refused to accept his baiting, or his desire to make us try to win over each other. We had an unspoken pact to support one another unconditionally, no matter what he said.

During my mother's illness, we had moved to a "Gone with the Wind" mansion in Scarsdale. The social life there was stultifying and humiliating. My father's friends and activities were in New York. And if your parents weren't part of the community, you were truly left out. I remember the sting of isolation when I wasn't invited to a dance. I had not realized it when I was at Dalton in New York City, but we were of Jewish origin. My father was an agnostic. We never went to a temple or met a rabbi. He had never even told us we were Jewish, not wanting us to bear the pain. It was during the Second World War. He tried to protect us from the horror.

I discovered at Rye Country Day School the outrage of anti-semitism. Much to my horror, they were prejudiced against me! I wasn't invited to the dance because they said I was Jewish. I was excluded, and suffered from this mindless, irrational rejection through no fault of my own. When I told my father about it he said, "You have no right to be unhappy. There are *real* problems in this world: sickness, poverty, war, and then there are *man-made* problems. Your problems are man-made."

My father was a second-generation American. He wanted to sever any ties to the limitations of his past. His message was simply, "You are an American. Do your best."

'At *what*?' I wondered. My father had grown up in Brooklyn with a sense of hope. If you were willing to work for what you wanted, he believed, anything was possible. He was one who "made it," a millionaire at thirty, founder and head of Louis Marx and Company. He was called the "Henry Ford of the toy business," being one of the first to mass produce toys inexpensively.

Of course, Christmas played a significant role in our lives. My father normally brought toys home every day, not only his own, but his competitors, to try them out on us. But at Christmas time, the quantity of toys we received was massive. Huge cartons arrived for each child. We had more toys than anyone could possibly want. I literally lived in a toy culture. But, nonetheless, as Christmas approached, my excitement mounted. I wanted the moment to come, yet did not. Once we started opening the presents, I knew there would be only a few hours, and then it would be over. Beneath the expectation was the foreknowledge of disappointment. Even worse, I did not really want those toys. I already had so many that whenever I opened the toy closet, they fell down on my head.

One Christmas I noticed my father wasn't with us; he was upstairs in his room. I was annoyed and went up to find him working. He was shaped like Santa Claus, short, portly, bald, with compact strength and a penetrating glance that could frighten or attract.

"Why are you working?" I asked.

"I'm starting work on next Christmas," he said.

I was amazed that anyone could be thinking that far ahead. But I suspected he still was enjoying the holidays more than I, because he already had something to do for next Christmas. That's when I first sensed that working for something was better than being given something. The problem was that I didn't know what I wanted to do. My father believed material security was the purpose of work. His motive was never again to be poor, to have to wait at the end of the line, as he put it. But he worried that in giving his children money, he was destroying our motivation. "If I give you this money," he once said, "you will never know the value of a dollar. You will grow up to be spoiled brats. I'm ruining you."

"Take it away then," I had answered, "I don't want to be a brat."

He shook his head. "That would be false. You know that if you really were starving, I would pick you up and save you. I'd rather you learn what it's like to waste."

So when I went to the movies with friends, he gave me ten dollars rather than five. I was ashamed to have more. In fact, I hid it, or wasted it on candy and then felt sick.

I was determined to find something to work for. But for me, it could not be more money, because I already had more than enough, just as I had too many toys. I was on welfare from my father, but any level of welfare is insufficient without a challenge for growth.

When I was fifteen, we dropped the atomic bomb on Hiroshima and Nagasaki. I will never forget the horror and the shock. Then suddenly, out of my stunned awareness of the pain we had caused, there arose in my mind the questions which have dominated my life. Where are we going that is good? What is the direction of life itself? For me, *the question* was, 'What is the purpose of our power?' I realized that I could not know what to do my best at, if I did not know where society as a whole was going. I unconsciously made the person-planet connection.

I could see that progress was not inevitable, that in fact, our power could lead to the destruction of the human race. Yet, at the core of my being, I was magnetized by an irrepressible, intuitive attraction toward something magnificent that was coming. There was a *meaning* to our power. I had to know what it was. I hungered for an unknown fulfillment.

At the age of sixteen, I began to read through literature. I was seeking a positive image of the future equal to our new powers in science and technology, and to my own feeling of hope, yet I could not find it. The Greeks looked backward to a Golden Age. The Stoics asked us to nobly accommodate to the current condition, whatever it might be. The Existentialists advocated self-assertion in the face of an inherently meaningless universe. Utopians conjured up societies which seemed to me static, boring and closed.

Then I read a book on the world's great religions, continuing my search, like someone starving for an unknown nourishment. And finally I found the first taste of *it*, the nameless attraction. "Behold, I show you a mystery, we shall not all sleep, we shall all be changed...the sufferings of the present cannot be compared to the glory which shall be revealed in us...the New Jerusalem, beyond sorrow, beyond death, in a universe of many mansions...." Yes! That attracted me. Something great was coming. My heart pounded with excitement. There was a reason for hope. The human race was going somewhere. This was what I was hungry for, a new way of being.

So I decided, at sixteen, to join the church. I went to an Episcopal church in Scarsdale, New York. I will never forget my first interview with the priest. "What," I asked him, "does it mean, 'We shall all be changed?' How? What shall I do to be changed? And when Jesus said that we could do the works that he did and even more, what did he mean? Is it true? What about the resurrection, the ascension and the Second Coming? Shall we have new bodies like his? Shall we overcome death?"

I was dying to know, literally. But the priest could not answer a single one of my questions to my satisfaction. "Barbara, your questions must come later," he said. I had the feeling he did not really believe any of it.

Sunday after Sunday I went to church. Once I prayed so hard I almost fainted listening for an answer from God to these questions. I heard nothing, absolute silence.

Beyond that disappointment, I was deeply irritated with the minister who preached that God was good and humans were evil. It seemed to me that Jehovah was more at fault than we. His behavior toward His children was unacceptable. There we were, weak creatures treated cruelly by a God who had all the characteristics of a male tyrant. 'It's not true,' I thought. One day I wanted to stand up in church and preach to the minister, 'If God is good, then as children created in His image, humans are good too! We are not passive children. We are responsible. We must respect ourselves, not hate ourselves.' But I did not dare. Soon, I left the Episcopal church.

While I "failed" at being an Episcopalian, I was a good student at Rye Country Day School. I loved to learn. Yet I longed for greater challenges, so I decided in my senior year to run for student president. My brother, sisters, and their friends campaigned for me: balloons, posters, cookie and milk strategy meetings. Since I had more siblings than the other candidates, I won. But I immediately felt let down. The victory had no meaning. I found I had nothing good to do for the school. After that experience, I decided never to win just to win. Competitiveness diminished in me, even though I came from a very competitive family and really did like to win.

I continued to have this uncomfortable feeling that I was missing something. I had my year as president and I graduated from school. I had done well enough at everything to know that more of the same would not suffice: more material goods, more winning, more popularity would not make any difference. My hunger increased.

I had been told that Bryn Mawr was the hardest of the women's colleges, so I chose to go there. I was seeking a challenge to draw me forth. Everything had been so easy for me that I could not feel my own strength. And the sense of need and hunger for something different was growing. There was no cultural affirmation for this unnamed hunger. I had been unable to articulate it clearly, even to myself. Yet there was an intuitive flash of joy when I would look up to the universe at night and realize that not only was there a lot going on in this world, but there were billions and billions of stars out there. I felt a part of that. During those flashes, I experienced a profound sense of unity with the universe. I lost consciousness of Barbara Marx and felt a strange oneness with the stars so far above. The fundamental similarity of our origins and composition, the unity of inanimate and animate, became clear. I could not understand why as a species we could not put our differences into their obviously superficial places.

'What is this centrifugal force that forever pulls against the centripetal force?' I wondered. I could not discuss these questions with anyone. So on May 27, 1948, at the age of eighteen, I started a journal.

I've waited far too long to begin you, my journal. Feelings, intuitions, ideas, have been lost irreparably. I have a desperate need to create. All my life I have absorbed. By using myself as a catalytic agent I hope to give pattern and form to the mass of sensations that have impressed themselves upon me. The power of intelligence is to connect, to relate, and to integrate impressions.

If there is a God, it is He who unites past with present and future, finite with infinite, truth with falsity, until all are more than a conglomeration, all is one and that one is far greater than the sum of its parts. That oneness is God's creation.

In looking over the catalog of courses at Bryn Mawr, my heart once again sank with depression. I realized I could easily get more knowledge in any of those fields: literature, history, science, politics; but they were broken into separate, unrelated courses. We were to select our major when we were still freshmen. There was no way for me to relate these separate boxes of learning to the much more general, profound longing for purpose, for relatedness to all of life.

My roommate and I chatted about our future after college.

"It would be fun to go to Washington and get a job," she said.

Thinking of nothing better, I agreed, "Why not?"

So we both majored in political science. The method of search for meaningful vocation at that period was given no significance. You were supposed to "know" what you were interested in. The courses were dry and detailed. Almost no one was interested in a philosophical search for greater meaning. Even more important, there seemed to be no genuine way to search for my own life's purpose, nor to find how that purpose related to the whole society of which I was a part. College was not helping me find what I was supposed to do.

I was very unhappy with the normal dating procedure. Blind dates were just what they were, blind! When I went out with young men, I asked them, "What's your purpose? What are you working for?" They had never even thought about it.

I found I could not learn through the general curriculum at Bryn Mawr. My moment of conscious detachment from the academic life occurred when we were studying Pascal's conversion from a skeptical mathematical genius to a passionate Christian. I read those pages with tremendous excitement. Pascal had found meaning through this conversion, a relationship to Christ, to God, an ineffable joy. I went to class in real anticipation of discussing this conversion. Did anyone else feel the need for such an experience? Had anyone else had such an experience? Was there any way we could have it? I raised my hand early to discuss it in terms of our own lives.

The professor just stared at me. "Mademoiselle, this is not a philosophy class; it is French literature."

My alienation deepened and I began to withdraw from Bryn Mawr. I decided to read on my own and take my exams when I had to, which I did. Reading Spinoza, Montaigne, Marcus Aurelius, the ethical and stoical philosophers, I looked for the essence of reality and a rationale to lessen the dependence on material possessions.

How can people live and not know why they're living? What is the purpose of life when you have enough things? I can pierce with the sharp eyes of intuition to the essences. Ever inward I am progressing, gaining that power which is life. As I become stronger in this kind of knowledge, my awareness of God increases. By feeling my own essence, I feel closer to God. To be at one with Him is uniquely to be myself. It seems to me that external possessions and attributes are worthwhile insofar as they are concrete representations of the intangible growth of our true powers.

I studied the early Greeks, Herodotus and Homer, and the pre-Socratic philosophers. Each was seeking the ultimate reality, in flux, in permanence, in fire, in air, in atoms, in numbers. My difficulty was that I could not find a way to get experientially to the ultimate reality. There was no method to connect that ultimate reality with the personal need for purpose. This hunger for purpose was felt, not abstractly, but as a deep, gut-level desire for some state of being that I sensed existed in the future. A knot of anxiety at the pit of my stomach ached just thinking about it. I sensed that there would be a total shared effort of humanity that would connect us to one another and to the universe. I felt that we would all feel this oneness together, and that there was something that I as an individual could do to help cause this experience. In the books I was reading I could not find any response to this passionate desire. I had tried religion and could not experience it there. Yet philosophy was disappointing as well, for the philosopher did not seem to know what was coming. I was reaching a dead end.

I was subtly disconnecting from the family I loved so deeply. None of them would work with me for that purpose; none felt the same need, and I no longer felt "at home" in Scarsdale. My father and brother thought something was wrong with me, that I was neurotic, trying to compensate for some worldly lack by my continued study of philosophy and need for purpose. My brother, who was at Princeton, popular, a good tennis player, effortlessly bright and easygoing, tried to get me to go out more.

"Barbara, you're overdoing this," he told me one day. I was seated on a couch, surrounded by books piled high on all sides.

He thought I was extreme. In fact, I *was* extreme in my need. I was starving. No one recognized that the need for meaning was primary. My culture simply did not accord my need as real.

Then I met a man in Philadelphia on one of those awful blind dates. He was a tall, virile, Gatsby type. Stanley Reese was his name. While all the other young men drove beat-up jalopies, he had a slick blue Buick, bought with money he had earned. His ambition was to be wealthy and powerful.

He called me the next day, and said, "I am going to take you out to dinner tonight."

"I beg your pardon!" I replied. "I don't want to go out with you."

"Yes, you do," he insisted, starting to laugh. "I am irresistible!"

I was irritated by his arrogance, and told my roommate that I would never go out with him. However, he arrived that evening elegantly dressed, buzzed my room, and said he was waiting. My curiosity prevailed and I went out with him after all. He tried every trick possible in the car to get me to kiss him, and finally succeeded, awakening in me, really against my will, a powerful sexual attraction. He repulsed but dominated me.

Almost instantly he fell in love with me. To him I represented a symbol of my father's success, his mythic dream of a princess to be won by the knight. He did not see me as a real person, and thought my philosophical quest naive and unrealistic. Before long he announced that he would marry me and with my love would become even wealthier than my father. God help me!

"Stanley," I argued, "you're trying to judge me by the wrong standards, and I won't let you. The life I long for is more than material power. If happiness is derived externally, then one must be dependent on external objects. I want to be *free*. The greatest joy I have known is feeling creative and connected to the universe by something I do or think. If you deny the reality of that joy, you deny what I am."

He fluttered his fingers, making fun of me as though I were a butterfly. He did not seem to understand a word I was saying. Even worse, he tried to make my own desires seem unreal, and it made me furious!

I was at a deep impasse. When I travelled home on the train from school for Christmas in 1948 I had a terrible, aching emptiness. A weight, like gravity, pulled me from deep within. Nothing I had found satisfied the hunger: having material well-being, having the love of my family, becoming an Episcopalian, winning everything easily, achieving cum laude at Bryn Mawr, having the love of a powerfully attractive man, nothing. As I experienced each of these situations, I became detached from them. The hunger for meaning and individual purpose continued to grow.

It was the Christmas of my sophomore year. I was just nineteen. My family was once again involved with the toys. There was the usual excitement and happiness, but I felt an uncontrollable, inexplicable misery in the midst of this loving, pleasant environment. I went upstairs and wrote in my journal:

> It's Christmas but I feel none of the mystery, the peace, or the warmth. All the beautiful feelings that come to one on Christ's birthday shun me. Instead I'm tortured with doubts, fears, and unhappiness. There's a constant pull in the middle of my stomach. I'm torturing myself to death. The cause is evident. In my own eyes I've achieved nothing, yet those same eyes have visions of untold glory. There's a key to my desires, which I hold but can't use. I must either lower my ideals or achieve them. I'm like a magnet feeling the attraction of another magnet, yet held apart.

I felt a direct pull at my solar plexus, a real force. I could neither see it, nor describe it, but it was there, and I felt it.

The atmosphere at school continued to depress me. At Rhodes Hall, where I lived, the girls stayed up late playing bridge, drinking coffee, eating candy, getting fat, looking pale. An aroma of perspiration mixed with the stale cigarette smoke in the large room. I could hardly bear to enter, yet felt sorry that I was not to be part of their lives, their companionship. I never was able to feel natural in the all-female social life, any more than I did with the superficial conquest and sexuality of the dating life.

By the end of my sophomore year, I realized that more time at college could not produce greater awareness of purpose or nourishment for my hunger. So I applied for my junior year abroad to Sweetbriar, and was accepted.

In the late summer of 1949, I went abroad, and Stanley followed. The girls were assigned to Reid Hall, the American women's dormitory in Paris. It was disheartening: American girls trying to talk French with each other! I quickly decided to move out. Through an ad in the *Herald Tribune*, I found a wonderful family, the Charles Merciers. Cultivated, kindly, they were relatives of the Cardinal Mercier of Belgium. I moved into their home and was given a small room on the fourth floor at 94 Avenue de Roule, in Neuilly, an elegant suburb of Paris.

I attended classes at the Sorbonne and at the École des Sciences Politiques, where they educated students for the diplomatic service. The students' knowledge was so superior to mine that I felt like an ignorant child. They had absorbed their history, music, and arts since childhood; their culture seemed part of their being. Moreover, some of them had gone through the "Sci-Po" several times. Because there were not enough openings in French society for people of their level of expertise, they were forced to repeat themselves while waiting for an opening. The brilliant potential of the European young was trapped in the mansions of the past.

In the great salon-like classrooms of the Sorbonne, the professors also were repeating themselves. I took a course with a famous professor who had given the same course on French history at the Sorbonne for at least twenty years. Complete outlines of his lectures and exams were available. I decided to read the lectures; there was no point being there.

If I had an academic purpose, I could have learned a great deal about French literature and culture. But my purpose was to look for meaning, not only for myself, but for life on earth.

I was very disappointed. Here I was in Paris, in the most romantic place in the world, and I was reading in my room and going to the movies with Stanley. Why wasn't something great happening to me? I felt this pounding, inner excitement and expectation. I feared growing old.

Oh, God, what if I feel this way when I'm forty. What will there be for me to do, bake bread? No! Never!

I felt I was failing to experience much life at all.

I was attracted to Gide, Rimbaud, and Valery, who were trying to break through rigid cultural and language patterns to find experiential reality. Since I had "failed at religion," I tried to live the philosophy of atheistic existentialism, where you assert your identity out of sheer, raw courage. You accept the "fact" that the universe is random, with no innate purpose; that life is a freak cosmic accident going against the stronger tendency toward disorder. You accept that humans are irremediable victims of irrational forces within and without; that our science and technology are leading toward Armageddon, with no God to guide us. You face it, stare your fate in the eye, and dare to be yourself.

I tried to be like the clusters of Americans who sat at the Café

Deux Maggots, but I did not seem to fit. They sat drinking absinthe, staring into space; young men living off the G.I. Bill, students, middle-aged tourists, all trying to recapture a style of life that had been exciting at the time of Ernest Hemingway, F. Scott Fitzgerald, and Gertrude Stein. The adolescent craving for manhood was simply pathetic in postwar Paris: bullfighting, drinking, amassing vast fortunes to attract unhappy girls. The *real* frontiers, the *real* challenges to human ability, were not apparent.

The most important result of my year in France was the end of my adolescent search for meaning through existing forms. I reached an awareness that something was breaking down. I had read, at least superficially, through most of the philosophies of the world, looking specifically for ideas of the future. I found they were either cyclical, stoical, static, or looking backward to a Golden Age or forward to collapse. Nowhere could I find any concept of the future that corresponded to the magnetic pull of hunger and attraction, except in the religious texts of the world.

I also was fascinated by the Eastern concept of physical reality as maya, a veil of illusion to be pierced. I sensed the desire to get off the cycle of physical lives into a new state of being, a conscious union with the All. But I could not make the mystical leap from my present condition to the transformed existence that would be achieved after death. Not that I did not believe it, I just could not experience it as a reality. I found no way, no steps to get from "here" to "there." Yet the hunger for meaning grew stronger. Since 1945, when *the question* first arose, it dawned on me that I was up against a genuine impasse: intellectual, social, and spiritual. I was in a real metaphysical bind, and could not find a way out through existing knowledge.

One raining November afternoon I separated from the rest of the students. It was the only day I had lunch alone while in Paris. I happened upon a little restaurant on the Left Bank called Chez Rosalie. There were two empty places opposite each other in the crowded room. I sat in one and ordered a small beef steak and a half bottle of red wine.

In a few minutes the door opened, and a tall, young American entered. He had a large aristocratic head, with thick, curly dark hair, and full lips. He was gaunt, with hollows at his cheekbones. I noticed his long thin fingers as he took off his duffle coat and hung it on the rack. His presence struck me like an electric shock. In a moment his eyes scanned the room and caught mine. I smiled and lowered my head, knowing he would have to sit opposite me, it was the only place available.

We introduced ourselves and began to talk. I told him I was interested in the meaning of life. Shyly, looking into his eyes, I asked him my perennial question: "What is your purpose?"

"I'm an artist," he said. "My purpose is to create a new image of man commensurate with our capacities to shape the future."

Instantaneously, the idea flashed through my mind, 'I'm going to marry him!' I smiled radiantly, and nodded my head. Tears came into my eyes.

He wanted to know what our greatness is now and how an artist could portray it. He said the last great image of man had been created in the Renaissance by Michelangelo in the sculpture of David, the great, noble, nude body of man, assured, humble, beautiful, divine. Since that time you could see a gradual disintegration of our self-image. He visualized a rapid film sequence, starting with David, through the gradual breakup into points of light in the paintings of Manet, Monet, Pissaro, through the fragmentation of the image by Picasso, the expression of anguish as in Rouault's Christ, and finally the smashing of the image in the explosion of random patterns in Jackson Pollock's monumental displays of splattered patterns, frantic streaks of light.

We talked all afternoon. The restaurant emptied and the owner swept the floor around us, benignly tolerating our total absorption in each other. By the time we left, arm in arm, it was twilight. The wood fires of Paris filled the chill November air with a delicious cozy aroma. For the first time in my life I had fallen in love.

I returned to Neuilly and announced to Madame Mercier, "I have met the man I'm going to marry: Earl Hubbard!"

"Where, dear?"

"In this little restaurant."

She was horrified. A French woman of a certain class simply does not just meet a person in a restaurant, and say, "I'm going to marry him." My father had been in touch with her and she felt a maternal desire to protect me from this idiocy. She asked me who his parents were. I had no idea, I had not thought to ask. He had no idea who my parents were. I had told him my father "made toys"; he had thought I meant by hand, in an attic. It simply did not matter to either of us. But this American way of behaving was appalling to Madame Mercier.

Earl was the first man I had met who had a purpose comparable to mine. He was a graduate of Amherst College, had been in the Air Force during the war, and was now writing, painting, and living in a tiny room in the Hotel des Ecoles. He lived on a small income that came from stocks his father had given him. However, I was still entangled in my relationship with Stanley. He was powerfully possessive and it was difficult to break the ties. Earl and I had made a date to go to a Christmas Eve party with some of his American friends. I had to make a decision between the possessive, dominating Stanley and Earl, who shared a purpose with me.

Stanley and I had a painful argument.

"Barbara," he pleaded, "this will destroy my life. I'll have to leave. I can't stand to have you go out with anyone else."

I was terribly torn between my hunger for purpose and my deep loyalty to him. Even given the desperate need for meaningful contact, I placed loyalty to the existing relationship over desire for the new. I had a horror of hurting the feelings of those I love. I gave in. Sitting on Stanley's bed, with his arms around me, I called Earl and said I could not go with him on Christmas Eve.

Earl was deeply hurt. His voice broke. "I don't want to hear from you until you know you need me; when you know that, call me."

By the time school was out, Earl had gone back to the States. I was to spend two weeks on the French Riviera at the Eden Rock Hotel with my family. In June they came to Paris to pick me up.

Stanley wanted me to stay in Paris to marry him. My brother Louis, then eighteen, told Stanley that if he loved me, he would never separate me from my family. He would trust me to go back to the United States and finish college. If we really loved each other, nothing would separate us. My brother's arguments were strong enough to give me the needed support to leave Stanley.

I said goodbye to him in a small Paris cafe, then went out into the brilliant Paris summer day alone, crying aloud and running down the streets. People stared at me.

Eventually the intense heat of the streets melted my tension. I began to feel fluid like a cat in the sun, stretching my whole body in gratitude. My heart began to beat rapidly, my cheeks flushed, and an overwhelming, violent joy lifted me out of myself. 'I'm free, I'm free, I'm free!' thundered in my head.

On the Riviera I hardly ate or slept. Late every night I sat with Louis and his Princeton friends, telling them of this fantastic joy. They did not understood it because they had not experienced the hunger. I arose at dawn to lie alone on the hot, sunbaked rocks.

Elizabeth Taylor was staying at Eden Rock also. I will never forget the day I saw her climb the jutting rock that served as a raft in the Mediterranean Sea. Her hair was wet and her bathing suit clung to her voluptuous body. Men everywhere swam in droves from all nearby waters to that rock. I swam, too, to look at her. Nature had outdone itself; the violet eyes and perfect skin were a glory. I loved her for that beauty and wanted to talk to her, to see if such a magnetic beauty felt the hunger. She had just married Nicky Hilton, the hotel heir. The only other time I saw her she was sitting forlorn in the lobby of the Monte Carlo gambling casino, too young to be allowed inside where her husband was gambling. I wondered how our lives would compare, since we were the same age.

During those short two weeks I was sublimely happy, through no act of will, effortlessly connected to the whole universe, I was free, free from Stanley, free from any man's domination.

But, strangely, before I left Eden Rock, I wrote to Earl, "I'm coming home." I knew what that meant. I would not have written to him unless I felt I needed him. I wrote without much of a critical analysis or decision making process. I merely wanted to be with him and felt that the purpose he espoused was related to my own.

I returned with my family and met Earl at the Waldorf where my father kept a suite. When Earl walked in, he looked to me like a Greek God; tan, confident, very handsome. He never asked me to marry him; it was just taken for granted that I would.

A few days later I met with my father to discuss my plans. I was sitting at the swimming pool, and he was eating orange slices after his daily jog, a bandanna tied around his forehead to keep the sweat out of his eyes. I told him I wanted to leave Bryn Mawr immediately, and not finish my senior year. But my father insisted I had gone this far and had to get the degree.

"Barbara," he said, "you're one hundred percent wrong. You know nothing about the world. You talk in glittering generalities, because you've never had to do a real day's work in your life. It's ridiculous to leave college your senior year."

"Dad," I argued, "*you* don't understand *my* world. They're not educating me at Bryn Mawr for what I need to learn. The diploma's a worthless piece of paper. I'm going to have to educate myself."

But to please him, I decided to do both, get married and finish college. For me formal education was so easy I really could do it with a minimum of attention.

My wedding was held in New York City at St. Thomas Cathedral on January 3, 1951, followed by a celebrity-filled reception at the Waldorf. The terrible thing was that I really did not want to get married. I was walking down the aisle on my father's arm with this voice ringing in my ears, 'Don't get married. Don't get married. I don't want you to get married.' But I could not stop myself. The scene froze in my memory like the instant before an accident; the smiling faces, my father's embarrassed grin, the unavoidable, flower-bedecked altar of matrimony toward which I marched.

From the moment the minister proclaimed the words, "You are now pronounced man and wife," I knew I was trapped in a relation-ship that was wrong for me. I was not trapped by Earl, but trapped in a socially enforced relationship in which I did not believe. I wanted to be Barbara Marx, not Mrs. Earl Hubbard. But I did not have the strength to struggle against it. It never occurred to me to live with him without marrying him.

I'm married, wrapped in bright, red paper with a big, yellow bow. I sit in a room with my husband, a cup of hot tea, Edith Piaff on record, the end of me alone, excited by my shadow. The sun is at full noon; the beautiful black shadow has snapped up. Together we look out - not at each other. The end of an invigorating romance. We must keep the sun straight overhead.

Every once in a while I realize that my life is at stake, my own growing, exciting, creative life. I'm sick to death of floundering about. I'm not in competition with Earl, but his creativeness is a constant reminder of my own death. His talent and fluency tighten up my own rather sticky abilities. I need warmth to make them melt. Without some challenge, the best of abilities retire, much less my lukewarm genius. I can't afford to let it slip away any longer. If I write every night, it helps.

Two

Confusion

When I realized I was pregnant, my first reaction was shock. I had thought, once finished with college, Earl and I would travel and I would be able to find the life I craved. But Earl persuaded me we would have to buy a home instead, because, after all, I *was* pregnant.

I did not want a diploma, I did not want to be married, I did not want a baby and I did not want a house. How did all this happen?

The current cultural patterns were ingrained in me. I was an innate seeker, not an innate rebel, so I did not think to cast off the social patterns the men in my life unconsciously imposed on me.

I am getting deeper and deeper
into the material world.

I became confused. I had decided to marry Earl for the sake of that hunger, but the personal entanglements of our relationship were taking over. When I got pregnant, I was bound by marriage and therefore felt required to make my husband happy, to do what he wanted. Furthermore, he was supposed to make me happy! I was soon in a state of complete disarray. I had lost my compass.

Of course, everyone else had the answer: "Well, once you have that baby and your own home, you'll get over this need." Unfortunately, I did not know how to protest, or what to suggest. I had discovered nothing for me in Paris or New York or Scarsdale or in any particular art or philosophical movement.

Earl, on the other hand, was exuberant with hope and a sense of his own role in making history. He often spoke to me in Churchill-like phrases: "Barbara, this is America's time on the stage of history. This is our indelible moment. Egypt, Greece, Rome, Europe, all have made great contributions. But Europe is now the audience, that's why we can't go back and live in Paris." I was uplifted, but wondered how I could be a part of this purpose.

Earl wanted to move to Maine as soon as I finished college, to be as far away from current society as possible. Even though I wanted to please him in every way, I had the strength to say no to that: "Earl, I've got to be near New York, to have some fun."

The sociable, witty, philosophical young man I had met in Paris, who painted charming paintings of French scenes as gifts for his friends, who conversed for hours in cafes, suddenly changed upon marriage to me. He became intense, seeking isolation, craving affirmation of his work.

When we first met, he had been attracted by some of the French painters, especially Matisse and Rouault, but in studying them he concluded there was no sense of direction in their work. He decided the new image had to be created by him. I agreed that someone had to create something new, because what was needed could not be found. Earl likened himself to Robert Frost, living on the soil of this fertile land to produce a new vision of humanity.

I still accepted the positive aspects of existentialism, that the purpose of anyone's life is to affirm existence and become one's own authority. It was a painful effort. Being a positive person meant that I could not become desolate, that I must be able to find joy in every minute by affirming myself and my family. So I decided even though I did not want to be cut off from Paris and New York, I was willing to accept a move in pioneer fashion to affirm life by the sheer power of self-authorization. I was looking at everything from the perspective of its own being.

We could have lived anywhere: a castle in Spain, Paris, or New York; instead we ended up in Lime Rock, Connecticut. It was not too far from New York, and Alfred Korzybski lived there. His seminal work on the "consciousness of abstracting," *Science and Sanity*, interested Earl, and Earl wanted to meet him. Korzybski's central idea was that the word we name an object, is not the object.

We drove to Lime Rock to see Korzybski in March 1951, while I was still finishing my senior year in college. We discovered that Korzybski had recently died. The weather was chill and dark, no sign of spring. On the spur of the moment we asked a real estate agent to show us some houses. At the end of the day we found a small, red, barn-like studio, overgrown with vines, on a hill on White Hollow Road. It had belonged to an artist and was more unusual than any other house in the price range we had chosen.

We planned to live on Earl's income, rather than use mine, because he felt a man should support a woman. This was ludicrous to me since his income came from what his father had given him, just as mine did.

Earl had been very distressed when he discovered my father did not make toys "in an attic," but that he was a millionaire and I was an heiress.

I was disappointed that Earl did not have enough confidence in our relationship to let go of the role of breadwinner. We argued about it, but in the end, I agreed to honor his feelings.

We bought the studio. It consisted of one big room with a giant fireplace, a small, decaying kitchen, and a tiny run-down bathroom, with a built-in bed next to it. We were to move there as soon as I finished college.

When I went back to school to finish my senior year. My friends asked me about my house. I was the first girl to get married or pregnant in our class. I wanted to sound enthusiastic about it: the charming vines, the fireplace, but I couldn't.

We were living near Bryn Mawr in Haverford. Each morning I left Earl reading Korzybski, and I drove to college with my brown-bag lunch. Then I came home to the apartment where I cooked horrible dinners of hamburgers and stuffed celery. I resented having to cook, although eventually I learned to enjoy it.

I had problems with the pregnancy. The baby was low in the womb. At college one day I began to bleed and was rushed to the doctor. I was told I must return to Scarsdale for complete rest, or I might lose the baby. So we returned to Scarsdale where I took my final exams and awaited the birth of my daughter, Suzanne. This was to be the only birth during which I was unconscious; the New York doctor believed in induced delivery.

One July evening Earl drove me to the hospital. The next morning I was given one drug to start contractions and another to help me "forget" the pain. Only with my subsequent pregnancies did I realize what a terrible deprivation it is to be unconscious at the birth of your child.

As soon as I saw Suzanne, I fell in love with her. We drove to our home in Lime Rock in Earl's old Plymouth with Suzanne in a basket and a poodle called Zipper in the back seat.

The house was not ready. So, I entered a period of trying to make a home for my daughter and husband. It became perfectly obvious that, as much as I did not want to, I would have to concern myself with stoves, dryers, washing machines, and refrigerators. I had thought I was getting out of the material world when I married a man of high purpose, but because I had a baby and because it was Earl's desire, I got deeper into it. I hated it, but kept telling myself

I always had the option to leave. The saddest part was I did not see what else I could do with my life. The exhilarated joy I had felt upon meeting Earl disappeared. I felt displaced, lost.

This morning I burst into tears when Suzanne's chopped carrots fell to the floor. I had left the dishes unwashed last night and faced a greasy kitchen, a cluttered living room, and a messy nursery when I got up. I didn't want to get out of bed to begin two hours of cleaning and cooking.

I feel terribly sorry for myself. Here I am, twenty-two years old, and how am I using what I have? Earl appears satisfied to do his work, care for the land, etc. but what is my work?

He seems to see nothing sad about my grubbing around in the kitchen. He repeatedly expresses an aversion to women who are active outside the home. I hate to admit it, but I'm bored. It seems an admission of stupidity. But I can't put down the all-encompassing surges of boredom. I wake in the morning with a quick kick of excitement, then poof! I say, what am I going to do today? Make breakfast, straighten the house, take a walk, play the piano, lie in the sun, write in my journal, play with Suzanne, bathe and feed Suzanne, make dinner, clean up, read, listen to the radio, take a desultory look at the stars, then go to sleep.

In the Lime Rock area, there was a group of young adults somewhat like ourselves, who were well educated and had some independent income. They, like us, had decided to live a new, noncompetitive way of life and to raise their children outside the "rat race."

Everyone I knew was having four and five babies (Margaret Mead later called it the "retreat into fecundity"). The women were hooking rugs, cooking, and planting gardens. The men were working outdoors, many of them buying cows and expensive farm equipment; others set up country practices as doctors and lawyers. Our purpose was to lead the "good life," enjoy ourselves and help our children grow into beautiful people.

It worked for a while, the way of life had real quality, the environment was pure, the people were kind and good. I went through it as best I could. I worked on all the committees: League of Women Voters, Housatonic Valley Music Association, the Sharon Playhouse, the Connecticut Mental Health Association, the Garden Club, the Film Society, the Salisbury Welfare Association, and the Sharon Ball

Committee. People said they were so busy they had "no time to think." Women complained about housework. A pose of weariness fell like rancid dew on fresh lives.

What can I give my children
if I don't give something to myself?

The concepts of Freud had taken hold of the American experience: any higher aspirations or growth need is rooted in failure to satisfy some basic deficiency, mainly sexual. Therefore, do not aspire. It is abnormal. When my brother Louis had said to me several years before, "Your desperation for a philosophy of life is a compensation for not succeeding in the world," that was a Freudian concept. He did not know it, but he was accepting the idea that the higher drives were caused by failure or repression of the lower.

In the Lime Rock community, the local psychiatrist was a Freudian psychoanalyst, a pale, effete version. His attitude was that anyone who wanted a higher order of satisfaction was to be snickered at. At parties, when I would try to share my need to affirm the meaning of life, he would look at me cross-wise and try to figure out what was wrong with my sex life. "Nothing is wrong with my sex life!" I finally told him. "I want something greater." He could not accept that.

Freud had a depressing effect. It was one of those blocks I was able to overcome many years later through the works of Abraham H. Maslow, the psychologist who founded humanistic psychology, which goes beyond Freudianism and behaviorism. Maslow had not studied mentally ill patients or rats in a cage, but healthy people: people at their best, people who experience life as joyful and productive, people who are loving and loved. He called them self-actualizing people. He identified a "hierarchy of human needs": basic, growth, and transpersonal. If your basic needs for food, shelter, sex, security, and esteem are not met, you will have problems. But once those needs are met, you will experience growth needs: natural desires that pull you toward goals that appear intrinsically valuable, such as knowledge, justice, and beauty. If you do not move from deficiency to growth needs, you become mentally ill. He also discovered that each healthy person had a chosen work he loved to do, a vocation. Further, each one experienced some connection with a higher order, whether it be called God, the universe, the Logos, or evolution. Transcendent or transpersonal needs also were met, through "peak experiences" which were flashes of joy, unity, bliss, connectedness.

Maslow saved my sanity when I had about given up and was ready to accept that my hunger was neurotic. But at this time, I had not heard of Maslow and my need of purpose aroused suspicion among my Freudian friends.

As each child was born, this need for purpose was accentuated in me. After Suzanne would come Stephanie, Alexandra, Wade, and finally Lloyd. Because of my primal hunger and restlessness, I did not consider myself a good mother in the ordinary sense of the word. But I loved my children deeply and spent most of my time with them. Unfortunately, the more time I spent with them, the more I added their needs to my need for purpose.

Only pregnancy seemed to solve the problem. For nine months I had a purpose, a significance; it was a blessed relief to have a child within me. But as soon as a child is born, it is a person apart and outside. The child requires attention, elicits love, but is never the answer, so I was left to face myself as I was before the child was conceived. As a mother, I wanted to give my children something other than this terrible hunger. Since I had not found it for myself, it lessened my courage as a mother. Each one of those lovely little people was driving another wedge in my heart.

Toward the end of each pregnancy, love for the coming child took over completely. For a few brief moments the hunger disappeared entirely. Just before birth, during birth, and immediately afterwards, I was at rest, at peace. In fact, I craved the first labor pain, eagerly anticipating the delivery, despite the pain, because birth was the only experience I'd had, except for a few moments of joyful unity with the universe, during which I was able to overcome the hunger.

At my first meeting with Abe Maslow, about ten years later, he made an interesting observation. He told me women were more likely than men to become "self-actualizing," fully functioning people. Most men, when interviewed about their "peak" experiences put sex and, particularly, orgasm at the top of their lists. But when Maslow interviewed "highly sexed women" (I don't know how he knew that), asking them which experience was more intense and fulfilling, orgasm or giving birth to a child, every one named birth. Certainly that was true in my case.

The loneliness and sense
of uselessness are deepening.

Earl did not know how to cope with me. My dissatisfaction and discontent mounted daily. I associated it with the isolation being imposed on me in Lime Rock where I was surrounded by people who had decided not to accept a challenge; people who purposefully took themselves out of the competitive world; people who had no new purpose, no new growth challenge, no vocation, who just desired more comfort and the creation of a benign way of life. The parties became awkward for me. Men became interested in other men's wives. Chronic boredom was setting in.

Earl was painting seven days a week, except for time off to break rocks to make a lawn out of the old New England field. I was deeply lonely, boiling with energy I could find no way to invest.

Every now and then my father would call and speak sharply to me. "You're putting yourself in a box! You've got to get out into the world." Then he would invite me to this or that glamorous event, a theatre opening, or a trip to Europe.

Earl did not want me to go. I used to cry after each call, wanting to go, yet feeling disloyal. My father was totally success-oriented and was scornful of any man who had not "made it." Much to my humiliation he would say so openly to Earl. It was unbearable. Earl had expected to become well-known, like F. Scott Fitzgerald, but it was not happening.

Occasionally I did accept an invitation. My father was a close friend of Dwight Eisenhower. Right after he became president we were invited to attend a gathering at Omar Bradley's house. My father had remarried and had several sons by his second wife, Idella. Each had a general as his god-father. Dad's idea was to have a family photograph taken with my half-brothers and the generals, including Eisenhower, George Marshall, Omar Bradley, Bedell Smith, and Emmet "Rosie" O'Donnell. The gathering included all of those men, my three half-brothers, along with the governesses, myself, Earl, Dad, Idella and other family members.

I always felt a surge of excitement whenever I was near political power, and Eisenhower's charisma was overwhelming. The attraction was so overpowering, I could barely speak in his presence. My heart sank as we drove home that evening. Walking into our tiny, isolated cottage was so depressing that I almost could not bear it. I felt cut off from life's energies by some mysterious disease.

Several months later, my father invited me to visit Eisenhower in the White House. I was thrilled and awed as I walked into the magnificent mansion, yet strangely, I felt at ease, almost at home. I had a premonition that I would be in this house again one day.

I was ushered into the Oval Office. There sat the President. He offered me a chair and turned toward me with his brilliant blue eyes. I looked deeply into his eyes for an instant, speechless, magnetized, when *the question* flashed through my mind!

"Mr. President, I have a question for you."

"What's that, young lady?" he responded.

"What is the meaning of our power? Where is the United States going that is good? What is your vision of the future?"

He stared at me in surprise, and remained silent. Shaking his head, he said slowly, "I do not know."

The thought occurred to me, 'Well, then, we had better find out.' But I did not say it.

The contrast of the excitement of these kinds of events made the evenings in Lime Rock all the more boring. I never knew what to do in the evenings there except read.

I read Thoreau's *Walden* in a desperate stand to affirm reality as it is, letting that suffice. I agreed with Thoreau that all these material goods of society are not the answer. It is possible to get deep into reality by becoming totally immersed in nature, recognizing that you are part of it. I knew worldly power in itself was not viable, but I felt, on the other hand, that trying to be at one with nature was not valid either, it was too passive. It also seemed impossible because nature, too, was engaged in a daily struggle for life.

> *Faced with the beauty of nature, I am thrown into confusion. I want to immerse myself in it, to become part of nature by simply being. All my thoughts seem frivolous in comparison. Yet, as I study the day more closely, I see that the glory of nature is not a unity but a composition of untold numbers of individuals. Each, as I, is striving to exist; each is in mortal danger; each is seeking the sunlight for the sake of its soul. Each blade of grass is as alone as I, even though, as I look across the lawn, I see a single carpet of green.*
>
> *I want to identify with the whole and forsake my individual needs. But I can not determine what the whole is.*
>
> *All the religions and philosophies refer to this whole with which the saint can identify, reaching beyond the "veil of maya," or separateness, to a reality that indivisible and eternal.*
>
> *I can not see beyond this veil. I see only the single blades of grass, and when I find something to relate to, it is to individuals who in their singleness are, like me, alone.*

Robert Frost, the stoic, had reached the point where he could look God in the eye, and say, "I know you are not going to explain yourself to me. I know I can never understand you. I'll bear the pain nobly, and do my best." My father's commandment echoes in my ears: "Do your best." I search for the courage to go on with my life, as Frost says in The Mask of Mercy, "The courage in the heart to overcome the fear within the soul and go ahead of any accomplishment." He was right. The fear is "eternal." This is my moment in eternity. If I lose my chance, I may have lost it forever. The stakes are everything. The gamble is absolute. The odds are millions to one. Yet, I have no choice but to do my best.

There was a certain relief in my acceptance that I could only do my best, that the chances are it will not be enough, but that I will do it anyway. Discouragement is so inevitable with odds like these that I could more or less ignore it. The courage Frost spoke of was the courage to "overcome the fear within the soul." What other way was there to overcome any fear than to face it?

I was profoundly distressed by the impermanence of everything. Words were my way of holding onto reality. I tried to put everything around me into words. One morning I awoke at the usual time. The sun was shining; the children were laughing; the birds filled the valley with song, but in my heart was a depression so deep it ached.

I went to the hill with my pen and pad to see if by writing I could dissolve the ache. I knew it came from that core of myself that demanded life everlasting; that core which happy children, loving husband, tender friends, could not satisfy. That core represented in me the most common, the most universal, ancient, prehistoric human possession: the spark of life, the difference between animation and inanimation, between being and not being. This vital spark at the core of my being gave me life and did not want to be put out. That was what ached, ached because I believed that since it soon would be put out, it demanded perfection, demanded that each precious, unique moment be perfect. However, each moment was not perfect; most moments passed unloved and wasted forever.

So that morning I quietly left the house to face up to life's demands, to write, because the word, once written, need never be destroyed. The deepest satisfaction I could bring to the demanding core of my being was that I recognize it and immortalize it to the extent of my ability in everlasting words. Instead of trying to cover it up, to lose the ache in activity, I decided to try to reveal it to myself, to learn to live with it, rather than fight against it.

I decided to write a book based on my life. It was called *Each Day at Dawn* and was about mustering the courage to face the meaninglessness. I was pregnant with my third child, Alexandra, when I started this. It meant survival to me, my way out of the trap of emptiness and into the world. But "no one can identify with this person," I was later told. A terrible blow. I had thought if I were not alone in my pain, I could somehow gather strength. But evidently I was expressing it so no one could identify with me. The loneliness and sense of uselessness deepened. I was incommunicado. I felt "no exit"; the wall of meaninglessness was closing in.

How can I trust myself when it seems I am always wrong? Does the higher meaning I'm after exist at all? Whatever wrongness exists in me is in so deep and down so far that it is me. If I'm wrong, it's my very nature to be wrong. There's nothing I can do to change who I am. I have no alternative being to turn into; I must live it out as Barbara, then die.

It is the fall of 1957, six years after marriage. I have come to the end of my endurance. No matter who I am with, Earl, my father, even my own children, I feel as though I were separated from them by this invisible shroud. I am able to converse, but not to initiate conversation. If they stop talking, I stop talking. I feel panicky; I search my brain for something to say, to assert myself, to feel alive at least, but incredibly, I can find nothing. Emptiness. I'm frightened. I smile and act as if this is the way I am supposed to be, this stone woman. I have no understanding of what's happening to me. I only know that the enormity of my failure overwhelms any tiny gesture I make to rescue myself. As I write this, there's a soul-moving yearning to believe it isn't true. To put it down as something outside myself is my only hope. It is impossible to purge yourself of a cancer. Surgery is the only hope, and I'm no surgeon.

Earl offered me the strength of his love and I've left him loving a figment of his imagination. I'm no longer the girl he loves. And he eventually will find out that I have nothing to give, that I'm stone and he's alone. He will take a while to realize it and when he does, he will find strength to bear it within himself. He believes that what he's doing is valuable. Thank God for that. I believe that everything I have done is valueless. And it is, except for the children, for which I have simply offered my body.

Every time I droned on in my journal about this wasted, withered person that I called myself, a voice of protest came crashing, surging up from the depth of me, calling out, 'No, no, it isn't so! You're alive and you have strength and I'll not let you die!' And I grasped at this voice to lead me out of darkness. I grasped and the hope filled me with a light, all the lighter because of the darkness everywhere.

For the first time I made a stand for life, for my own life. I said to Earl, "We're going to New York City. I have to get into an environment of action." I chose New York because it was the only place I knew, and it was the center of the art and cultural world. He didn't want to go; the children didn't want to go; but I said, "I'm dying. I'm going to New York, and if you want to be with me, you'll follow." It was the first time I made a decisive, selfish act, and his self-assertion collapsed in the face of it. When I became a causal factor, initiating not submitting, he became submissive. I was amazed at the power of the will. Yet, I knew if I "won" my life at the expense of his, I would destroy our relationship. I wanted to grow without destroying.

"We can go to New York," Earl said, "but what's going on there is a funeral; you and I both know they are having a wake for the past image of man."

"You're right." I agreed. "But I would rather be where there are people than rotting in Lime Rock alone."

So we went to join the funeral. Our moves were very costly in energy and money. We had four children then and needed a large apartment. Each move meant shifting furniture, decorating, concerning myself with those things I did not care about.

When we finally were settled in an apartment, I got up in the morning and could not think of what to do. I spent several hours a day at the New York Society Library, reading again, this time works such as the life of St. Paul. Something had happened to him on the road to Damascus, and I longed for something like that to happen to me, something that would me blind me with light, set me on the path of right action, give me a direct signal. But I heard no "voices," saw no light, was given no clear direction or signal.

Here I am at my desk again, alone in a sea of silence. The children are the only rafts in sight. They are always there to do something for. There's nothing I can do for myself unless I find ways of doing something for others. I want to give what only "I" can give. The egoism is extreme. I don't want merely to serve. I want to give something that's uniquely mine. But give I must.

We returned to Lime Rock for the summer. The hunger now was quite literally at a point of desperation. I was totally absorbed, waiting, searching. I was, you might say, in a state of constant prayer, attuned to hear any sound, see any sign.

In the early twilight of the summer evening it is hard for me to believe that the sun isn't going down, that instead I am turning away from it. It is also hard to believe that the sun's light doesn't go out when I can't see it. I had to be told that. Instinct can be very misleading. I feel no movement at all. I close my eyes and focus my attention that I might sense the earth moving in space, to try to feel that I live and move in the universe.

No universe exists for my senses. But there is one. There is an outer one, and an inner one inside me, fabulous systems moving independently according to laws I never made, as do the stars. I also know there is an inner-inner universe, working in the deepest secret, entirely beyond the reach of my sensual instruments, the atomic universe, stars within stars within stars.

This afternoon I stood under the apple tree, wondering. An apple fell at my feet; the ground trembled. That small tremor I could feel, but the earth turning away from the sun I couldn't feel, nor the blood in my veins, nor the whirling of atoms, and beyond that, there was so much that I could never feel, could never know. My human limitations thrilled me with a certainty: Everything is more miraculous than I can comprehend, including myself.

The focus on self seems a dead end for me, as does the focus on the world. If only I could bring the inner and outer worlds together, my work might live.

Whenever we were in New York, Earl's misery deepened. "I have no roots. I can't live here," he told me in real anguish.

His work was not succeeding in the soil of the New York art world, and to him his work was his life. I could not bear to see him suffer, so I agreed to move back to the country. His relief was so great that he offered to cash in his fortune to buy a small apartment in the city for me to use whenever I wanted to visit. We put the large apartment on the market and began to look for "my place."

In October of 1961, during our early venture to New York, I became pregnant again, my fifth and last pregnancy. I had not meant to get pregnant. I had just barely started my search for a new life.

As with the first pregnancy, it came not only as a shock, but as a seemingly lethal barrier to the development I needed to live. If abortions had been legal, I would have considered one. I went to my doctor and told him I did not want this baby; it was going to ruin my life. He said, "That doesn't make the slightest difference; it's illegal." Since I had agreed in principle to move back to the country and it was apparent that the Lime Rock house was too small for another child, we decided to sell the studio-house and purchase a beautiful estate which had just come on the market in nearby Lakeville. It would be wiser than building on once again. The Lakeville property was beautiful, with a studio for Earl, a garage-guest house, a pool, a tennis court, and a large Georgian house with a view toward the magnificent foothills of the Berkshire mountains.

Once again I became embroiled in an orgy of materiality: settling Earl, the children, and myself into our new home, while I kept experiencing the weird sensation of not belonging anywhere.

The children were a stabilizing joy, because their lives obviously required my attention. I had taken my journal with me during each birth; they had to forcibly stop me from writing as I was being wheeled into the delivery room. I often glanced back to relive those moments. I had recorded the character of each child at birth, especially each child's response to frustration, which I considered a key trait. I felt if you give up or become enraged easily, you will never realize your potential. The first frustration is birth itself. How does the baby handle the strain of breathing, nursing, coordinating?

Because I was under sedation, I do not know Suzanne's earliest reactions to life. But several hours later she expressed a deep intensity, as though searching for inner signals to act upon. When she first studied the Old Testament at school, she said, "I'm glad I didn't live in the days when God was boss! Why did he keep hiding behind bushes and clouds?" She also insisted she did not start out as a fertilized egg. It was undignified, she said.

Stephanie, a beautiful, perfectly formed, blue-eyed, dark-haired baby, was born with a strange lack: she did not respond to being held. The others instinctively were comforted by cuddling, but Stephanie continued to scream, wide-eyed, not sensing love. For several years she had trouble receiving nourishment from love and became self-deprecating. However, she eventually grew into the most openly loving child, constantly injecting the rest of us with shots of cheer, love, hugs, and kisses. Her experience of lack of love had motivated her to give love and to support each person's self-esteem.

Alexandra was born enormous, and worried: her little brows furrowed, filled with tension. When she was three years old I watched her swinging from a willow branch, her black hair glittering like silver in the sun, defiantly asking me, "Mummy, which would you rather spend your time doing, having babies or dying?" When I told her I would rather have babies, she said, "So would I, but I'm not going to die either!"

Wade, my first son after three girls, was born so fast I barely made it to the delivery room. I had no drugs at all. I remember screaming to the doctor: "I'm not ready, I want to escape," to which he calmly replied, "You can't escape, Barbara, there's nowhere you can go." So I decided to try to feel the pain with my whole being, and it abated almost instantly with my decision to go with it rather than against it. Wade emerged rapidly and immediately accepted the world as it was. When the breast was first offered to him he took it without hesitation and nursed contentedly to satiation, burping, then going right to sleep. Once when I was carrying him through a doorway, I put my hand on the back of his head to protect him, and suddenly found his baby hand on the back of my head, protecting me.

Lloyd was born with the need to understand. When I first offered him the breast he screwed up his little face, pursed his lips tightly, and refused the unwanted intrusion into his private world. This behavior continued for several nursing attempts. Finally when the nipple was presented to him again, he stopped in the middle of a scowl, opened his eyes wide, and with his clenched fists splayed out like sudden stars, he bit into the nipple and nursed for dear life. It seemed that he could not do it at all until he "understood." As he grew up, he kept everything to himself, until the point when he would make an inner decision and follow it through implacably.

I reread my notes on each birth and felt the driving hunger within me. Here I was in Lakeville, one husband and five children later. I knew where I was, but the question that nagged me relentlessly was, where am I going?

Three

Nourishment

Earl had a good gallery in New York, the Rehn, where he had one exhibition in 1960 and another in the fall of 1962. He was portraying the individual as incorruptible and strong. His style had developed from abstractions, to patterns, to stoic portraits of the individual asserting his own right to be in total freedom. Faces and bodies of light broke out of backgrounds of earthy browns.

At that time, "abstract expressionism" was popular in New York. It was America's contribution to the breakdown of the past image of man. Few people came to Earl's exhibitions; they received almost no attention from the critics or the public. His works were totally out of fashion.

During Earl's second exhibition in November 1962, we visited the Museum of Modern Art to see a collection of recent acquisitions. A key moment of my liberation from the "self-concentration camp" occurred that day. There was a line queued for admission tickets.

"Reminds you of the Rehn, doesn't it?" I said, smiling at Earl, thinking of the stark contrast between our empty gallery and these crowds. He grimaced. Still cheerful, I gazed at the people, somehow unprepared for what I was about to see.

There, being guarded by uniformed men, were the recent acquisitions of the world's greatest modern museum. Vast canvases hung empty on the walls: one, all grey; one, barely touched by some frantic wiggle, like the trail of a worm; another, so full of orange it looked empty; still another, a panel encrusted with charred, jewel-like bits; then, a plastic hamburger; next, a few rocks on sticks; nearby, a medicine cabinet; finally, some nails in plaster.

I was shocked. "My God, Earl," I cried. "Where are we? In a mad house? Who are these people staring sheepishly at all this?"

Earl shook his head.

"We should all rise up and take those dreadful things off the walls. Not only do the artists describe the death of the mind and spirit, the people like it. They must delight in dying, look how the artists enjoys spitting on the corpse. It's perverted, Earl. In fact, it makes me sick.

Take me out of here. This is an insane asylum, but no one knows it. And the critics said, 'Another interesting show at the....'"

"Take it easy, Barbara." Earl clutched my arm, guiding me out.

"I can't take it easy, Earl. Look at the people; their faces show nothing. Don't they see these artists are dancing on their graves? Well, I'm not dead; they'll not dance on my grave!"

Suddenly I was shouting, I wanted to make a scene. I recall a guard stiffened to attention, protecting a plastic hamburger from me.

"Earl, people must not take such insults passively. We should hurl these paintings from the walls." But no one else felt insulted. That was the worst of it.

"Someone has to say what's going on here. This is a death feast. The victim is humanity, and the killer is dehumanized man, who, God help us, has become the fashionable artist. They're not *commenting* on the destruction; they're *doing* it."

Earl nodded and tried to pull me along.

"And the museum is helping, guarding the grinning killers while they hack away at the victims, praising the artists for every wild and eager stroke, all in the name of art. Earl, what we're up against is insane." I was trembling with anger and frustration.

"Barbara, you mustn't get so upset. It's not important."

"It *is* important, Earl, because it's everywhere."

"Barbara, these artists and their work will be forgotten in ten years. We've got to get together enough work in the meantime to hang on these walls then."

For the first time in my life, I felt it was not just my life, but life in general, that was being attacked. The powers of the modern, intellectual culture machine were being used to affirm meaninglessness, and make people accept it as the nature of reality.

Out of the depths of my being, I heard a voice: 'I will not accept this,' but now it was not just for myself but for the rest of society. 'We are going to have to fight back. We have to find a way of new hope.' With that sense of attack on humanity itself, I began to have the directed energy to enter the public world.

I am developing the first link
of that essential bridge between
a meaningless and a meaningful life,
a sense of vocation.

I had found the thread of something unique to do, something truly needed by others: to act as an advocate for humanity, for the possibility of meaning, values and the improvement of human behavior. For the first time, with this anger against death and this response for life, I felt a sense of myself, a clue to my identity.

I questioned Earl deeply about the future, and asked for his ideas on specific projects to help serve as "advocates." Thus, we began our dialogues at breakfast. His fertile mind sprouted thoughts, and he was glad to give me ideas to pacify my desire to do something. However, his energy was still totally invested in his painting, while mine was on the loose. Daily I was taking the children to the park, reading, and writing.

Once he gave me a long lecture: "I never again want to hear that you're unhappy. I'm sick of miserable wives! Every woman I know is unhappy. None of you has been happy since World War II when you were in the factories riveting. Don't you know your job is in the home, loving your husband and taking care of your children? Don't you realize the influence you have through motherhood?"

"Earl, that may sound good in theory, but in practice, day by day, it doesn't work for me. It's too restricting."

So half in jest, half seriously, he challenged me to be the one woman he knew that wasn't complaining. I rose to the demand!

At his suggestion I asked my brother Louis to start a small foundation - the Deerfield Foundation. He agreed. The first thing I did for the foundation was to bring some voices of hope to the theatre, to the stage of the Poetry Center in New York, famous for presenting the great poets of modern times. Dylan Thomas, T.S. Eliot, Robert Frost had all read there.

I commissioned Agnes Moorehead to do a dramatic reading from the journals of Wanda Landowska, the superb harpsichordist who lived in Lakeville near us, and whose journals were being edited by Robert Hawkins, a teacher at the Hotchkiss School. The reading was beautiful in Agnes' queenly rendition. It came to life on the stage as the voice of a powerful woman who had overcome all obstacles to bring the music of Bach in its original form to the world. Agnes became my friend and asked to work with us on other projects.

Then I thought it would be interesting to do dramatic readings from other great journal writers: Emerson, Thoreau, Montaigne, Pascal, etc. The idea broadened as I realized that throughout history there have been "possibilists" who affirm life and "impossibilists" who deny it.

To help bring forth the reservoirs of human greatness for our age became my first calling, my vocation. It was not easy, because the contemporary cultural scene was dominated by despair. I groped for a way. I gave a little grant to help finance a series of readings of younger poets. However, I stopped when I realized some of them carried "cultural diseases," spreading the virus of hopelessness. It was like paying for the spread of a tuberculous germ.

Soon I began to feel energized, liberated from my absorption with my own lack of purpose. I began to grow. As Carl Jung said: "True personality always has vocation: an irrational factor that fatefully forces a person to emancipate himself from the herd and its trodden paths.... Only the person who is able consciously to affirm the power of the vocation confronting him from within becomes a personality."

In preparation for my vocation as an advocate for humanity, I decided to study, once again, humanity's image of itself as it has evolved, starting with the pre-Socratic. Just as I started that scan through literature, looking for the crucial self-image, John Glenn was fired into space from Cape Canaveral.

> *As the giant rocket rose in a blaze of pure energy, I saw it as a supreme ejaculation: humans sowing their seed farther and higher than ever before.*
>
> *It is a rare experience to watch a species at the precise moment of change, of evolution, most of which has been buried in the imperceptible crawl of time past.*
>
> *It is interesting that many intellectuals don't consider the adventure into space important. They say it will never change humanity's condition. It's as true as saying the discovery of fire made no difference, or the rising from all fours to an erect position, or emerging from the sea to land was insignificant. "Just another technical gimmick," they must have said.*
>
> *Of course it will change our condition. It will change humanity itself to have done this. How else are we changed than by what we do and where we do it? Anyone who remembers we were in the Neanderthal era 60,000 years ago can't discount change.*
>
> *The concept of life as an evolutionary process has subtly taken hold of me. I don't live in a static eternity but in an evolving universe. I'm going somewhere. Being of the race of human, not animal, for the first time in history there's an opportunity to choose, at least a little at a time, where and how.*

I realized at the Museum of Modern Art that the way we see ourselves influences the way we act. If we continued to see ourselves as faceless, ugly victims, the image would become a self-fulfilling prophecy. But images are conceived by people and can be changed by people. This modern image could be transformed into a new one, if we could see the new direction of hope.

I set myself the task of discovering the new images and ideals that were emerging. The thinkers were easier to find than the image makers; I began to piece together the beginnings of an new evolutionary philosophy.

Abraham H. Maslow provided the psychological basis in *Toward a Psychology of Being*, the book that had saved my sanity at a time when I considered myself abnormal and neurotic. Through him I realized those high moments of joy and unity were not freakish but true health. Once I affirmed the normalcy of my hunger, I could work to fulfill it with genuine confidence.

Teilhard de Chardin provided the cosmology for the evolutionary philosophy. In his great work, *The Phenomenon of Man*, he traced a unifying pattern in all existence, from the original creation to the present. There's a basic attraction, he called it love, that brings particles together to form bodies of ever greater complexity: the atom, the molecule, the single cell, the multicellular organism, humans, and now humankind. At each phase of increased complexity, a synthesis occurs; a new "whole" system is formed that expresses higher consciousness, purpose, and freedom. Now, we, humanity, are in the process of forming ourselves into a synthesis, a planetary organism, humankind. We are the planet becoming self-aware!

He wrote eloquently about Omega, a point of synthesis, the "christification of the earth." He said we were creating the "noosphere," the thinking layer of earth, comparable to the biosphere, the hydrosphere and the geosphere. At some point, the "noosphere would get its collective eyes." We would see together what none could see alone.

He foresaw a time of actual experience of oneness. My heart beat with excitement. Here was the magnet that attracted me, which I read about in the Bible but could not find in the church, portrayed as a natural evolutionary next step. My passion for something new coming was affirmed, not only by my intuitive faith, but by a scientifically-based observation that nature is forming a new whole system through us, on earth, now!

The third key thinker in my philosophy of hope was Buckminster Fuller. In his *Utopia or Oblivion*, he revealed that the universe is designed to be an ever-regenerating system. It is not going down to an inevitable fiery death through increased entropy, but rather upward to ever greater synergy, ever greater intelligence and capacity to work with the laws of the universe. Humanity is designed to know the design. Fuller stated that we were to be stewards of "local universe." We now had the technology, resources and know-how to make humanity a 100% physical success.

The individual has unused potential and the planet is evolving naturally to a higher state of being. Humanity has a conscious role to play in its evolution, and we have the technology to make the world work for everyone; if we cooperate with the design of nature.

Finally, the picture of a positive future began to emerge. I felt like a seeker on a treasure hunt for the most valuable jewels of life: purpose and a vision of the future that could attract us.

These thoughts excited and nourished my hunger. It meant that our generation had a role to play on a planetary scale, a role in understanding how "the system" works, in coordinating our diverse parts, in emancipating the new level of potential of all members of the body. It also indicated we were to keep going onward, because evolution is by its very nature progressive, a continual movement toward higher and higher states of being. John Glenn's flight helped me realize that one of the next steps of evolution is to develop our capacities in the universe. We were not an earth-bound species.

Ever since experiencing the hunger for the first time, I expected something "new." Evolutionary thought affirmed this expectation. Quantum leaps are traditional. The evolutionary spiral - from the origin of the universe to the creation of earth, life, animals and humans - is factual evidence that new forms emerge out of the old. This awareness confirmed my early perception that more of the same would not suffice. The tradition of nature was transformation. Holism, or the tendency to form whole systems, was inherent in the nature of reality.

I did not know how to participate in the quantum leap from divided humans to humanity, from earth-bound to universal, but I knew it was happening. Having experienced the instants of joy, the oneness with all humanity and the universe, I sensed that the physical step into space was a natural aspect of the quantum leap.

Joy is becoming my compass.

The joy I felt at the lift-off of John Glenn was irresistible. All during the dark days of meaninglessness, I had unknowingly followed the flickering light of joy, in faith that it was real.

The combination of the discovery of the evolutionary mode of thought, the portent inherent in John Glenn's flight, and the overwhelming dead-endedness of our contemporary life in the arts and in philosophy deepened my sense of vocation. When I recognized there was something I could do for others that I needed to do for myself, I began to grow. This was the evolutionary connection, the link between our own evolution and the evolution of the social body as a whole. The dichotomy between selfish and selfless was transcended. I was "self-actualizing," and it felt good. I began to be happy, awakening with that leap of expectation. My behavior was not idealistic; it was self-fulfilling.

This was an important revelation. It negated the existentialist view that "I am sufficient unto myself," that by self-affirmation and self-service, I could be a moral and useful being. That does not work. The self cannot affirm itself; it has to realize itself through the affirmation of its connectedness with others and with the All. For me, vocation was the connection with others and with the All. I experienced psychologically the All as the evolutionary process. For me, it was not a theory. Where I had "failed" at traditional religion and at existentialism, I began to "succeed" at evolutionary action.

I have found a vantage point from which to direct my life, to view the course of history and therein my own. I took a reading of history that made the future a contingency not an inevitability, and myself a formative part of a formative process. This is making all the difference for me.

With this excitement, I started writing letters to everyone I could think of to ask them to dramatize the evolutionary idea, or to lecture at the Poetry Center. People began saying yes. I invited directors, TV stars, actors, and heads of foundations to lunch. Much to my delight, they came.

Then during one of our long dialogues, Earl said, "Barbara, everything you're doing takes you away from me. Every idea I suggest works for you, but not for me. You're the joy of my life, but you're moving away from me. I can't stand it. I'm the genius, not you. Your main function is to love me."

"Earl, I do. But somehow I must find the way to work that helps us both. I'll die if I suppress my desire to do something on my own."

So I continued. One of the people I contacted to dramatize the evolutionary ideas was Jacob Bronowski, who had written an excellent survey of ideas: *The History of the Western Intellectual Tradition.* I wrote to him asking him to compose a dramatic script on the "dialogue between the possibilists and impossibilists" throughout history, concluding with a basis for modern hope. To my delight he wrote back immediately that he was interested and would stop in New York on his way from England to California.

When he came to visit in the spring of 1964, the family had returned to Connecticut; our apartment was being sold; I was alone.

I had been memorizing my points to convince him all morning: erudite quotes from Pericles, Seneca, St. Paul, Erasmus, Luther, and the like. I was very excited. He was a brilliant man. If he could dramatize the voices of hope, people would see and everything would change!

I was naive, not realizing the weight of fatalism and pessimism in which our age was floundering. I overestimated the rapidity with which change could occur; it was so alive in me I thought the minute someone else saw it, the whole world would see it and everything would change the next day.

When I opened the door I saw a small, witty, highly intelligent man. Instantly I felt shy. Here I was, all by myself in a large apartment in New York.

"My dear, I expected a rather dotty, sixty-year-old dowager, instead I find you!" he said with a debonair smile.

At this time I was thirty-four. I realized I could use charm for my purposes, not his, and my purpose was to get him to write the script. This was my first encounter with someone who was involved in the evolutionary life to some degree. He was a man of brilliance and ego. He wanted to conquer everything and everyone in sight.

But he agreed to do the script, with very little quoting from me. All I remember saying was: "Dr. Bronowski, I think the development of humanity is threatened; we must come to the defense." The rest of the conversation was me listening to him. Before he left he told me he was on his way to the Salk Institute.

"What's that?" I asked.

"This place Jonas Salk is starting..."

"The Jonas Salk?"

"Yes. You see, we all know something new has to occur, a new basis for values. I'm going out there to do this for him. It will be a place to study the whole human, from the cell to the self-image we create in the arts. We are going to put a scientific basis under human values. Through learning how nature works, we're trying to learn more about how human society works."

This interested me immensely - a new basis for values! I had not found it in current religion; I had not found it in secular society; I had begun to find it in evolutionary thought but there was no cluster of people to work with. I felt alone in the bowels of "realism" in New York, always one out of hundreds, always losing. Finding and working with Bronowski, someone who related to the evolution of humanity, was tremendously important to me. I had been looking for an "evolutionary cluster" my whole life. When he said Jonas Salk was creating an institute where people will gather...*people*! Human beings together! In touch with each other to do this work! I immediately wanted to go, too. I became more interested in this than Bronowski's script. I said I wanted to know everything about the Salk Institute.

Bronowski sent Gerry Piel, publisher of the *Scientific American*, to see me. He was forming a society for the institute. It was to be made up of laymen who wanted to discuss how to use science to create a humane future. I offered to help him.

"Gerry," I said, "the Salk Institute should create a 'Theatre of Humanity' to dramatize emerging values based on our knowledge of the evolution of life. We're becoming responsible for our own evolution. Without a sense of the past and a direction for the future, no one will know what to do."

He asked me to write all this down. I had been "writing all this down" in my journal for years. This was the first group of people I had ever met who were interested in anything I had to say. My joy was overflowing. As I rode home on the train, I let my mind relax, gazing at the summer earth, the woolly sheep adrift among the flowers, the cows standing still, almost rooted to the ground. My eyes filled with tears. 'Oh, earth,' I thought. 'Oh, growing things, I'm one of you now. I'm home at last. Joy is the best compass. It alone can point the way to go.'

When I returned to Lakeville I went to my "thinking tree," where I had sat, day after day, year after year, looking at the clouds and the mountains, seeking a single sign of meaning. I wrote this letter to the Salk Institute:

"I realize after my brief association with a few people from the Salk Institute that its approach creates an atmosphere of hope and possibility, which is extremely precious in our society. It is the leaven that can raise the loaf....

"As the *New York Times* quoted President Johnson this morning: 'The most prosperous, the best housed, the best fed, the best read, the most intelligent, and the most secure generation in our history, is discontent. The reason? In our national character, one trait runs unbroken. That is the trait of putting the resources at hand to the fullest use, to make life better tomorrow for those who follow.'

"I believe the president is right. We are imprisoned by unused or misused resources....

"Most problems facing humankind today are profound, so general as almost to escape definition. Yet people active in public life are confined by circumstances to cope with symptoms. There should be meetings, 'evolutionary clusters' as Margaret Mead calls them, where leaders of society can meet with scientists to confront the maze of problems with general, unifying solutions, the only kind that are practical today. Everyone knows, for example, you can't solve the problems of cities by more police, more parking lots, more social workers; or the problems of a life of leisure with more hobbies.

"Concerning a possible Theatre of Humanity: I believe that the long-range purpose of such a Theatre should be to dramatize the new concept of humanity which is emerging. This concept is based upon new knowledge of humans and their evolution in our age. Let us begin a Theatre of Humanity."

Later I visited the Salk Institute offices in New York. A secretary informed me that Dr. Salk had seen the letter and had read it on the way to the airport one day when he was in New York. The man who had shown it to him was in the office.

"What did Dr. Salk think of it?" I asked.

The man smiled and replied, "He took off as though he had found a kindred spirit."

"He has," I said.

*Something is happening
and it's not just happening to me.*

I was sitting at the pool in Lakeville in the sublime beauty of a hot September afternoon in 1964. The trees were dry and beginning to flame and die; the lawns simmered with visible heat waves. The cutting garden was wild with marigolds and chrysanthemums, the flowers falling all over each other in abundance. I basked in the beauty, my whole body alive with a deep expectancy. The children were splashing in the water.

It was a time when Suzanne, blond and olive-skinned, and Stephanie, fair and dark-haired, at thirteen and eleven, were passionately in love with horses, which were grazing in the field beyond the pool. Alexandra at seven and Wade at five, on the other hand, were in the snake and salamander phase. Baby snakes were found in bedroom slippers; white mice scurried through the house to escape being fed to the snakes by Alex, to "keep the balance of nature," as she told me. (I secretly helped the mice in their desperate desire not to serve nature quite in that way.) Lloyd was barely two. He had learned to walk with great caution. Whenever I caught him walking alone, he quickly sat down and pretended not to have done it. He apparently did not want to be held accountable for giving up crawling before he fully understood walking.

The poolside phone rang. I picked it up and heard a voice at the other end saying, "This is Jonas Salk. Is Barbara Hubbard there?"

"Yes! She is. I'm she!"

His voice was deep, resonating, laughing, lively. "I loved your letter. It was great."

"Did you really?"

"I could have written it myself, but you did it better. It's amazing. I guess you're another one who's been bitten by this desire."

"Yes, I am."

"I would like to take you to lunch. I'll be staying with Warren Weaver in New Milford next week. I could drive by and pick you up, and we could go on to New York together."

For the next week I lived at a height of expectancy that dominated every thought. I couldn't sleep or think of anything else. The morning of his arrival I watched my clock crawl minute by minute. I was amazed to feel this way about someone I had never met, but I knew with certainty that something was about to happen.

By now the New England fall was in full glory. The trees were orange, red, gold, purple; the grass was glimmering emerald; the foothills of the Berkshire mountains were blue; the sky was white with heat. The smell of cut grass and flowers, the caw of the sleek black crow, everything was ineffably beautiful.

He rang the bell, I ran downstairs and opened the door. His eyes had an instant warmth; his smile was radiant and magnetic.

He looked around the property. "This looks like the Garden of Eden. It's just like paradise here," he said.

"It is, it really is." I nodded, thinking how the beauty practically drove me out of my mind until I found something of my own to do.

We got into his rented car. Warren Weaver, chairman of the board of the Salk Institute, a distinguished, elderly man, was in the back, Jonas and I in front.

I did not think of it then, but going out to lunch with him was Eve stepping toward the Tree of Life. When Jonas said this is the Garden of Eden, and I said, yes, and joyfully followed him out the door, I was moving closer, taking a step toward the humble and obedient, not disobedient, eating of the fruit of the Tree of Life. It meant learning how to become a conscious participant in the designing process of life, discovering the laws of the universe, lovingly and with humility, and learning to cooperate with "the gods" in the process of evolution.

I stared at Jonas, my facial muscles lifted into a childish smile like those half moons children draw. "Jonas, do you believe Teilhard was right about humankind uniting into one body, a new organism progressing toward an unknown future?"

Again that radiant smile. "Yes, of course, that's natural."

He magnetized my being, as though he were a momentary personification of that great, invisible, mysterious "magnet" that had pulled at my solar plexus as a girl. I felt the attracting power. He embodied evolution, the biologist who studies how creation works: life, the cell, the gene, the building code of our minds and bodies, were his objects of interest. He had touched the branches of the Tree of Life. He yearned to know the processes of life in order to work with them consciously, to help guide human society toward its next step.

We let Warren Weaver off somewhere and were alone in the car. As the inner voice had raged in anger when something was dying, it now burst with joy that something new in me was living. I trusted it implicitly. I was so happy. I cried in the car, blowing my nose and pretending to have hay fever.

He took me to lunch at the Carlyle Hotel, where he usually stayed. We sat at a small table in the corner of the elegant gold and white dining room. I told him, "Jonas, I want to help bring forth in the arts a new image of humanity commensurate with our capacity to shape the future."

"Barbara," he said, "You and I are scooped out of the same genetic material."

"Oh, yes, that's true. Maybe that explains how I know I have known you forever."

"We're psychological mutants," he said. "Every now and then

evolution produces precisely the right type of person for the needs of the time. You're such a person: a bearer of evolution. It's all in you. You've got the script inside, the attraction for the future, the desire to be responsible for the whole, your willingness to learn, to connect separate disciplines and people. You're a bi-valent bonding mechanism. You've got hooks at both ends!"

I laughed. "Thanks for the compliment!"

He told me about his own strange journey. The great victory of the Salk polio vaccine, the birth of an international folk hero, the antagonism of the scientific community, and then, his dream: a new, beautiful place for the biological sciences to share the wisdom of life with all other fields, to build a new philosophy for the age. He bowed his head wearily. "You can't believe what I've suffered. They kill you when you try to do something new."

"You are not alone," I said.

"I know, but how few. Over a quarter of a century of looking and I've only found a handful. I'll introduce you to them."

"And I'll help you find more. Together we'll do it. You remember that beautiful phrase in the Bible, 'Wherever two or more are gathered in my name, there I am,'" I said. He nodded his agreement.

When I left him that afternoon I was filled with joy. We had vowed to work together. Unformed plans flooded through my mind. As in the past, I was ready to trust my intuition.

I am unable to refrain from being exuberant and euphoric, unable not to expect the vital sense of the future that's in me and Jonas to light a flame in every heart we meet, kindling in them the thrill that I feel, of being poised at the brink of a new development in humanity. Separate members, individuals, have longed since time immemorial for union, We can now join in a new organization. Everywhere we look is chaos: from the Republican party to New York City to the Communist empire to the old ideal of the individual in isolated freedom. (Freedom does not lie in getting away but in getting together.)

My life is in upheaval as though from the depths of my being a new mountain range were heaving itself up. It's really not "I" that is acting self-consciously, in that painful way I used to, hearing my own voice in my ears, watching myself act aimlessly, like a private and continual Italian film.

I included Earl in these new and exciting events. My work with

Jonas accelerated my desire to help Earl express his new images. My loyalty and love for my husband deepened now that I felt affirmed in the essence of my being as an individual.

To be needed for the action I had already chosen to undertake gave me for the first time in my life a sense of personal identity. The identity problem was over from that day onward. I knew who I was: a member of the human species and planet earth learning to evolve consciously, becoming aware that we are now able to change and therefore take some responsibility for the direction of change.

I wrote in my journal the Christmas of 1964, sixteen years after the miserable entry of 1948:

> *This Christmas of 1964 is the best of my life, not because I've achieved my ideals, but because the problem of identity has disappeared. I can never again say as I once did, "in my own eyes I'm nothing," for, as all people are, I, too, am the inheritor of the evolution of the ages. In my genes are the generations. Every cell in my body identifies me with the great and terrible adventure of inanimate to animate to human and every desire of my being sets me passionately to work to further the rise of humaneness out of humanity. I am what was and what will be. If I am nothing, life is nothing; that it cannot be - and be.*

I received a call from one of Jonas' friends, another "scoop" of the same genetic material, Al Rosenfeld, science editor of *LIFE* magazine. We immediately began a discussion as if we had known each other all our lives - that strange phenomenon of recognition. Over the phone I had pasted Teilhard's description of homo progressivus because it inspired me. I read to Al from the quote.

"Al, I'm going to read you a description that sounds like us. Teilhard is describing a new type of person, one who experiences this evolutionary pulse. He says, 'This type of person is new because its only been two hundred years that even the notion of organic evolution of the world in time had any reality in the human mind. This new human type will be found to be scattered more or less all over the thinking face of the globe. Some apparent attraction draws these scattered elements together and causes them to unite. You have only to take two people, in a gathering, endowed with this mysterious sense of the future. They will gravitate instinctively towards one another; they will know one another....No racial or social barrier seems to be effective against this force of attraction....'"

He laughed. "I know. I've had the feeling."

"Al, you know Jonas wanted us to meet, to link together somehow. What do you think is the purpose of the Salk Institute?"

"I don't know, Barbara, but I think about it all the time. I think the social seas are now comparable to the chemical seas on the early earth," he said. "They're getting 'hot.' We're disorganized. New social clusters are going to form and self-replicate, just like the first cells did. The Salk Institute might be one of those early social clusters of different kinds of people to make a new social whole."

I became a conscious evolutionary, and I began to reach out to others in whom this flame burned. Sometimes I imagined what it would feel like to be a daffodil coming up in spring, pushing your way through rocky soil and frosted ground, pressing your little green shoot up into the light. Onward, all alone, not knowing where you are going, then suddenly developing a blossom, looking around, and discovering thousands of daffodils in bloom, all nodding in surprise.

Jonas invited me to visit the Salk Institute as soon as I could. I accepted his invitation for the end of January, and began, at the same time, to work on a new kind of book for Earl. I told him that his images and ideas belonged together and should be juxtaposed in a sort of documentary book of all his paintings. I typed every idea of his I had written in my journal to make the beginning of an evolutionary text. I announced to Earl that I would take it to the Salk Institute where Jerry Hardy, the publisher of *LIFE*, and Al Rosenfeld would be meeting during January. Even though Earl was deeply hurt that I wanted to go, he could not help but be fascinated as I pieced together his work in a new synthesis. I believed that Earl's genius was the source of my own. As I became activated, my admiration and love for him was strengthened.

The trip was discouraging. Jonas was preoccupied, burdened with a thousand details of setting up a new organization. I wanted to work for the Salk Institute, but it wasn't even finished. It stood on a beautiful Greek-like promontory overlooking the Pacific in the dry, clean air, an organic structure designed by Louis Kahn, rising like a new temple to the emerging capacities of humanity.

Jonas wanted to bring the finest molecular biologists from the world to the institute to do research into the basic knowledge of life; then the humanists and the artists were to follow. But he had not finished the buildings, and already I was designing the first play on the stage of the Theatre of Humanity. I was ahead of what could be done. Furthermore, many of the outstanding molecular biologists were not evolutionary personalities. They were scientists concerned with a specific aspect of nature, exclusive in their interest. Not only were the molecular biologists in general not entranced by evolutionary philosophy, many believed it was unscientific. They subscribed to the view that there is no predictable progressive patterning process in the universe, no intelligent energy at the core of the designing system, no increase of information, consciousness, and order to counteract the increase of entropy and disorder, the physical death of the universe.

Evolutionaries believe that there is an innate pattern and tendency in evolution toward higher consciousness and greater freedom through more harmonious union. By loving all people as members of one body, recognizing the oneness of humankind and our earth, humanity will be able to gain an understanding of how our planetary system works, care for all our members, coordinate our functions as one body of almost infinite diversity, limit destructive growth, and move toward the next phase of human development.

At a party at Jonas' home in La Jolla in January 1965, during my first visit to this "hallowed ground," I was distressed by the attitude of some of the biologists. One even claimed that "as a scientist" he could not say Hitler was wrong because science does not enter the field of subjective values.

"It's objective, value free," he said.

"Can you go so far as to admit that as a scientist you must be an advocate of life?" I asked.

His answer was, "As a scientist, no; as a man, yes."

Others had a revulsion against the idea of individuals becoming responsible for the evolutionary process, particularly themselves. They were changing all life by discovering how the cell works, giving the power to control life to society. This responsibility was a burden.

I understood their reluctance. Many nuclear physicists had entered the age of responsibility with the explosion of the nuclear bomb. Now it was the biologists' turn. Soon, in fact, we all would have to realize that the essence of evolution is that every act affects the future. Jonas knew this, of course, but not all his scientific colleagues did. In fact, they resisted it on principle.

In my effort to build an evolutionary philosophy to counteract the value-free objectivity of some scientists, I read Lancelot Law Whyte's *The Next Development in Man*, and found it to be a great work. It described the fact that the formative processes of nature were at work in us and we were part of that formative process. This deeply verified my intuition that I was part of the process.

I wrote him, congratulated him on his genius, and asked if he would come to the Poetry Center to speak about where we are now in evolution. He accepted. Our first meeting was overwhelming, the same magnetic attraction that I had felt with Jonas and Al. Lance was sixty-eight, an integrative personality born in a disintegrating society. I returned from New York with a link forged forever between Lance and me.

I remember one particular conversation with Lancelot. We were sitting in the Edwardian room at the Plaza Hotel on a beautiful May day, looking over Central Park. "Barbara," he asked, "how in the world did this happen to you, your sense of your role? Very few women have had such vast opportunity. If you don't squander your energy, and if you have good judgment of people, why, my dear, it staggers me to think of what you may accomplish. How did this happen? You're not just 'facilitating' anything, not just doing good like so many others; you've selected this unifying, organic role. How did you find it? Who influenced you the most?"

"My husband," I answered. "He made me aware that humans have changed and that a new image is needed, that we are responsible as artists for building the image." It did not occur to me that I had any genius of my own. "But," I told him, "I think I became emotionally involved when I felt humanity was being attacked, and I had to do what I could to help. You see, as a child, I took it for granted everyone was for humanity, for life."

"But that's not true," he murmured. His face was so surprisingly unromantic, yet his eyes so lit with love. It was love for the desire in me. My desire and his were identical, we fused our deepest intentions for the emergence of a loving world.

The same flame of expectation burned in each of us and it got hotter as we got closer. We had a common cause: to spread the awareness that each person was potentially totally alive and growing within the whole universal process. Not only did we empathize with each other, but we loved the world and wanted to work together for the world. We pledged our lives to our common dream.

I was being transformed by these new relationships. I tried to make Lance believe that all these ideas were Earl's. He totally rejected this assertion. I wanted him to love and admire Earl, too, but he wasn't interested. And I pleaded with Earl to read Lance's books and to become his friend. But it did not happen.

My growth seemed to be separating me from my husband, yet my joy was overflowing. The very fire of life lifted me beyond my former role of wife and mother.

> *If I were to die tomorrow I have had enough of heaven on earth to last me forever. To have been completely engaged in the process of life, even for six months as I have, is to have tasted nectar and ambrosia. I haven't "succeeded." I have grown. The anxiety that gnawed away at me has been replaced by the fullness of love and joy. How? By relating to people for a purpose - or rather, relating to people by means of a shared purpose.*
>
> *Robert Frost said, "My life was a risk - and I took it." Thank God, I did, too. It now feels natural to do something totally beyond my capability.*

During that wonderful fall of 1964 I appeared on a television program, "Open Mind," to discuss "the arts and the foundations" with Huntington Hartford, the wealthy heir to the A&P stores, who had built a beautiful museum at Columbus Circle in New York: the Gallery of Modern Art. His purpose was to present art that was affirmed meaning, beauty, dignity. He did not like abstract expressionism, nor the other versions of modern art promoted by the Museum of Modern Art and most of the chic galleries. McNeill Lowery, then head of the Ford Foundation's arts and humanities grants program, was another participant.

I suddenly cared about my appearance. I splurged on a beautiful Balenciaga dress and had my hair done for the show. Earl walked me to the studio. My heart was pounding with hope. I wanted desperately to do something for Earl, to help him come into his own. We were seated around a table, the lights glaring. In stature I was like a gnat beside an elephant, the large foundation executives and me. But because of this evolutionary fervor, I started making mighty pronouncements: "The Deerfield Foundation will never fund an artist whose work asserts the irremediable evil of humanity!"

McNeill Lowery, whom I mistakenly kept calling "Mr. Ford," turned to me in anger. "Are you trying to play God, Mrs. Hubbard? Who are you to judge whether an artist's personal philosophy is right or wrong?"

I said, "I honestly believe it is my responsibility to discern what is constructive or destructive. If I were the only foundation in the world, or as big as yours, Mr. Ford, I might not have this problem, but being as small as I am, if I didn't discern I would be reneging on my responsibilities as a human being. I consider it wrong to persuade people that life is hopeless. Therefore, the Deerfield Foundation will *not* fund anything except that which can affirm life, Mr. Ford."

"My name is *not* Mr. Ford."

"Well, it might as well be," I said. Lowery is one of the "cultural valets," a high-level professional servant, hired by the very wealthy to disperse funds "objectively," with no personal involvement. They tended to resent genuine evolutionary motivation, maybe because it involved one totally. "If your criterion is not whether a person is constructive or destructive, what is it?"

"Talent," he said.

"Well, now, talent is for something. What if you're good at killing? What if you're creating images that make people feel insane, despairing? You can be very talented at that. I think it verges on the criminal to support it. I would not suppress it, but to support it borders on being diseased yourself."

After the program, no one said anything to me. I left thinking I had failed, downhearted.

The broadcast was aired weeks later, the Sunday before Christmas. Earl, the children, and I were sitting in my little study before our TV set. I was amazed to see myself on television. I really liked it and kept nodding my head in agreement with what I was saying, as though I were another person.

The minute the show went off the air, the phone rang in the study. "This is Huntington Hartford." His distinctive, aristocratic voice startled me. "Mrs. Hubbard, I liked what you said on the program. Would you serve on the advisory board of my museum?"

I could barely keep my voice from breaking with excitement. "Yes, I would be delighted. Your museum is the one place in New York built to show a new kind of art. Who else is on the board?"

"General Eisenhower, Salvadore Dali, and now, you."

I laughed. "Oh, no! What a combination!" I thanked him and said goodbye. He told me the museum's director, Carl Weinhardt, would be in touch with me soon. It was what I had longed for.

I turned to Earl, smiling. "Well, darling, we now have a museum!"

Coincidentally, at that time the children had blossomed into artists. This began the second phase of motherhood for me, which was much more natural than organic motherhood. My children, stimulated by our efforts, began to create artistic representations of the evolutionary way of being. My excitement stimulated them. For all the anxiety I may have caused them as I spread my wings in the world, I also provided an example of a woman, then thirty-five, continuing to grow. They knew from my example that there never need be an end to creativity.

Earl and I began to consider what a museum dedicated to the new challenges might do. Of course, we wanted to have an exhibition of his work, also a "TV documentary arts center." The real goal, though, was to create a "museum of the future of humanity" to show the evolution of forms from atoms, cells, animals, humans, and cities, to the new bodies science is building, our human extensions: the rockets, the bulldozers, the microscopes, the telescopes, etc. We wanted to develop the Theatre of Humanity at the lovely theatre in the museum. We talked for days, listing ideas.

The first step was to put together an exhibition of Earl's paintings. I decided to redo the documentary book as an exhibition. There should be words next to each painting, an excerpt of the text to dramatize an idea the painting seemed to symbolize. We realized there was no text for the modern age, no body of writings commonly accepted to represent our view of the nature of reality, no story to symbolize our struggles. Nor was there an acceptable image. There had to be a new image, and a new story.

Earl began to develop one such image. First, he gradually eliminated the body, because the body of man/woman no longer is in our own skin, but rather is enlarged through our extensions, our machines, that with which we move and fight and plant and build. These were the instruments of action, not the physical body alone. We saw the personal body as becoming even more "the house of thought." The mind was becoming increasingly important as the creator of the instrument of action, and as the center of values, and intuitive connection with the larger processes.

As the body was disappearing in his paintings, the background was opening out toward the universe, as we had seen during the flight of John Glenn. The background became black, the color of the universe, with the emphasis on the face, the color of starlight, a synthesis of all colors; it represented individual awareness.

"From the new perspective of space," Earl said, "humans become humankind: one body on earth, alone, reaching out to make contact with another living planetary body; just as we now hopefully seek voices other than our own, intelligent signals from outer space. We'll grow together as we reach out together for new life in the universe. Going out into the strangeness of the universe will make our earth 'home' and all people brothers and sisters."

After several months of work, and private meetings with Carl Weinhardt, I set up a meeting between him and Earl. Earl's rendezvous with destiny was arranged. At lunch Carl offered him a one-man show at the Gallery of Modern Art during the best season of the year, November 18 to December 18, 1965. Then, miracle of miracles, he went on to say the gallery would be proud to publish Earl's book as a catalog. The next day I was playing around with the title. I looked at the phrase "The challenge of freedom."

At cocktails, I asked Earl, "What do you think of *The Challenge of Freedom* as a title?"

He nodded. "It's true; the challenge is freedom."

"That's it! That's the title," I cried. "That's what your book is saying, that's what your work means. We have the power; we're free to shape our destiny. We have to wake up to our new capacities. That's up to the artist, the architect of the image of humanity!"

I redid the book of paintings and ideas. When I read it to Earl, he said, "Barbara, it's even a challenge to me. You've made this whole thing possible. I just don't know how to tell you how much I admire what you've done."

We planned to hang the paintings in the large exhibition room with printed quotes next to each painting, such as "The concern of humanity is the future of humankind. We can build for no other time. The meaning of every act lies in its effect upon the future...."

As the day of the opening approached, Carl, who had been very helpful to us, became increasingly nervous and ill. Huntington Hartford was an unreliable head of a museum. His ideas were excellent, but he did not live them in his personal life. Occasionally, I had to call on him in his lush apartment at Beekman Place. Late in the morning he would still be in his bathrobe, his face unshaven, his eyes sunken, eating corn flakes, with one phone nestled by each ear. Sometimes he would keep me waiting for hours while he took call after call. Once I simply got up and said I would never speak to him again until he unplugged the phones. He did. But it was painful, they were like his defense system against having to concentrate directly on a person. He withheld funds from Carl and often turned functions over arbitrarily to unknown people. It really was a tragedy that a man with so much vision had succumbed to an undisciplined, disorderly life.

As Earl prepared the paintings, I sent out news releases, wrote the invitations, put together a mailing list, with no help from the museum. It was a real amateur effort. The next day the art critics came. They could make or break an exhibition with the stroke of a pen. We were not permitted to meet or talk with them. I felt like the Flying Wallendas on a tight rope above an abyss. We were on a high wire of life or death. At the opening that evening, quite a few people came, including my father, brother and sisters.

Saturday night before the reviews were to come out in Sunday's *New York Times*, I was sitting alone in my Lakeville study, writing in my journal. Earl was asleep. The phone rang; it was our friend Warren Steibel in New York, who had gotten me on "Open Mind."

"Barbara," he said, "I have very bad news. John Canaday's review is terrible." He read me one of the most vicious, humiliating pieces I have ever heard.

Canaday said it was ridiculous to assert that humans were becoming responsible for their own evolution; the paintings did not communicate the ideas; the words were presumptuous; the philosophy stupid; and the show a disaster for the Gallery of Modern Art. We had entered the jaws of the enemy. We were on their territory and they killed us. Rage engulfed me. Canaday clearly had murdered us in the art world.

After a few days in the museum, talking with the people, not the critics, I began to feel differently. Although the effect of this blow was at first shocking, eventually it was liberating. Walking through the forest of life, we found that one path had been momentarily closed off to us: the current art world. This negation was complemented by a new path, a positive one which was being opened to us: the way of the morally and spiritually motivated.

A group of nuns came to the museum to see the exhibition. One said, "These ideas are so much like Christianity." She pointed out that Christians speak of the body of Christ. "Every person is either part of that body or potentially a part. It's so much like what you call the body of humankind."

I had noticed this before. Earl used the body image continually. He spoke of the awareness of our position as humankind in space, locking his fingers to symbolize us merging together into one body.

After that, surprising things began to happen. We had looked to the scientific and intellectual worlds for sanction, but the people who responded were from the Church. I'd had no contact with organized religious groups since I left the Episcopal church in Scarsdale so it was only through the exhibition that we discovered there was a new reformation stirring in the Church, an awareness of a deep sense of responsibility for the future. They had gone through radical theology, the death of God, the "secular city"; they had discarded past images of God. Some believed God was calling upon humans to mature and live the Christian life through rebuilding this world.

We discovered among some clergymen a profound search for a renewal of the story of Christ. What does it mean that Christ was born? What does it mean to be a Christian? There were few answers coming out of the Church; but of all the institutions of our society, they seemed at that time to be willing to ask the great questions as a matter of life and death. I was astonished at their openness.

We met Dr. Gerald Jud, director of the Division of Evangelism of the United Church of Christ. He came into the exhibition and immediately invited us to a Belief Crisis Conference. We all met in Hillsboro, New Hampshire, the summer of 1966. The conference was held in a camp-like retreat.

The first night at dinner a man turned to Earl: "Can you imagine, this group represents the leadership of the United Church of Christ. Most of us have two or three degrees; we've been to the seminary; we have big churches; and we don't know what we believe. Why, if you knew as little about your work as an artist as we know about ours, imagine where you would be!"

In my working group two ministers called themselves cynics, and the other two felt at a loss to define themselves at all. The most active ministers were in the streets, looking to Robert Kennedy and Martin Luther King as leaders.

The depth of the upheaval is profound. The earth upon which these men so firmly stood as ministers has slowly buckled up. A new mountain has arisen. They stand at the foot of it, ready to climb, but unprepared.

The depression deepened, but curiously, surrounded by these openly seeking Christians, I felt my faith deepen too. I told them that Bishop John Robinson wrote in *Honest to God* that whenever he watched TV debates between a Christian and a humanist, he found himself siding with the humanists. "Well," I said, "I find myself in the opposite position from the bishop. As a humanist, I discover myself siding with the Christian, because in Christianity there's a vision of the future in all its newness, and the humanists have only utopias that would bore us to death, literally, the day after we achieved them."

I asked the ministers about transcendence, about immortality and the resurrection of Christ, what that meant in relationship to leaving the planet alive through the space program and learning how to change our bodies through understanding the DNA, the genetic code. Almost no one had thought of these questions. I answered them myself.

"As an evolutionary being, I love Christ," I said. "He embodies the new humanity. He did not try to reform this world. He transformed himself into the next stage of humanity: an ever-evolving being with full mastery over the material world through love of God and knowledge of himself. He told us we could do the works that he did. We can. We can be a universal species. That's our destiny, and that's the only real solution to our problems on this earth...."

This hypothesis hung in the air, past the grasp of the ministers.

Gerry Jud told me I was "the beyond in their midst." He said he had a few free pulpits and if I should want one, to let him know!

> I believe, as they do, that there's an intention of creation. Evolution isn't utterly random. There's a formative pattern in the process to be discovered, a pattern which humans didn't choose, but that we're free to express to the extent we're aware of it. This intention, this formative force, which might be called the direction of evolution, is the transcendent in our midst. It's in us as well as everything else. It's "God's will."

Although the Church was more responsive than other institutions, it was not our ground. We were always invited guests and had nowhere to stay. We did not intend to become Christians in the traditional sense. We were not about to form a new church. We were outsiders to every institution. I realized institutions were not set up to carry forth this kind of discussion or action for the future, and I could see the Salk Institute was by no means ready for the Theatre of Humanity. Science, at its very best, of which Jonas was a prime example, would take some time before it would welcome this dialogue into its bosom.

No one path seemed sufficiently strong; some synthesis was needed. After the exhibition I scanned the horizon to see which step to take, which direction to go. I entered a period of taking long walks alone every day after lunch and putting a question to the evolutionary process, or to myself, or to a force that was beyond me. I can't say exactly who I was putting the question to, but it was always the same question: What is the next step?

I asked myself the question and began to take walks around the top of Wells Hill, where I would fall into a state of total contemplation or meditation, entranced by the beauty of nature, unconscious of myself as I was walking around the path. It was as though I was on an auto-control system of some kind because I wasn't self-conscious and I had no sense of the passage of time. By the time I would complete the circle on the hill, I would have an answer to the question. Sometimes it was a simple answer; other times it was an amazing response that would shape my whole life.

I was suffering because of my desire to build the Salk Institute and my recognition that it was impossible. My emotions, stimulated by the spiritual hunger, sensing nourishment, almost drove me out of my mind. To maintain my balance I had a dialogue with those wild uncontrollable horses of desire, day after day: "I'll try to fulfill you. I know you're aiming for a deep satisfaction, but if I follow you, you'll destroy us both." I really felt there were two voices: my emotions and my self.

Then I had a remarkable dream. I dreamed I was in bed when I smelled smoke coming from downstairs. I got up and went to the living room. Flames flickered up between the floor and the wall. I rushed to get the fire extinguisher and put the flames out. But I heard the seething crackle of a conflagration beneath me and realized that the flames I had extinguished were but the top-most part of a bonfire in the cellar.

I went to the cellar and my fears were confirmed by a blast of violent heat and fire. I rushed upstairs to awaken Earl to tell him to put out the fire. "Hurry, before the flames reach the oil tank and destroy the house. Hurry!" But he was very calm and reassured me that it wasn't possible because the oil tank was not in the cellar. I was afraid, and rushed to get the children out of the house while he went down to the cellar. Then I went back for the paintings and my journals, and finally down to the cellar with another fire extinguisher.

By that time Earl and John, our gardener, had put the fire out. Both were resting on the damp earthen floor (which our cellar in Lakeville did not have). The cellar had become a primitive dirt floor place, like the cellar at Lazy Day Farm where I spent my happy childhood summers.

My relief was immense. But then the fire brigade arrived and started to dig up the earthen floor, saying they had to find the cause of the fire.

In the dream, panic overcame me. I remembered I had accidentally murdered a child, and buried it in the cellar, as deep as I could, so it would never be discovered. The corpse would be unearthed.

I watched, paralyzed with dread, as their shovels dug in the precise spot where I had buried the murdered child. One of the shovels hit something hard. My heart almost stopped beating. Earl said: "Oh, maybe they've found some toys." But I knew what it was. Relentlessly, they dug and uncovered a dark, moldy coffin. One of the men bent down to lift the lid. We looked in and gasped in horror. There lay a corpse seething with worms, a revolting mass of putrefaction.

'Oh, God,' I thought, 'it's not a skeleton yet. They will know it's not an ancient crime. They will know it happened while I lived in this house. They will know I murdered this child.'

Then the writhing mass of worms rose slowly. The worms fell away; the flesh returned; a smooth, rosy-cheeked, brown-haired child smiled, stood, and walked out of the coffin.

'She will tell on me,' I thought. 'She will give me away and incriminate me.'

But no, she smiled gaily and took my hand. I looked at her closely. There was something very familiar about her. I racked my brain to remember, and suddenly I did: I was that child, at the age of twelve, when I had been for the last time until now, fully alive and happy. She did not blame me for what I had done to her. She was simply happy to be free. She joined our family and we walked together, hand in hand.

Once I awoke, I realized that the child that I had murdered was myself, who had been so happy until the age of twelve, when my mother died. "I", the questing, hungry self had destroyed this joyful child. Now that I had rediscovered my joy, she, my child self, arose and joined me as my partner in this fabulous process of growth.

Four

Epiphany

My attraction for an evolutionary life became a living, breathing force within me. I wanted immediate fulfillment. Yet the process was long and complex. I could not find a direct path to gratification. I was always helping someone else: Jonas, Earl, Lance, which I was happy to do. But I was beginning to feel that I could not continue just to help others I considered greater than me.

> *I must rally my own strength now, remembering that everything that rises converges. I must take all the straining tentacles of desire and twine them around each other to make a central pillar of aspiration attractive enough to draw all of myself willingly upward toward a higher union. I must convert desire to aspiration. I must be sublime - sublimated.*

In time I learned to discipline my emotions. I found I could use emotional energy to do my work. Like a spiritual athlete, I trained that wild power to perform precise acts of concentration.

I began to restudy the Gospels, looking for my next step of action. I found one of the qualities of having an evolutionary nature is that I needed to invest my high energy in intense action or I felt I would be blown up by it. I was seeking a way toward total involvement in the world.

I also was moving into a new relationship with my brother and sisters, one that was a little estranged. Louis felt my ambitions were inordinate, crazy! He expressed irritation at my lack of "normal" interests. Jacqueline listened passively, but seemed to make every effort not to be with me. Patricia told me I tried too hard to convince others.

One day in his office Louis chided me: "I know you and Earl are basically right. You want to *do* something about the eight hundred million starving Asians, and all I'm doing is making more money that I don't need. But for Christ's sake, Barbara, give it seventy-five percent of your time. Save twenty-five percent to wonder whether

Aunt Tilly is well and what's the latest movie."

"Louis," I said, "I know I must seem strange. I love you so much. You have been so good to me. But, Aunt Tilly bores me and I don't care about the latest movie. Perhaps there are times for intense effort, when, if you're going to make it at all, every ounce of energy is required. Well, Earl and I are at such a stage. Later we will be able to act in ways more normal to you, maybe." I hugged him, wanting some of his sense of security, well-being, normalcy and success to become part of me, too. Yet, at a deeper level, I felt normal, and others seemed abnormal.

There was no doubt in my mind that my intensity was alienating some just as it was attracting others. I was reaching for a "new normalcy" in which a real sense of relatedness would unite those "tentacles of desire."

One fateful afternoon in February 1966 I was taking my walk. It was a freezing day. The trees stood black and brittle against the winter sky. There was no sign of life anywhere. I wrapped my scarf around my face to protect me from the bitter wind and walked with my head down to avoid the cold.

I had been reading Reinhold Neibuhr on the subject of community. He had quoted St. Paul's famous statement, "All men are members of one body." I was thinking about that idea and feeling a deep nameless frustration in my own body, as though an awareness were poised, flickering just beyond the periphery of my consciousness, attempting to enter my mind. I felt envious of the Gospel writers. They had a simple story to tell. A child was born and from that all the rest followed. Peasants and kings could understand it. Western civilization was built on it. One story!

Unexpectedly, a question burst forth from the depth of my being. I spoke it out loud, almost in anger as though I could not live without knowing the answer. Lifting my voice to the ice white sky, I demanded to know: "What is *our* story? What in our age is comparable to the birth of Christ?"

I lapsed into a day-dream like state, walking without thinking around the top of the hill. Suddenly, my mind's eye penetrated the blue cocoon of earth and lifted me up into the utter blackness of outer space. A technicolor movie turned on.

I felt the earth as a living organism, heaving for breath, struggling to coordinate itself as one body. It was alive! I became a cell in that body. The pain of the whole body was flashing through the mass media, the nervous system of the world.

I felt children starving, soldiers dying, mothers crying, people burning. The agony of our earth was mine. Her polluted waters, her clogged air, her depleted soil, the destruction of her forests, it was all happening to me! She and I were one. There was no other, no outside. We were one body, literally.

Then the movie sped-up. I saw something new. A flash of extraordinary light, more radiant than the sun, gleamed in outer space. Instantly, all of us, collectively, were attracted to the light. We forgot our pain for a moment. We stopped crying and together we saw the light. It caught our attention for one brief instant.

With that moment of shared attention, empathy began to course through our body. Wave upon wave of love flowed through all people. A magnetic field of love aligned us. We were caressed, uplifted in this field of light. Joy began to pulse through our bodies.

We felt light rising from within. Miracles and healing occurred. The blind could see, the lame could walk, the deaf could hear. People flooded out of their houses, offices and buildings, meeting each other in ever-growing gatherings, embracing, singing, loving one another. We sang together in spontaneous harmonies, a planetary choir of voices all singing out loud for the first time. A chanting rhythm beat through the earth, synchronizing our heart beats.

No division of race, color, nation or class held against the pressure of attraction. The ancient human feelings of separation and fear dissolved as waves of love attracted us to each other. Our hearts opened. Our thoughts connected and we experienced the awesome intelligence of ourselves as one living body.

I saw the weapons melt. The air cleared, the waters purified, the land renewed. I could breathe again. Food coursed through the body, reaching all our members. The pain of the earth dissolved. The mass media pulsed with light. As it carried the stories of our transformation, it was transformed.

I saw our rockets rising majestically, penetrating the blue sky of earth, silver slivers of life, reaching beyond our terrestrial home to the place where my mind's eye resided, in the universal dark, carrying the seed of humanity in peace to our cosmic destiny as children of the stars. As the rockets penetrated outer space, the earth coordinated itself as one body. Reaching outward and coordinating our body were one gesture in time. Just as a baby's reach for an object outside its own body helps it coordinate, so our reach into space was speeding up the integration of all our systems on earth. I felt it in my own body.

With each wave of harmony, the glowing light surrounding us intensified. As we coordinated as one, the light became brighter and seemed to fuse with the light within each of us. Each of us was a point of light, growing brighter as we joined. As we connected on earth, millions of distant points of life-like light became visible in the universe, surrounding us. As we harmonized, they became more visible. As we became one, they became real.

We heard a tone, a vibration that oriented us in one direction. The entire human race was magnetized by that sound. We were listening together to hear our first word. The glowing light around our planet seemed to be intelligent, loving, familiar. It was about to speak with us directly. We were straining to understand, yet too immature to fully know the meaning of the sound.

Then I heard these words clearly: "Our story is a birth. It is the birth of humankind as one body. What Christ and all other avatars came to earth to reveal is true. We are one body, born into the universe. Barbara, go tell the story of our birth!"

With those words, billions of us opened our collective eyes and smiled a *planetary smile*! It was like the first smile of a new born baby when her little nervous system finally links up. She opens her eyes, sees her mother and smiles that amazing, radiant smile. Somehow she knows her mother, even though she has never seen her face to face before. As that baby knows her mother, so humankind knows the light. Even though we have never seen it together, each of us in a secret place in our hearts has experienced the light. Now, for the first time, we were seeing it as one through our collective vision. Ecstatic joy rippled through the planetary body.

I was enthralled. I shouted to myself upon the hill, "We are being born. It is true! Our story is a birth! I know it because it is happening to me right now." A sense of overwhelming gratitude filled me.

Then the whole story of our birth unfolded within me. I felt myself tumbling through an evolutionary spiral. With each evolutionary advance, I felt a new turn on the spiral. The creation of the universe, the earth, single-cell life, multi-cellular life, human life, and now us, going around the spiral once again. It all raced before my inner eyes.

First I heard music, a silence more profound than quietness. Then came the awesome thunder of creation. The same tone that had coursed through the planet aligning us at our birth, sounded the note at the beginning of time/space.

I felt the coming together of clouds of hydrogen, bursting into supernova, giant stars fusing within their heart of heat, the materials of our earth, the minerals and metals that make up our bodies now.

I felt myself as a large molecule floating passively in the seas of the early earth, suddenly swept up into a new, more complex pattern of life, a cell. I could see! I could move! I could act! I could replicate myself! We continued dividing to reproduce, semi-immortal creatures who did not die. We consumed the nutrients of the terrestrial seas. We began to pollute, to over-populate, to stagnate. We were reaching a limit to growth, coming to the end of the dominance of single-celled life.

Then I felt us coming together as multi-cellular organisms, joining with one another to face the crisis, fusing into new bodies, transforming from single cells to plants, insects, fish, animals and birds. We invented photosynthesis and built the biosphere; we colonized the once barren earth; we filled every nook and cranny with life. And we learned to die so that our offspring could live on.

Then the first humans appeared. We felt strange in the animal world. We recognized our own death and sought to overcome it. We heard voices of gods, we buried food with our dead, we reached for the stars. Then we humans began to replicate ever more rapidly. We spanned the earth, learned to mimic nature, and to build technological extensions of ourselves until we started to over-populate, to pollute, to deplete the resources of our mother earth. Our current crises appeared. Limits to growth! Don't be fruitful and multiply! Cooperate or die! We began to repattern ourselves, fusing into networks, clusters, new units of social life. We reached beyond ourselves into the seemingly barren environment of outer space to find new life, new resources, new energy, new knowledge, born as a living body, opening our eyes into a universe full of life and light.

Then, as suddenly as it had begun, the technicolor movie of creation stopped. I found myself upon the frosty hill in Lakeville, Connecticut, alone. There was no sign of what had happened. Yet, I knew it had been real. The experience was imprinted forever upon my very cells.

I had found my vocation. I was more than an advocate, I was a story teller! I stood upon the hill and thanked God. The endless hours of asking, searching, reading, praying had been answered. I made my life commitment, "Yes, I shall tell the story of our birth, and when this experience actually happens to all of us, I shall be ready to offer calm and comfort, so that we will not be afraid."

So I proclaimed upon the hill to the forces of creation, to God, who had answered my question so fully, so beautifully, so indelibly. My personal purpose was revealed to me as a vital function in the life of the planet as a whole.

Overwhelmed with excitement, I ran across the top of the hill, past the frozen trees etched against the sky. Tears were streaming down my face, freezing in the bitter cold. Finally my mind had opened to a larger reality. I had heard the inner voice. I had seen with my inner eyes the glory which shall be revealed in us in the fullness of time. I ran home from the hill, arriving at the house with my lungs burning with cold.

How would I tell my family that I was to go out into the world and tell the story of our birth. Suddenly I felt shy. It would surely sound strange to someone who had not experienced it. How would I convey the experience?

Earl was in the studio painting. I wanted to rush in and tell him, but something made me hold back. I was in a vulnerable state. What if he did not understand? So I went alone into the house. The children were still at school. I entered my studio, lit a fire and made a cup of steaming hot tea. I sat before the fire, staring at the flames for hours.

Everything I had ever known, read or thought about was integrated by my cosmic birth experience. It all made sense. We have had a fifteen billion year period of conception, gestation and birth. I saw that we are being born. Our problems are the problems of birth not death. Our situation is dangerous but natural. We must stop growing within the womb, clean up our own wastes, restore our mother, develop renewable resources, coordinate all our members on a planetary scale, and above all else, reconnect in our consciousness, overcoming the deadly illusion that we are separate from each other, from nature or from the patterns of creation.

I saw that one of the major dangers is that we do not know we are being born. Our interpretation of events can engender so much guilt and fear, that we might kill ourselves. Imagine if we were seeing a baby being born for the first time, and did not understand what was happening. We would get hysterical! A new self-image is vital if we are to survive and grow to be a universal species. I felt that if we could get through this dangerous moment of our birth, then we will discover we have the capacity as humankind to feed, house, clothe, restore, educate and begin our life in a universe of immeasurable dimensions.

I sense that if we could all share in this birth experience together, at one moment in time, we would not have to go through the violence which had been foretold in the doomsday predictions. We could have a gentle birth. I felt I had a planetary precognition of the coming fulfillment of the human race. I was motivated to "tell the story" as quickly as possible. I felt there was an organic timing in a planetary birth, as in a biological birth. If we did not know our own story soon, we might suffer from radical birth trauma and be damaged forever.

I remembered my favorite phrase from St. Paul: "Behold, I show you a mystery, we shall not all sleep, but we shall all be changed." Of course we shall all be changed by the coming events. I imagined for a flash what we would actually be like as a planetary species with all our new capacities - personal, social and technological - operating harmoniously, resonating as one being, in love with ourselves as one body. My God! Of course it was glory untold, as the mystics have said for eons of time. The promise was being revealed in us now!

I wondered if all those flashes of UFOs, angels and spirits which people from all cultures have seen through recorded history, were "pre-natal" intimations of the many dimensions of reality. It became clear to me that our maturation is the key to the next stage of awareness. What mystics and saints of all the world religions have experienced and told us about, we would now know collectively and personally. The religions held the promise. Now we would experience the fulfillment. And once we experience this expanded reality together, nothing on earth would ever make us separate again.

As I drank my tea and warmed myself by the fire, I realized that I had experienced what Teilhard de Chardin called "Omega," or the "Christification of the earth." He foresaw that we would all love ourselves as one body. The noosphere would get its collective eyes. St. Paul also had said it, "Now we see through a glass darkly, then we shall see face to face." All this happened to me during the birth experience. 'My God, these prophesies really must be true,' I thought with amazement.

The question I had asked Eisenhower in the White House twenty years before was answered at last. What is the meaning of our power? The meaning of our power is to carry us to the next stage of evolution as universal humanity. It's not adaptation to limits, it's not defense or accommodation or consumption, it is transformation. We shall all be changed! I saw that caring for ourselves and our mother earth is not the end. It is the beginning. In a state of prophetic knowing, I felt sure we would discover that we are not alone in the universe. For the first time I felt a deep, personal longing for real contact with other life.

As the fire turned to embers, I fell in love with the human race. As a mother "forgives" a new born child its "faults," I forgave us our errors and ignorance. I understood all our tragedies. We had suffered from the illusion of separation in the womb of earth; we had felt alone, divided, afraid, but we were being enlightened now. I saw our greatness, our goodness, how it had not yet been revealed to us, but soon would be. And I was to tell this story! My joy was boundless. I knew what I was to do. I would piece together the story of our birth and I would write a book.

That evening I dressed as for a ball. I put on a long robe, played my favorite Frank Sinatra record, "Strangers in the Night," lit the fire and paced the floor as I waited for Earl. How would I tell him? My heart was beating with anticipation and nervousness.

He came in and made himself a drink, looking tanned and handsome after his evening exercises. This was the first time I told the story. I described to him my experience as best I could, trying not to be overexcited, but even speaking of it made the technicolor movie start within me again. As I spoke I became radiant, as the words reignited the living memory of our birth. He nodded yet remained passive. I was disappointed. Yet I felt compassion for him. He used to be the one who got me excited by his ideas. Now, I was excited by my own experience. Perhaps he felt rejected, unneeded. Along with my concern for his possible loss, a deep exhilaration warmed my heart. Something was happening to me that was not dependent on his genius, or any other man's. I was galvanized to take action on my own behalf of my own vocation. That made all the difference.

How do you tell the story of the birth of humankind?

I began to organize all the materials I had developed for *The Challenge Is Freedom*, deciding to index every idea, then piece together the story of the birth of humankind. I would work in dialogue with Earl, thinking of each question as a magnet to draw out from him yet another small but brilliant insight to place it in the dazzling whole. Every morning, after the children went to school, we sat at the breakfast table in deep conversation for hours. It was thrilling, the best times of our marriage for me.

I would question him. He responded with insights; then I again took the initiative in directing further questions, organizing and editing the material, communicating to friends, finding publishers, and, at last, acting upon the vision. He was deeply appreciative of my questions and I of his insights. We had a true, co-creative partnership, a union which was producing something unique and different from either of us as a child is from its parents. This relationship was a genuine fulfillment of our marriage.

I spent the entire summer of 1966 literally on the floor of my study, kneeling over hundreds of pieces of paper, each with a separate idea, since no table in the house was large enough to hold them all at once. I could see the pieces fitting together into one great synthesis of the multiplicity of events occurring today on planet earth. My happiness came from seeing meaning in everything, with the expectation of sharing that meaning and connecting with others through that act of sharing.

I began to read again: cosmology, geology, biology, anthropology, art history, current events, science fiction, sacred texts to piece together the story of our birth and to envision our future as a universal species. Everything fit. All knowledge was part of the *process* of our birth. Our new capacities in science and technology were not meant for an earth-bound humanity, but for a cosmic one.

I saw the destiny of the United States, in cooperation with all other nations, to be an evolutionary goal: to meet the needs of all people, restore the environment of the earth and to free the human race to realize its vast creative potential, on a universal scale.

I've gained access to emotional contact with the body of humankind. I'm in touch. Thinking of those I love throughout the world, at work far away, I feel nourished and energized, even though they aren't in communication with me. The good they do is done to me, and whatever I achieve is theirs.

My oppressive need to be in direct contact with certain people has been fulfilled by the awareness that everything I do touches them. To the extent I achieve the aims of my work, Earl, Jonas, Lance, and all the others, are facilitated. And visa versa.

If we are one body, then, we are one body!

I now had five children to care for. With the discovery of my vocation, I realized I had to have help with my them. My entire passion was directed to action. I felt like a spring that had been compressed for a long time. I had to be free or I would explode.

I put an ad in the *New York Times* for a governess. Within a few days I received a call from Mademoiselle Jacqueline Baldet.

She had a soft melodious French accent. I asked her to come to see me. It was love at first sight. She reminded me of Mary Poppins. She was at ease with the children and had a special sense of humor that enchanted the whole family.

She became a second mother, taking the children on hikes, excursions, day long picnics, things that I did not presently have the patience for. My vocation was not motherhood, while hers was, yet she had no children and I had five! We complemented each other perfectly. She became my friend. We often spoke to one another in French and I often spent hours sharing with her the ideas of the "story of our birth."

Then at night, after she and the family had gone to bed, I would return to the living room, relight the fire, turn on some Beethoven, and pace the floor for hours, looking at Earl's paintings of people's faces as starlight against the infinite darkness of the universe. Tears of joy filled my eyes as I thought about the past goodness of humankind: the struggle out of the caves, the raising of children in the deserts, the mountains, the snows, the storms, the animals, the plagues, the pain, the diseases, the constant death, death, death. The nobility of the struggle to survive exalted me. Then I thought of the glory which shall be revealed in us, the birth toward universal consciousness and action as we coordinate our internal systems and become a universal species. It was the birth experience relived and relived until it became a normal state of consciousness. I was reprogramming my own mind.

I live in cosmic time.

One day, as I worked on the story, I began to feel in my own body specific details of humanity's struggle to survive. "I" was struggling; "my" life was at stake. I sensed our electronic nervous system flashing signals of pain around our whole body. Once again, for a terrible instant, I felt a searing, unbearable anguish, the pain of each member of humanity: hunger, torture, cancer, paralysis, burns, brutal accidents, people in solitary confinement, soldiers with their eyes being blown out, mothers with their children dying at birth. I could not stand it.

I began to sob hysterically and ran from the house to my thinking tree, where I sat and cried and meditated. Deep inside I knew the suffering would end. There would be new challenges, new pains, but not these, dear God, not these. We were evolving to a new stage.

I transcended the pain by feeling myself to be a vibrant part of the body of humankind which was being born. I kept re-experiencing the great events of our evolution. As a cosmic being my life span was the billions of years of creation. My past was the history of the birth of humankind. I was created at the beginning of the universe. The original hydrogen atoms that gathered together in clouds and condensed by attraction into supernovas and exploded to form the heavier elements in our sun were my process of formation in the womb of the universe. Those atoms were in my body now; the salt of the early seas of earth ran in my blood now; those seas flowed in my veins; the minerals formed my bones.

I felt the awakening of all members of the body to their own growth within the whole. The Civil Rights movement, the various protest/liberation movements against injustice and dictatorship, were our own protest against loss of potential in any of our members. Every one was needed now to actualize their specific genius within the new born planetary system. The personal growth movement was the unlocking of that dormant potential in each person.

> When I click into the state of empathy, of feeling with the whole body, I am it! I am living the experience, not thinking about it, or telling it - I am it. When I am it, it has an irresistible reality. I'm not yet strong enough to stay in this state of empathy, but I have learned to enter the empathetic state of consciousness whenever any person talks to me who hungers to connect. It does not matter who the person is: a child, someone on a bus, a professor. I feel exactly the same with all people who experience the hunger for union. In this state of consciousness, there is a new awareness of equality. If the person is with you and you are wholly with that person, there is no judgment, no comparison, no separation. I am possessed by my own desire.

As I worked on the book, my sense of mission grew. I entered a different state of being. I was no longer self-conscious; I was on a different time scale, not worried about anything; all fretfulness was gone; I was in a state of joy, every day alive with fulfillment.

I would call Jonas or wait for his call; I would call Lance or wait for him to visit; then I would share the book with them. This interaction was vital to my creativity, like oxygen needing hydrogen to make water.

Lance Whyte came to visit in Lakeville when I had just about finished *The Birth of Humankind*. I read portions of it to him, as we sat on the couch in my study. He got so excited he moved farther and farther forward in his seat and finally fell off.

He said it was authentic, essential, wonderful. "This is your work?" he asked.

I shook my head. "No, it's Earl's. The words came out of Earl's mouth through my questioning and probing and trying to find all the pieces. He has a powerful capacity to make images. This is really his work; I'm just editing it."

Lance became furious with me and did not want to discuss it with Earl. I couldn't persuade him that Earl had truly said these things. I ran into the same problem with Jonas. He identified the words with me. This was painful because it wasn't fair. Earl originally said the words and the words became flesh for me. I lived and breathed and felt every minute of the day and night the birth of humankind and the excitement of the next step. My role as editor was for me a highly creative act.

Lance's appreciation of me and my own personal way of telling the story made me realize that I had a greater role to play, yet my conditioning was so deep that I genuinely could not acknowledge to myself that I possessed genius of my own. As others related so deeply to me, I found myself trying to make them respond to Earl as well. When they did not, I felt disloyal, as though it were wrong to be appreciated for my own qualities. In retrospect, I am amazed at the depth of my unconscious self-image as an extension of Earl rather than as an individual in my own right.

Earl was continuing to develop the image of a face, the color of starlight, against the background of black. He used me as a model. I sat for a photograph in the breakfast room, looking up to the sky, and thinking with all my being: *'We are humankind, born into the universe, seeking a greater awareness of the creative intention.'* He did a portrait from that photograph, a portrait of a state of consciousness, the expectation of universal life, a face the color of starlight looking outward to the infinite black of space. Some days, when working on the book, I would stare at it for hours. It helped me relive the cosmic birth experience on the hill.

We were developing an image and a story of our cosmic genesis that might become suitable for the first universal age. Meanwhile,

Jonas was embroiled in the struggle to create the institute, to raise funds, to handle the human conflicts that arose out of doing an utterly new thing. I looked upon his institute as a place where this image and story might be developed. He reported to me often from California. But it had become clear that I could not work directly with him. The institute required large-scale funding that could only be done by professional fund raisers.

The scientists themselves were not attracted to the vision of evolutionary transformation. In fact, many of them were narrow-minded, ego-centered, and against Jonas' vision. They argued over research grants, secretaries, paper clips! I represented something disruptive to Jonas' effort, because I found myself in philosophical argument with them. I had such a powerful drive to "tell the story of the birth of humankind" that I was no longer driven to help someone else anyway. I began to feel that the message of the birth was as important as what he was doing.

I finally began the subtle shift from being a feminine dependent, needing a man to express myself in the world, to a whole woman, a feminine co-creator, imbued with the force of evolution itself, attracting Adam to the *second* tree: the Tree of Life.

I began the laborious effort of trying to get the book published. It was like trying to get a bright but unusual child into school. The amazing difference in response to *The Birth of Humankind*, from Lance's falling off the couch to total lack of understanding, had to mean something. It was a signal.

In a flash of excitement I decided to start my own publication. I would find people all over the world who had the joy inside, write to them, ask their ideas about the next step for the future good, and offer to publish excerpts of their thoughts in *The Center Letter*, to share with others on the same frontier. From the day of my experience on the hill, I wanted to link with others who shared a similar experience. I felt that the electric current that expanded my individual consciousness would become continually available if enough people connected and formed a group channel of receiving and communicating awareness. I listed everyone I had ever heard of who was interested in the future. I anticipated a quantum leap when enough people who experienced this instant communication of which Teilhard had spoken were linked with each other.

I wrote to Abraham Maslow, telling him his book *Toward a Psychology of Being* had saved my life. I told him how I wanted to identify others throughout the world so we could be in closer touch with each other. He wrote back immediately that this was essential and that he would like to meet me.

He came to lunch at the New York apartment. He was tall, slim, with a moustache and a wonderful, wise, weather-beaten face. He had a deep curiosity about what made people good. He questioned me at length about why I was doing all this. He kept nodding. He said I was an example of his theory of self-actualizing people. He had a pronounced goodness, but was tough, a fighter for life.

"One thing I've learned, Barbara, is that you have to fight back. You're right not to let the bastards kill you. You can't permit those who would degrade man to prevail." He told me he wanted to start a publication called *Assent*, and he talked about the vicious destructiveness of some academic liberals. "They want to *prove* that we're rotten." He encouraged me to bring together the "good."

He offered his Eupsychian Network, a list of the "good people" he had collected over a lifetime, those who would form the "Good Society." This was before the human potential movement had surfaced. Abe was very open about good and bad people. Although he affirmed the growth potential and tendency toward goodness in all people, he also stressed that people who don't start growing, once their survival needs are met, get sick. How well I knew that! Five more years of nongrowth and I would have been an embittered woman. These nongrowers were probably the people whose behavior tended to be "bad" or destructive to their own and other lives. The Eupsychian Network were people in the growth mode. Many were humanistic psychologists founding growth centers, such as Carl Rogers, Victor Frankl, Michael Murphy of Esalen, to help people move toward full health. Jonas, Al Rosenfeld, Lance Whyte also gave me names. My list soon totalled over 1,000, each one a precious being, sensitive to the emerging civilization.

In August 1967 I sent *The Center Letter* to this mailing list, telling of my feeling that a profound change was occurring on planet earth. Homo progressivus types, those in whom the flame of expectation burned, were spreading throughout society, in all cultures, races, nations, and backgrounds. I invited them to correspond with me and each other. Then I waited in excitement for their response, as though we were lovers.

The response to *The Center Letter* was thrilling to me. Within the first few weeks, I received hundreds of letters from all over the world, from well-known people like Lewis Mumford, Father Thomas Merton, and from unknown enthusiasts. In the second letter I chose key excerpts from those first responses. In the third, on humanistic psychology, I published Maslow and others from the Eupsychian Network who had responded. People started passing the letter from one to another. I received word from an African chief who offered to circulate it through Africa. Someone on a bicycle was carrying it to people in New Delhi.

Then in the fourth letter I decided to include excerpts from *The Birth of Humankind* and to print one of Earl's paintings of human-kind as a face of awareness in the universe as the centerfold, to see if this concept appealed to the people who liked *The Center Letter*. I had originated the letter in the asking, receptive mode; I had created a context and hoped that through it people would be able to piece together the new whole. But it did not work that way.

After the fourth letter I received a long, cruel response from Lancelot Whyte saying he was withdrawing all support for and contact with me. He charged I had lost my integrity by putting Earl in as a central philosopher of the age when I had said I would seek out the best ideas. He practically accused me of being an intellectual fraud, which was really unfair; he always knew precisely how I felt about Earl's work. I wrote back affirming my intention to seek the best, and saying that, as a friend, I did not understand how he could possibly deny all contact. But I never heard from him again.

As *The Center Letter* progressed in popularity, activists wrote proposing their own policies to improve the world. Each had a fragment of the whole; each put his or her own view first, downgrad-ing the importance of the others.

I telephoned Anthony Sutich in California, who published the *Journal of Transpersonal Psychology*, asking if I could write an article for him on the relationship of the space effort to the development of human potential. Abe Maslow had given me his name, calling him a hero. Tony is totally paralyzed from the neck down. His body, Abe said, "is turning to stone," hardening at the joints with some spreading disease. He lies immobile on a stretcher, able to raise only his head, and from that position edits magazines. 'My God, what courage,' I thought, as I waited for the sound of his voice; it was only slightly blurred. We had a pleasant conversation, but he warned me that although he would like to see the article since I was a friend of Abe's and he admired *The Center Letter*, he was against the space program. After receiving my article he wrote back saying he saw no relationship between the step into the universe and human growth; moreover, the space program was drawing funds away from vital programs in development of inner awareness.

I asked Father Thomas Merton what he thought of the step beyond the planet in relation to religious development. He wrote back: "Frankly, Mrs. Hubbard, I never think about the space program except occasionally when I pick up a magazine in the dentist's office. I don't think it has any relationship to religious development."

Space scientists did not respond to *The Center Letter* at all. It wasn't in the language of their discipline. In fact, I found no advocates who were holistic: seeing the importance of both their position and, concurrently, the others. No one could appreciate anyone else's viewpoint, especially if it seemed to be in opposition to their own.

I visited Maslow several times during *The Center Letter* period at Brandeis University. He had written from his hospital bed when he thought he was dying from his first heart attack. The message was scrawled by hand on green steno paper: "When I thought I was dying, I thought of you. You represented life to me. I want to tell you to keep going, never stop. You represent life."

On a visit just before he died, I asked him what he thought about going into space in relation to the great potential of humanity, particularly in the field of transpersonal growth, the greater connection with the universe, toward cosmic understanding.

"Barbara, as long as you don't impose it on anyone, everyone can do what he pleases. There will be those that want to go into space; there will be those for whom it isn't valid, for example, myself. I can get into a state of universal consciousness through meditation; therefore, I have no personal interest in the space program, but I'm not against your being interested in it."

"Abe," I said, "it's more than my being *interested* in it; I believe it's a natural organic step if humanity is to become operative in the universe. Space exploration is the outer expression of the inner state of cosmic consciousness. The human potential movement, the environmental movement, human rights and space development are all related."

He did not disagree. He just nodded, but he did not care.

One hot summer afternoon, Jonas and I both had a few hours free in New York. He called and asked to come over to my apartment. We relaxed on the big, white couch, sipping iced tea and watching the Central Park trees flutter with green and yellow dappled light. Earl's giant portraits of the faces of starlight against the background of the universe glowed like black holes in the white walls, so concentrated as to absorb all energy.

Jonas was the opposite of Earl. Earl was angular, a minister of space. Jonas was warm, seductive, a lover of earth and flesh and life, able to make you feel as if you were the most indispensable person in the world to him, that his whole effort would collapse without you. He made everyone feel that way: secretaries, cleaning ladies, chairmen of the boards. I deeply enjoyed talking with him. He had the mind of a poet, amazing me with his analogies between biology and sociology, the behavior of cells and human populations. To him, everything was meaningful.

During the afternoon I innocently brought up the subject of the aging process, mentioning how Al Rosenfeld had told me that many scientists believed aging was a "degenerative disease" that could be overcome, *soon*. I told him how appropriate such knowledge is. "It's necessary to extend our live span if we are going to live and work on a cosmic time scale. Will your work on cancer help toward the extension of the life cycle?" I asked.

He amazed me by suddenly becoming enraged. I think it was the first time I had felt his anger. He rose in wrath against me like a biblical prophet. "Death is essential to life!" he proclaimed. "If the individual doesn't die, the species can't go on!"

My heart contracted. I felt attacked. "Well," I said, "you better get out of that laboratory and take off your white jacket, because you're working to understand the cell, and its time clock for death is surely not inevitable. There was no scheduled death when life was a single cell; it divided to reproduce. Death came in with multicellular systems and sexual reproduction. They're historical events, not eternal verities." I gave him a lecture for a change, shifting from a demeanor of appreciation to cold disappointment.

"It is possible that the mammalian death cycle will be changed," I insisted. "Extended life would be disastrous for an earth-bound species, but we're not earth-bound. We can't be compared to fruit flies. We are the only species able to leave this earth alive. Once we learn to live in the universe beyond our mother planet, we will be on a cosmic time scale, not an earth time scale. We will need increased individual development, variety and depth of wisdom and experience, rather than the reproduction of multitudes of the same type of individuals.

"If it's true that the potential of the human mind has barely been tapped, that unused capacity will be required for the development of our universal step as well as to care for life on this earth. We must live longer when we leave this earth. I don't think it's an accident that rocketry, genetics, cybernetics, and the recognition of the limitations of our finite globe all occurred within the same generation. It's natural!"

He disagreed violently. He even said if he thought he were contributing to that possibility, he would leave the laboratory. The strength of his anger shocked me.

As I probed Jonas' emotional rejection, it turned out to be more a matter of his not wanting this future rather than rationally proving to me it was impossible. Neither of us had proof, since the step had not occurred yet.

A while later, I had another meeting with him at the Westchester Country Club. He had been thinking about our conversation. Being a constructive man, he had a solution for me.

During our first conversation, I had said, "Jonas, you realize the sun is going to expand and destroy this earth. It's many billions of years away, but I can't recommend as a pro-life policy that we just sit here and wait to be destroyed when we know we have the capability of transcending the earth. How can you say that we shouldn't if you know the earth is going to be destroyed?"

His solution to my need for life everlasting, in reality, not in metaphor, was this: "I think it will be possible to transform the cycle of the sun so that it won't destroy the earth, so that we can stay here without being destroyed."

My heart sank. It was as though my parents had said to me when I was two years old in that crib, shaking the bars: "Dear child, you will be able to stay in the crib forever; don't worry; you will be taken care of; there's no need for you to get out." I felt as if he were putting a plastic bag over my head, slowly suffocating me.

"Jonas, the point is, I *want* to leave earth." I was amazed at my own words. Until pressed, I hadn't put it that way, even to myself. I reiterated. "Yes, I love earth. It's my first home, my mother, and I will cherish and care for it always, but I still want to leave it. I am a star child."

He was astonished, and so was I. "If it's possible in my lifetime, I intend to go and live beyond planet earth. What's more, I would like to keep going; I don't mean just to circle the earth in a capsule, I would like to go beyond the solar system. I want to meet other life. If scientists or psychics learn how to teach us to extend our lives, I'll extend mine. If it becomes possible to change the corruptible flesh to incorruptible, as St. Paul said, I'll do it. If it's possible, I'll not sleep; I'll be changed, and 'death shall have no dominion.'" Jonas was shocked.

We were both stunned by the conversation. Later I told him it was like a Greek drama between earth people and cosmic people. Possibly we were witnessing the natural diversification of the species at this phase. Some will meet the requirement to be attracted to new and vital tasks of restoring, nurturing, tending, and bringing harmony to earth, what Teilhard calls "the agents of planetisation", the "builders of the earth." Some will be attracted to going beyond earth to build new worlds, and be transformed into new beings (extraterrestrials and new terrestrials), builders of "new heavens and a new earth": new worlds on earth, new worlds in space. The diverse groups will be complementary and mutually supportive.

I learned from Jonas' rejection of universal life, and Abe Maslow's disinterest in the physical aspect of universal development, that a philosophy was needed that included their aspiration, even though theirs didn't include mine and those like mine. Through the challenge of those men, whom I so deeply admired, whose work is seminal in their fields, I found myself trying to develop a philosophy of synthesis, inclusion and empathy for those of different inclinations and temperaments. I tried to gain an emotional stand toward the various functions, roles, and characters of people, which did not require them to accept my vision of transformation in order for me to accept portions of the vision they saw. That is, I tried to identify emotionally with the all parts of humanity, no matter what they thought of each other or of me.

I began to feel I was taking a broader focus than anyone I knew. It was hard for me to accept. I was so accustomed to looking upon experts as superior. Each great man I knew: Jonas, Abe Maslow, Earl, Lance Whyte, closed some doors in his mind that were open to me. I saw connections everywhere. I related the parts of humankind to the whole of humankind, and humankind to the whole evolving universe. I saw everything in terms of phases, of processes leading to major evolutionary changes. The integration of society on earth, the care of basic needs of all people, the emancipation of individual potential, the restoration of earth, the expansion of our consciousness, physical life extension, and extraterrestrial development were all natural characteristics of a planetary species at the historical point of transformation from its earth-only phase toward its global/universal phase of development.

My intellect was racing to catch up with my intuition, always lagging behind the "signals." The hunger of Eve had led me toward a holistic vision. It dawned on me that there might be some comprehensive enabling role to play.

This attitude was strengthened by the developments in *The Center Letter*. The responses reinforced the recognition that people were seeing fragments, and I was publishing fragments, even reinforcing fragmentation. I did not have the strength to communicate a holistic view in that letter. I had so far failed to create a context in which people could discover how the parts fit into the evolving whole. I found that the essence of the experience of being part of the body of humankind was not communicable by the written word alone.

> *I have been completely transformed*
> *by an inner motivation.*

I brooded deeply about why I could not continue to receive direct signals. I'd had the cosmic birth experience, but all the other signals were so unclear. I was denied their kind of continuity of mystical experience, which I longed for in the hope of being absolutely certain I was under the commandment of God and not my own selfish whims.

Yet, when I look back on my whole life, I have been completely transformed by an inner motivation. A pattern of life guided that girl in Scarsdale to become a new being. I had learned no reliable skills of meditation or yoga. I was learning the way of evolutionary creation through vocation, or chosen work.

Maslow had told me that there were two factors that helped people move from basic need motivation for food, shelter, security and self-esteem to growth need motivation for meaning, beauty and purpose. One was meeting at least one other human being you admired who could affirm your higher state of being as real and needed. For me, that was Jonas. The other factor was a peak experience, a transformational moment of joy, union, ecstacy and grace that provided the intimate knowledge of the reality of a higher state of consciousness. Of course for me, that was the cosmic birth experience on the hill.

Late in 1968, I decided to stop publishing *The Center Letter*, although I was enjoying the personal satisfaction of meeting people. Correspondents were in touch world-wide. When they came to New York we would meet; I had a series of auto-intoxicating encounters.

We affirmed each other, but the results of our meetings were short-lived and finally appeared to me as self-indulgent.

I prepared my last letter in December 1968: "The Cathedral of Action." I felt we were really building a Cathedral of Action but could not see it, because there wasn't any structure to fit our separate acts together. I envisioned a structure with three pillars of action converging at the peak like the spire of a cathedral, or a rocket: freedom, union, and transcendence. I saw every act that enhanced freedom, or created greater unity, or helped us transcend some limitation, as a jewel in the Cathedral of Action. I wanted people to see the beauty of their acts put together like the Rose Window of Chartres, with each pane of glass seen as contributing to the whole.

This letter was by far the most effective in the series of eight. It was more appealing than *The Birth of Humankind* for most people, because I did not try to force anyone to accept anything, yet I created a context in which each of their acts were included. They were not required to like each other or agree with each other. People sent for copies from all over the world. Mrs. Aldous Huxley bought a hundred for Christmas cards. It was a celebration of the beauty of each act as part of the whole. But, still, nothing happened, or so it appeared to me.

In retrospect, I am sad that I discontinued *The Center Letter*. My response to not achieving immediate success, or to meeting obstacles, was to stop rather than to persevere. When the empathy disappeared, I lost energy. I was very consistent with my over-all purpose, but inconsistent with the actual projects to fulfill the work. When I met up with complexity, anger or disappointment, I went on to something else. I deeply regret this trait.

If more people were for people....

That Christmas season, 1968, Apollo 8 circled the moon. Frank Borman read from Genesis: "In the beginning God created heaven and earth...." For the first time the world saw itself as one body with the same eye at the same time from the same place. It was a profound moment for humankind, and it was experienced throughout the entire body of earth, bringing us closer to a cosmic birth experience than any other event. It caused some people to experience what I had: our oneness and birth into the universe.

That same Christmas Eve, Earl, the children, Mademoiselle Baldet, and I were flying to New Mexico for a meeting of Up with People, a group of young women and men, assembled from many nations, who were composing and performing a new music of hope.

A year before, our eldest daughter Suzanne had decided to join Up with People. They had come to sing at Hotchkiss in Lakeville. Suzanne was then at Fox Hollow Boarding School in Lenox, Massachusetts. A neighbor had called me, asking if I would put up two or three of the young people at my house. I said I would be glad to. She wasn't sure who they were, except they were travelling the world, singing about the future and the potential of people. I was immediately interested.

I found in the young women an element I had not seen before in any group. They were totally positive, full of confidence that people could create a new future. They wrote their own music to celebrate possibilities. They did not seem to be following a particular dogma or religion. (Several years before, the group had separated from Moral Rearmament, a Christian-based movement attempting to save the world by following the ethical commandments of Christ.)

I was excited by their hopefulness, so I called Suzanne and asked her to get excused for the concert. "I have a feeling it's something you should hear." She managed to get away, and we picked her up and went directly to the auditorium at Hotchkiss. Suzanne was then sixteen, restless and rebellious at Fox Hollow. Yet the alternative schools experimenting in various life-styles, were turning out serious cases of psychological breakdown - people who couldn't tolerate the frustration of the world at all. As far as I knew there was no school that taught a student to become a part of conscious evolution, a builder of the future. I had an intuition that Up with People might offer real opportunity for her.

The Up with People cast came charging down the aisles; they ran onto the stage and began to sing their theme song:
   "Up, up with people,
   you meet them wherever you go;
   up, up with people;
   they are the best kind of folks you know;
   if *more* people were *for* people,
   for people everywhere;
   there'd be lots less people to worry about
   and lots more people who care...."
   © Up with People
The magic was the genuine motivation and the irresistible beat of

enthusiasm. Suzanne was excited by the spirit. After the performance, we talked to members of the cast who circulated among the
faculty and young men of Hotchkiss. Suzanne asked, "How do you
join?" The adults who were organizing the event said, "We need
you. Just come with us." That was amazing. No red tape, no
credentials, no qualifications - only motivation. Yet the young people
of all colors and backgrounds looked healthy, vigorous, clean,
exuberant. They were travelling all over the country in buses; it was
obviously a major organizational effort. Suzanne immediately asked
Earl and me if she could join them, and we agreed to let her go.

She joined a "sing-out" and invited us shortly after to join her and
Cast A in Milwaukee. Earl, Wade, Alex, Stephanie, Lloyd,
Mademoiselle, and I attended a large performance of several
thousand people in the Milwaukee Stadium that night. It was brightly
lit as if for a baseball game. The cast of young people were the
players, pushing their energy to the limit to reach the hearts of their
audience with the basic message that "within every person there is
someone bigger who wants to be born."

Suzanne's description of the interpersonal relations among the cast
made ordinary classroom relationships seem barbaric. "At school we
were always working to get credits," she said, making a face, "or to
get better marks than someone else, but here, we forget about self
and think about reaching out to others. Everyone helps everyone
else. And we advise each other without worrying about hurting each
other's feelings."

She took us to a "Green Room" meeting of the cast. Various
young people got up to encourage the whole group. Then one of
the "superstars," as Suzanne called the great singers, said, "Let's
have a minute of silence and try to harness our thoughts into one."
We bowed our heads, and I felt the power of united aspirations
linking me to these strangers and to my own daughter in a way I had
never experienced before.

Suzanne introduced us at one of the cast meetings. Standing up,
unasked, she said, "I want to introduce you to my parents, who are
the most wonderful mother and father anyone could have." Then
Earl made a speech on the artist as a maker of images of transcendence. He said that to him, Up with People was representing an
"evangelism of the future."

That night Suzanne talked to us for hours. She said her desire to
star, to lead, had been given a good outlet. "I had to decide whether
I was going to be the 'naughtiest kid on the block,' or do my best.

It was a life-or-death decision. The minute I saw the cast come on stage at Hotchkiss, I knew that was my chance for life. I decided to do everything I could to get it."

She told them about our work; I mailed a copy of *The Birth of Humankind* to Blanton Belk, the head of the organization. They were immediately responsive to the philosophy of birth and hope, and invited Earl, myself and the children to join them in New Mexico, where Suzanne and hundreds of others were congregating for the Christmas season. They invited Earl to speak there.

It was a significant cluster of events to me: Apollo 8 was circling the moon and for the first time we were invited for the sake of our own work to meet with a group of people dedicating their total energy to awakening in others hopeful action for the future. Also, "The Cathedral of Action" was out in the world, my first effort to synthesize the action for change into a new whole.

Earl gave his speech the first evening we were there. As he arose, they began to sing directly to him, for him, celebrating his work on behalf of humankind. Earl, who had been working with only me by his side for so many years, was deeply moved and gave an extemporaneous talk plus questions and answers, which finally became the introduction to *The Birth of Humankind*. When he finished they sang to him again.

The next day Buckminster Fuller spoke. He walked to the stage, a small man in a halo of light. Before he could speak, they began to sing one of their great hits: "What color is God's skin? It's black, yellow, red, it's brown and it's white; everyone's the same in the good Lord's sight." Every time I think of this I cry. Bucky stood there in silence, tears running down his cheeks; he simply could not talk. Finally, in a voice barely audible, he said, "I want you to know, there *is* a God."

I had never read that word in his writings. Clearly he was deeply moved to speak from the depth of his being. He was affirming the faith of the young people who were affirming his work. Fuller was notifying humanity that our destiny is to become a total success by working with the laws of the universe. We, humanity, can understand evolutionary processes and co-create a world system in which every person will be free to emancipate their creative potential, to become universal citizens, stewards of evolution, both on this planet and in the "local universe." That night he, like Earl, was in his element, surrounded by others who shared the same vision of humanity. I felt the irresistible magnet of shared purpose empowering us all.

Up with People offered total affirmation of the reality of hope. Coming from the young in music, it reached directly to the heart. Words and philosophy communicate with the mind and are essential, but they don't touch the emotions, particularly abstract philosophy such as Buckminster Fuller, Teilhard de Chardin and Abraham Maslow wrote. This total affirmation in music was overwhelming to those in whom the flame of expectation burned. Audiences as a whole wept. I have seen adults in Italy, France, Germany, completely transformed by this joy, which is spiritual and evolutionary, joining us to each other, to nature and to God.

Up with People invited us to travel abroad with them to Italy. The following spring we accompanied them to Europe. We went in a large jet financed by some corporation, with all their guitars, musical instruments, costumes, lights. Up with People groups were forming throughout Europe. The Americans learned the language of the countries, to sing in Italy, Spain, France; then the young people of the country would form their own Up with People song groups. I remember one tiny town in Italy, not far from Milan. There was to be an Up with People performance by Italian youngsters in a small hillside village outside Milan. We drove with an older couple to a village schoolhouse in the hills. We walked in and the music began; it was in Italian, the same experience there. The power of that affirmation was tremendous. I wanted to be able to give everything I had to broaden that simple message in song to include philosophy, science, and politics.

They indicated they were going to use Earl as their spokesman to the press and elsewhere. However, it did not turn out that way. This was another instance of something almost clicking. Earl spoke with each group (three casts were touring Europe). He told them that in Europe a spark of freedom had been ignited that had now travelled around the earth and was moving forward toward the universe. He spoke magnificently. But whatever the reason, perhaps the philosophy was more specific than they were ready to espouse, we were not given the opportunity to speak to the press for them as promised. I can understand that in retrospect. They were winning support from everyone through stimulation of feeling, and they were successful with that approach; why should they risk it with a philosophy that was controversial?

There was a scene I will never forget at a large square in Italy. Two main buildings stood on either side of an immense piazza. On one side was the Catholic church, and on the other was the Communist Mayor's residence. The red flag of the Communist party flew in front of the Mayor's office on one side of this ocean of space; on the other continent was the cathedral. The young people were singing on the steps in front of the Mayor's Building with the red flag flying above them. The square filled with multitudes of people from the village.

When they began, "What color is God's skin?" the bishop in his red robe stepped out the cathedral, and the mayor appeared at the same moment. Both joined in singing "What color is God's skin?" in Italian. A Communist mayor, a Catholic bishop, all the Italians, and all the young Americans, the agnostics, the atheists, the different religions; it did not make the slightest difference, because the truth was greater than any of those divisions. You could see it there in that picture of the Catholics and the Communists and the young and the old and the black and the white; it made no difference. They were one, we were one. We have a common future. When that music played, I do not think anyone could have resisted it. The feeling created a magnetic field of unity that I have come to experience time after time in certain situations. This was the first time I recognized others feeling the same sense of being part of the evolutionary process and of mankind.

Then something happened to Up with People. They became popular. Their songs were excellent, their performance outstanding, stars were born among them. They took anyone who wanted to go. They weren't looking for talent, they were looking for motivation. Some of the most beautiful young singers I have ever heard surfaced. They were on television with Bob Hope, sponsored by Coca-Cola and Pan-Am; they were recognized. The astronauts came to see them. The raw talent that came off the streets and the schools was being transformed into a highly professional singing team. They developed a rock beat instead of the straightforward gospel beat of rising hope. When I saw them subsequently, I felt that some of the rising power was gone. They had become too perfect, too professional. It was as though the meaning was bleached out of them prematurely.

However, it was a tremendous experience. I know as time goes on, there will be meetings and places and times to celebrate this oneness and transcendence. The new rituals of this age are being created by such groups as Up with People.

After our exciting meeting with Up with People, I sent *The Birth of Humankind* to Stewart Lancaster, editor of *Pace* magazine. (*Pace* was published by Up with People.) We received a letter within the week: "This is a magnificent book, we would be proud to publish it." Earlier, when I was starting *The Center Letter* in late 1967, I had met Ed Cornish, who founded the World Future Society and publishes *The Futurist*. Ed and I moved into the public area at the same time. He was working for the National Geographic Society as a science writer. He started *The Futurist*, circulating a mimeographed sheet mainly to people in business management, general systems, urban planning, technology assessment, forecasting, and those interested in the future in general. It was a different kind of group than *The Center Letter* correspondents: technologically oriented, "pragmatists," and preponderantly male. He invited me to be on the board of the World Future Society, along with Carl Madden, chief economist of the U.S. Chamber of Commerce; Nobel prize winning physicist Dr. Glenn Seaborg and Michael Michaelis of Arthur D. Little, the consulting firm; Arnold Barach, editor of *Changing Times*; Orville Freeman, who had been secretary of agriculture under Kennedy. I was the only woman, and also the only nonprofessional person on the board. I asked Ed why he chose me. "You have a different kind of wisdom, which I think we need," he replied.

Ed was one of the few people I know who took a leap without being sanctioned by any other authority. Shortly after he started *The Futurist*, he was offered a more secure job with the National Geographic Society. He had to make a choice, if he took the more secure position, he would have less time to work on building the World Future Society and publishing *The Futurist*. With no independent income, and no guarantees, he left the National Geographic and gave his full time to building the World Future Society; his wife, Sally, worked devotedly with him. Ed was modest, mild, unassuming, and had a single purpose: to provide a forum for ideas on the future. He did not take a stand on ideas.

We were complementary but different. My desire was to advocate a future based on global society and universal life. His desire was to provide an open forum for all concepts. Both were necessary. *The Futurist* became the outstanding publication in the field.

Both he and *Pace* published excerpts from *The Birth of Humankind* before it became a book. (*Pace* changed its title to *The Search Is On: A View of Our Future From the New Perspective of Space.*) Excerpts were also published in Clarence Streit's magazine *Freedom and Union*, the publication of his organization Federal Union, which promotes a federal union of the democracies as the next political step toward freedom and order on a global scale.

Once I had completed the book for Earl, I decided to do for myself what I had done for him. I went through my journals and typed by hand eight hundred pages of excerpts, only one-fourth of the total verbiage! As I went through my own life, typing what I considered to be the nuggets, I relived it.

> *I feel united with my own past. I'm grateful to the girl that I was, that she never gave up. If she had given up, I wouldn't exist. I am different from that person who went to Bryn Mawr, who lived in Lime Rock and Lakeville. She was trapped in an old concept of reality. I am free to evolve a new concept of life. My gratitude to her endurance is boundless. I am detached from my past but love it. I love myself but, in a strange way, as though I am loving someone else.*

After typing the eight hundred pages, even I knew it was too much. I met a soulmate, Eleanor Garst, who had helped me do some of the reading and editing for *The Center Letter*. I asked her to read through it and help me edit the excerpts into a book. Eleanor took a suitcase full of the typed material and together we edited *The Chosen Life, an Experiment in Freedom*.

I started the usual efforts to get published and met with the usual rejection. Finally I found a publisher that expressed interest in it, a West Coast publisher of mystical works. I hesitated, not wanting to be identified with occultism of any kind. Just then we received word that Earl's book was to be published, so I decided to hold back on mine, since having it published by a mystical press at that time might be harmful.

Earl and I had become accustomed to in-depth dialogue in the development of the first book. While I was editing *The Center Letter*, doing my own book, and meeting all these people, I was continuing my dialogues with Earl. A new book began to emerge in my mind for him: *The Need for New Worlds*. I finished that one later, but I never had it published; I never tried. Subsequently Earl revised and elaborated on the manuscript. Then it was published in 1975 as *The Creative Intention*.

However, events overtook both my efforts to publish *The Chosen Life* and *The Need for New Worlds*. It was 1969. NASA was preparing for the lunar landing. I had become evermore interested in the space program as an expression of the physical aspect of universal life, as a complement to our psychological/spiritual growth.

When the landing on the moon occurred, I, like millions of others, stayed up all night. My experience in watching the rocket take off on television was one of absolute joy, completely beyond the ordinary. I identified with the rocket! I felt myself rising in space, breaking through the cocoon of the sky and moving into the universe. I had felt the same joy at the birth of my own babies. I cried uncontrollably as it rose into space, the words 'freedom, freedom, freedom' pounding in my head. I was so embarrassed I had to leave the room. It was the middle of the night in Lakeville; the capsule had landed on the moon; the door of the lunar module opened and Neil Armstrong backed down the ladder, toward that famous first human step upon a new world.

Even the mass media responded. Walter Cronkite was thrilled. This event seemed to break through the infantile nervous system for a second, although they reported it as an exciting, costly spectacular. Man-in-the-street interviews were given around the world. The major excitement was expressed by the "common citizen." The intellectual was holding back, saying, "Well, this money could have better been spent on earth; here we are with the Civil Rights movement, people starving, and the United States spent this money to show off," or "How dare we put an American flag on the moon," or "This was just an act to beat the Russians."

That very day, July 20, 1969, *The Search Is On* was published. That was a remarkable coincidence. The birth experience was affirmed on the very day the book was born into the world.

Five

Totality

I was overjoyed at the lunar landing. At last, the story would be known. We had all experienced our oneness and birth. We had come through the danger. The placenta had been pierced. The waters had broken. The rocket had risen, spewing fire and water, a tiny sliver lifting from the giant, magnetic hold of earth. The cosmic child had touched the breast of the moon, that wonderful ancient rock, so full of minerals and resources, that would soon provide a new source of nourishment as we stopped depleting our mother earth.

But, after the first few instants of feeling the joy of oneness, the pain of oneness intensified. Humankind screamed. Bad news flashed through the nervous system. Everything hurt. The birth was a mistake. NASA spent too much. We should be minding our business on earth. The sense of defeat and despair deepened. The Civil Rights movement was increasing in intensity; flower children were taking drugs; students were rioting, locking up deans and sensing loss of relevance. Political leadership was floundering instead of announcing a new age of cooperation that required the involvement of all people. Some prophets asserted that knowledge, science, technology, the rationalism of the West, and civilization itself were wrong. We should withdraw and return to some past state. Perhaps the whole enterprise of humanity was a failure. The voices of hope were silent.

*When I become totally committed,
I become totally free.*

Everything I had done seemed pitifully ineffective. I felt a failure. I had to think of something new to do. I worried that humankind might destroy itself for lack of awareness and hope.

Once again that blessed driving anger fueled me with the strength for action. As at the death of my mother, as at my own psychological death in Lime Rock, as at the slaughter of hope in the arts at the Museum of Modern Art, now again the rage for life took over. I sensed humankind like a newborn child being whipped before my eyes by those who said we could not make it. My response was instinctive: I rushed in to help.

Since I had already experienced the personal connection between myself and humankind, I did not even feel I was helping someone else. Self-preservation, not self-sacrifice, was the motivation. If humankind self-destructs, all its members suffer: To care for yourself, pragmatically you must care for the whole.

That anger, born of love for life, caused me to open to an even broader channel of consciousness. I felt empathy for the whole body, which activated within me a total commitment to help humankind get through its critical infancy as a global/universal species.

I took a walk on the Lakeville hill and spoke out loud to myself, a clear dialogue between a guiding voice and a responsive servant. The guiding voice within me spoke: 'You'll commit yourself totally for the life of humankind. It's not enough to tell the story of our birth at luncheon parties. You have to go out into the world and find out how to communicate with people. You've got to *do* something. You have to put everything else second: children, Earl, money, your own comfort. Go forth and tell the story!'

"All right, I will. I want to. I know it's right," said the responsive inner servant.

I told my children that their mother was a pioneer. I had to create a new way of being. They could come if they wanted to, as soon as I had created an open place. Their response was heartening. One night, as I was tucking my nine year old Wade in bed, I told him, "I'm afraid I may appear to be a poor mother for some time, but I want you to know I love you."

Wade quickly put my fears to rest. "Mummy, you're doing what a mother's supposed to do. You're making the future for us. That's what mothers are supposed to do. And we know you love us."

Earl, however, tried to persuade me I was mistaken to try to become an organizer. "Barbara, we must be *used* by organizers to give them ideas."

"But, Earl, no one is asking us! We could sit around and wait the rest of our lives to be asked. No! We've got to take the initiative. You're wrong to want the world to come to you. We've got to reach out to others."

I felt I had earned the right to this total commitment. I had been constant in my dedication to Earl and the development of his ideas. The hardest part of executing my mission was the thought that I might neglect my children. It was easier for me to separate psychologically from a man I loved than from the children I had borne and cherished.

Suzanne already was out in the world public arena. By this time Stephanie had decided to join Up with People also. Wade, Alexandra, and Lloyd had Mademoiselle Baldet as well as me, so they were never at any time afraid of being left alone or rejected. There were times, however, when they would resent my pre-occupation with my life's work. Occasionally I resented it too. Sometimes I asked for release, for rest, not to feel the pull, but it never went away. I could not concentrate for long on anything but this strange mission.

I realized I was developing an additional role. While I was still their biological mother, I also was taking on a larger, more holistic motherhood. It was impossible for me to say I was working for anything but the whole of humanity.

I did not know what I was going to do, but I knew I had changed, that I would never be the same person again. I would never be bound by any pattern that prevented me from doing my best to bring options of hope into the communications system. There was nothing else I wanted to do. I was in a wonderful, coherent state of being. I experienced a depth of freedom I had never known. I was free of self-doubt, self-constraint, confusion, pride, fear. This freedom came from opening myself totally to the full force of the unique life urge within me, the part of my being that knew who I was and that connected me to the larger flow of planetary changes.

There was something ludicrous about a woman with no professional skills and no reputation, deciding to tell humankind that it was one body being born into the universe. The immensity of the task, its unusual nature, and my inadequacy struck me as ridiculous. But it did not matter. That was another part of the freedom of total commitment. I did not have to forge my reputation with the powers that be. I did not have to prove to the intellectuals that I was smart. I was freed from all that. I was under a new dispensation.

I racked my brain about what to do. NASA, the great agency of transcendence that Earl called "our stairway to the stars," was being maligned. The genius of engineers, scientists, astronauts, systems, was being scattered. The skilled builders of new worlds were fired, unemployed, driving taxis. Most people did not understand what they were losing: their arms, their legs, their eyes, for universal life. Their future was being taken away. The earth-oriented humanists, and spiritually-minded activists were rejecting space. I felt both were needed during this period of our birth. At least, that is what I had experienced in my epiphany upon the hill.

There was one woman I knew who might help (Though I knew that space and global oneness were not her interest.): Lady Malcolm Douglas-Hamilton, an American widow of a Scotsman, who lived in New York. She had organized Bundles for Britain during the war and was now setting up The Center of American Living, in order to affirm cultural excellence in the United States.

I took her to lunch at the Westbury Hotel on Madison Avenue. "Natalie," I said, drawing a deep breath. "I have made up my mind that the future of human culture and excellence requires the continuation of the space program!" An odd idea for 1969. "We've got to do something!"

She responded immediately. "Why don't we have a space meeting? Let's get the leaders of the country together with the space leaders and initiate a new national commitment to continue going forward."

"Great, Natalie, let's do it! We'll put Earl up there with the space leaders to talk about the need for new worlds, since they'll never do it on their own."

I hugged her, and we ordered a bottle of wine to toast "Victory in Space" (her title). Then we hurried to her apartment, got out the card files, and began to make lists of heads of such organizations as the General Federation of Women's Clubs, the Church Women United, the Boy Scouts and the Girl Scouts. I listed Werhner von Braun, Neil Armstrong, Frank Borman, John Glenn though I had never met any of them or even seen a rocket in the flesh. She wrote to the civic leaders and I wrote to the space leaders. I went home then and triumphantly told Earl what I had done.

"It'll never work," he said. "Those people won't accept me."

"Earl, stop thinking in such narrow terms. We're trying to make something happen, not get you accepted."

I remembered the exciting days of the discovery of the evolutionary idea as I wrote to everyone in the aerospace field, inviting them to participate. One of the letters fell on the desk of Colonel John Whiteside, who was the Chief Officer of Information for the Air Force in New York City. John was asked to look into the conference to see "if there is something for the Air Force in it." He turned the assignment over to a captain in his office, William Knowlton. Bill, it turned out, was a neighbor of ours in Lakeville, Connecticut, and that weekend he came to visit us. We discussed with him the meaning of space and future of humankind. He was excited by the ideas, and said, "You've got to meet my colonel. He's a spellbinder, and maybe he'll help." He told John that we should meet.

On September 25, 1969, Lt. Colonel John Whiteside came to lunch at the New York apartment. My meeting with him was similar to my first meeting with Jonas. He opened the door; we looked directly into each other's eyes, and there it was, instant recognition. He was wearing an Air Force uniform and had an extraterrestrial look in his eyes; yet also had a worldly air about him.

John was medium height and solidly built, with the strong body of a man who had worked on a farm and in a coal mine during the depression. He came from West Frankfort, Illinois, from a Southern Baptist family. At forty-eight his face was weathered, lined, masculine and sexy. There were no other words for it. He was a man who knew women easily. His look of self-confidence, intelligence, exuberance, and natural leadership charmed me. He had the top non-Pentagon position as Chief Officer of Information in New York, where he worked with the mass media, NBC, CBS, ABC. His life was in the mainstream of national affairs.

During lunch Earl spent most of the time talking. After lunch we sat in the living room while Earl continued to eloquently describe the meaning of the space program.

John and I sat side by side on the couch, Earl was facing us in one of the upright Spanish armchairs, lecturing at us with his brilliant yet formal tone. I caught John's eye once or twice and smiled at him. I felt a surprising attraction for him. Finally, I interrupted Earl and said to John, "You know what it's really like," I said. "It's like birth. We're going to be universal."

Those grey-green, all-knowing eyes softened. "That's right, we are." He smiled. "It's amazing." he said. "I spent years down at the Cape, I've seen hundreds of launches; I got the live coverage accepted. I knew, most of us knew, that what we were doing meant something. But no one could say what. It's like reporting the birth of Christ in terms of the labor problems at the inn, the cost of the food, and how much the baby weighed. But how did you come to this? You don't know one end of a rocket from the other."

"Purpose," I said. "I discovered it through my search for meaning. But now I know it's not enough to talk about it. People like us, outside the space program, citizens, have to act. They have advocates for every disease, every need, but not for the future of humanity. We have got to learn how to communicate meaning for the future."

He nodded. "That's very interesting. During the sixties we knew how to communicate ideas in the Air Force, but ever since Woodstock, something has changed. People have different antennae up, it's more selective. They're tuning out what they don't want to hear and listening for something new. You don't even need a high energy signal. If it's the right message, it'll get through; if they don't want to hear it, they don't." He laughed. "You know what I'm trying to communicate now? The C-5, the F-111, and the Vietnam War! I have to sneak my generals out back doors. There's no credibility."

I could see he had come to the end of his rope.

Bill Knowlton called after the meeting and said that Colonel Whiteside wanted twelve copies of *The Search Is On*. I called John then, and asked him to help us with the space meeting.

He agreed instantly. "Let's do it, Barbara!"

I knew I had found the person I needed: an activist who knew the ways of the world. We began to work together. He took over the organization of the meeting, the invitations, the media contacts.

My life transformed again. The meeting with John occurred three months after I had made the total commitment. We had a long talk one November afternoon in the St. Regis Hotel. I told him of my vocation, my mission to tell the story of humanity's birth. I told him what a struggle it was, and how I needed his help. "John, you can do this; it's in you," I said.

He knew that was true, but he said, "I don't feel I have the character, the high standards of morality, the background, to undertake a task like this."

I disagreed completely. "I think your so-called worldly weaknesses may prove to be a strength. No one is going to think you're self-righteous and perfect." He had all the typical attributes of his way of life: drinking, partying, women. But, somehow, I knew that would be a help. Also, I had been surrounded by self-righteous men and had come not to admire that kind of perfection.

John struggled both to accept this totality and not to. But in some strange way his life had been a preparation for telling the story. He had accumulated a remarkable set of talents. He had wanted to be a minister, but could not get a "sign from the Lord." He went to Southern Illinois University for two years and married a college friend, Francis. In World War II he entered the Air Force, believing deeply in the defense of freedom and in the morality of our efforts in World War II. Then he set up his own successful advertising firm. In a search for commitment he had tried Communism and Alice Bailey-type esoteric philosophy.

Called back during the Korean War, he reached the top of his profession in the sixties as public information officer. He told the media the truth, and they trusted him. He went beyond his authority to press for live coverage of the Apollo shots, and succeeded. Now the meaning had run out of his life. The space program was misunderstood. The military had lost its purpose of defense. It was the age of overkill; the game became obviously insane.

John was driving himself to slow destruction, squandering his energy, because, like me, he could not live without meaning. We began to be ever more closely attracted, working together continually on the space meeting. Obviously our effort would have to extend beyond a single event. The more we did together, the harder it became for him not to be as totally committed as I. My loyalty to Earl was so deep, and my genuine admiration for him was so great, that I did not want to acknowledge to myself that I was falling in love with John, but it was happening nonetheless. I hoped I could love him, while maintaining my relationship with Earl. John was married too, and I respected fidelity. I chose to maintain a platonic relationship with him.

On Christmas Eve, 1969, I was standing by the fire in Lakeville, surrounded by Earl and the children, sorting out the Christmas stockings, looking at the Christmas tree we had decorated on December 22, my fortieth birthday. The phone rang, it was John.

"Barbara, I have decided to do it. I am going to give my life full time to this."

A great weight lifted from my shoulders; I could feel the sense of lightening. My shoulders straightened, and I breathed deeply and stretched my body to full height. My eighteen-year-old fear of being forty and having nothing to do but bake bread flashed through my mind. "Thank you, John. I knew you would." I could say no more with everyone there. Gratitude flooded me, and, as at all moments of great happiness for me, I started to cry.

The children clustered at my side. "What's the matter, Mummy?"

"It's nothing, children, except I'm so happy, and I love you all so much." I put my arms around them in an awkward embrace and would not let go until they practically shouted to Earl for help.

Earl, John and I went to the space meeting on February 18, 1970, at the Roosevelt Hotel in New York City. On the platform was Frank Borman, the astronaut who had circled the moon; Krafft Ehricke, philosopher and long-range space planner of North American Rockwell (now Rockwell International); Dr. Harold

Ritchey, president of Thiokol Chemical Corporation and developer of the solid fuel propellants for the rockets; Chester Lee, who was later Apollo mission director and Skylab director; Hugh Downs, the TV star; Bob Considine, the columnist; and Earl Hubbard. In the audience were 200 heads of national organizations.

The meeting was a disaster. Civic leaders did not understand the language of the space leaders; the space leaders spoke in quantitative terms in the language of their discipline; they did not know how to relate their great act directly to the needs or imagination of the other people in that audience. Earl, who had been placed on this platform by Natalie, John, and me, was unknown to any of the space or civic leaders, and came from a totally different background and way of thinking. His language was so different from theirs that his speech, "The Need for New Worlds," hung like an unattached jewel in space. None of the space leaders were saying we needed new worlds; certainly no civic leaders were concerned with the need for building new communities in space, much less universal life.

When the speeches were over, Hugh Downs asked for questions: there were none; people were too stunned or bored or both. Hugh asked and answered a few questions himself to overcome the embarrassing pause. I was a nervous wreck, thinking once again that this was not the way. There was no communication between the languages of philosophy, science, and civic affairs.

Directly after the meeting, Jim Sparks, who had been working with us to put together the meeting, whispered to me, "Invite Dr. Ritchey to dinner."

I had never even talked to Dr. Ritchey. He was a distinguished scientist, head of a large corporation, an abstract speaker. Not knowing what else to do, and having no reason not to, I went over to him: "Would you come to dinner?"

He immediately said yes. "Not only that," he said, "I'll bring some of my acquaintances who are here."

Dr. Ritchey invited others including Karl Harr, head of the Aerospace Industries Association, a public relations lobbying arm of the aerospace industry. We also invited Sister Fidelia, a nun; Ken Delano, a priest who was interested in astronomy; Natalie; Earl; myself; John; John's wife; and a few others. I raced to the apartment to pick up some cold cuts, and within half an hour, about twelve people had gathered. We had drinks for a while and began to relax.

When we went in for dinner, Dr. Ritchey surprised everyone by standing up, lifting his glass, and saying, "I would like to give a toast to our host. I was sitting on the platform today, and I heard Earl Hubbard speak of the need for new worlds. At first I thought he was completely wrong, but I haven't been able to get it out of my head all afternoon. The more I think about it, the more I think he's right. Not only *can* we work to develop new worlds in space, but we *should*; we *must*. I would like to drink a toast to the concept of taking the next step forward to build new worlds."

For the first time I sensed the excitement of creating our own ground, not standing on someone else's purpose. This toast unleashed an outpouring of high feeling. I responded with a toast to Dr. Ritchey, saying it was men like him that were providing humankind with the tools of transcendence. Sister Fidelia congratulated everyone on the magnificent possibilities for the future. Earl made a heroic toast to the universal age. Everyone became very excited, except Dr. Harr, the man hired as a public relations lobbyist for the aerospace industry: "The public will never buy this," he said.

After dinner Sister Fidelia and I persisted with Karl Harr. He looked to me like a Roman in an old gladiator's outfit, exhausted, with a headache. He finally said, "Ladies, I give up! If people like you think it's important, you must be right. Maybe the public will buy it." Of course, in his heart he hoped we were right, but he had been so hardened and probably wounded by the difficulty of "selling" space from a vested-interest point of view that he could not believe in our innocent motivation. It never occurred to him that people who were not paid to be a part of the space program would care.

The evening was a surprising success. Several days later, Dr. Ritchey called, wanting to know when we could do it again. He thought we lived like this every day! He never dreamed it was the work of a lifetime just to have achieved even this beginning. He said he would like to give a dinner and have the same experience.

Of course, he believed deeply in what he was doing, but there was no particular joy in the aerospace industry. Its workers had not received the moral sanction of the public. They had no verification that many felt that they made a great contribution. And no one in the industry had affirmed the meaning of his act in relation to the whole of society.

Dr. Ritchey decided to give a dinner a few weeks hence. He wanted all the same people to be there and a few more. John Whiteside said, "I'm going to invite General Joseph Bleymaier, who developed the Titan III rocket." John called the general in Los Angeles, and said, "General, there's a dinner I think you should attend." Bleymaier came without question. At the party John said to me, "Barbara, your target is General Bleymaier." I asked him why. "Because he's the man who could lead the mission to new worlds."

Dr. Ritchey once again started a toast. The excitement spread, almost like a biochemical reaction. One after the other arose to propose a toast. For mine, remembering my instructions from John, I turned to General Bleymaier, a handsome Texan, a retired Air Force general, and said, "General Bleymaier, do you think you can build communities in space?"

He looked up, and said, "Yup! We have the technology to live and work in space. The important thing is the *timing*. If John F. Kennedy had said we're going to the moon 'sometime,' and not, 'within this decade,' it wouldn't have happened."

So General Bleymaier suggested we set a time frame for the first colony in space. After dinner, we invited most of the guests back to our apartment. I sat next to General Bleymaier, and said, "General, we'd like to form some kind of committee or group to bring these ideas into action. Would you help us?"

The general, not known for his loquaciousness, said, "Yup."

For the first time I sensed the step to new worlds actually might happen. I had already sensed the psychological process of evolving toward a new state of being, but when we started planning with the man who built the Titan III rocket, and he said yes, we can do it, and yes, he could do it, and we need a time frame, the reality of humankind's integration and birth took on a new dimension.

The idea of forming some kind of committee to rally the ideas and people for an open "new worlds future" percolated in our minds, as we tested the receptivity of audiences and groups throughout the country. Earl was the spokesman. He had a powerful eloquence. I edited speeches for him out of our breakfast dialogues and passages from the books. Then we took him to Dayton, Ohio, to speak before the Engineers Club. John set up meetings for him with the press, and arranged talk shows and interviews. But we had difficulty. Earl's absolutist, perfectionist, elegantly tailored personality cut off the tender stirring of new action that "the idea" stimulated. After Earl left, John and I were always picking up the pieces, seeing what people were capable of doing and assuaging hurt feelings. However, the "new worlds" movement began to be nurtured and to grow through tending to people and expression of ideas in gentle inter-action, starting from felt needs and proceeding to the larger goals.

John introduced me to his associates. One day he took me to the

Pentagon and dropped me off at various offices of his colleagues, saying, "Tell them about new worlds, Barbara," leaving me with some startled and uncomfortable officer at the other side of the desk. One man was Billy Greener, who subsequently became Assistant Secretary of Defense for Public Affairs. I plunged right into the case for space now in terms of the human potential: It could convert weapons spending to life-oriented technologies; it could provide an opening frontier and a nonmilitary, productive competition between us and our adversaries, as a transition to a peaceful world, it could provide employment, new methods of environmental protection, new knowledge and a deeper sense of purpose for all. I told him we wanted to establish a United States initiative for an integrated earth-space program. We established a rapport. When I told him that John was retiring from the Air Force to "take on this mission," he shook his head in amazement: "Well, he's a wizard. Anything he's ever decided to do, he's done. If he thinks a new worlds' goal can be established, he's probably right."

In the book *The Need for New Worlds*, which I was still working on with Earl toward the beginning of 1970, we were outlining a case for a new national and global goal: new worlds on earth, new worlds in space, new worlds in the human mind. We felt that if we did not start in our generation to build new capabilities in space as well as restore the environment on earth, some dire possibilities would occur. We believed the goal to establish the first space community should be started in 1976, because it seemed to us that time was not on the side of waiting. The finite resources on this earth were being used up. There would be more people whose needs must be met. Remaining fossil fuels should be used both to meet immediate needs and to establish the foothold in the universe. Renewable resources of energy - solar, geothermal, wind, and so forth - must be quickly gained or we might run out of energy before we secure our opportunity for universal life. We sensed that we are given a few decades of evolutionary grace.

I kept reexperiencing my cosmic birth experience, the transition from womb to world, the gasping for breath, the reaching out for life, the coordination of our internal systems. I could *feel* the irritation running through our planetary nervous system, the media.

The first major response to the crises we faced came from The Club of Rome, formed in 1968 by a group of European industrialists and scientists. They laid down the gauntlet to the human race: "You are in a finite world; limit growth or die!" But the limits to growth perspective denied the human race a choiceful future. I felt that if we followed that approach, we would be incarcerated in a closed system of increasing controls and depletion of resources. Given the fifteen billion year history of transformation, it did not seem natural for evolution to stop at some point and aim at balance. What is natural is synthesis and transcendence, the creation of new forms out of old systems. From the womb perspective of a finite, earth-bound species, the Club of Rome was right: cybernetics, genetics, astronautics appear unnatural. But from the point of view of our future potential, these were the natural necessities for the next development of life : a universal species.

Krafft Ehricke told the story of the erudite "fetal scientist" who's a cell in the womb of a baby in the seventh month. He predicts that, from current growth rates, by the eighth month there will be severe overcrowding and pollution; by the ninth month there will be massive starvation, suffocation, revolutions; by the tenth month die-offs will occur in most of the poorer nations of the world. The problem is, the fetal scientist knows nothing of the coming birth, and its suddenness. It cannot be predicted from the womb perspective. The limits to growth advocates were the erudite fetal scientists, extrapolating from the past, with no positive vision of the future, no sense of the transformation of ourselves into a universal species.

Out of such thoughts as these, we began to formulate a case for new action. This case offered so many options and benefits that we decided to form a group of diverse people who could develop the goal: "new worlds on earth, new worlds in space, new worlds in the human mind." We hoped to bring it into the public arena for discussion and action.

John was a great new factor in my life. He was trying to make something happen for this purpose and not for some other. We went to various friends and acquaintances, such as Dr. Ritchey, General Bleymaier, Sister Fidelia, Natalie, and others, and invited them to the first meeting in Lakeville, Connecticut, in June of 1970, to found The Committee for the Future (TCFF).

We developed the concept of a new, long-range, global goal of building: "new worlds on earth," (by meeting basic needs, restoring the environment, rebuilding cities, etc.), "new worlds in space" (by converting our military-industrial war economy both toward immediate human needs on earth and toward the peaceful, cooperative development of outer space), and "new worlds in the human mind" (by educating ourselves to recognize that we are one global family, living on one planet, in which each of us is a vital, creative member).

We saw this new worlds goal as a way of attracting the people of the United States and other countries to work together, to create a future of truly unlimited possibilities for all. It was an evolutionary scenario beyond the current mentality of the Cold War or the various strategies of adaptation, reaction or withdrawal. It responded to Maslow's hierarchy of human needs: basic needs for survival, growth needs for self-actualization, and transcendent needs for connectedness with the larger whole, both physically and spiritually. It provided an incentive for defense industries to become new world builders instead.

The Lakeville Conference itself was glorious. Finally, the beautiful house and grounds were serving the emancipation of humanity rather than feeling like a place of incarceration to me. John developed what we called "The Green Book" (because it had a green cover), which laid forth a strategy to bring this case into the public arena in time for a presidential candidate to carry the message in 1976, the bicentennial year. He thought The Committee for the Future should be a "nonorganization," calling upon individuals of different fields to do what they could, where they were, when they could. But the climate of opinion in the early seventies was not favorable to this goal. We were out of fashion: The campuses were alive with protests; if you did not have some issue of pain to put forward, it was hard to get a hearing.

This first year was a floundering search for what to do. George Van Valkenburg, one of our original founding members, a film producer in Los Angeles, came up with an extraordinary idea in the fall of 1970. He pointed out that two Saturn V rockets would be left over from the Apollo program. TCFF could initiate the first "citizen-sponsored lunar expedition," using surplus NASA hardware. It could pay for itself through the sale of lunar materials and the various television and story rights that would be involved. There could be a global subscription; people could subscribe either as they might to a great National Geographic expedition, or with some further interest in the development of space, which they could participate in later.

One of the factors that convinced me to undertake the citizens' mission was my father. I lunched with him after the founding of TCFF and described the difficulty of getting the new worlds' goal articulated and discussed. He agreed it was necessary to go into space. He saw that the future of the human race depended on a broad arena of action. He was not attracted at all by the back-to-nature movement and suspected others felt as he did.

But he said, "Philosophy will get you nowhere. Unless people feel they can own a piece of the new world, you'll never make it."

I said, "But people can't buy land on the moon; we can't sell anything. However, maybe we can find some way whereby people would buy a ticket for a journey that might occur for their children. If new facilities for human life in space are developed and implemented, these first subscribers to the citizens' mission would earn some access to the new adventure."

My father said he would back me in this plan of research and development for what came to be known as "Project Harvest Moon." He gave me $25,000 to get started. His reservations about the fantastic scope of the action did not stop him from helping. He had faith that great new things could happen, and he was willing to act on his belief. His gift was of vital importance to me, not only because it was the first contribution to our first concrete effort, but because my love and admiration for my father was now able to express itself in such a way that he could participate with me. This project was something worth working for, something worthy of doing your best for. The issue he had posed to us as children: "You'll all be spoiled brats because there will be nothing worth working for," was one to which I had found an answer that he actually believed in. I was going to work as hard as he did, not out of the need for money, but for the larger purpose of a positive future for all people.

Telling the story became doing it!

I have to step forward and carry
a primary responsibility.

Late one Friday afternoon John and I went to see Werhner von Braun, the handsome, brilliant father of the Saturn V rocket. Just back from the dentist, he sat unsmiling, his jaw stiff with novocaine. We went into his office, sat down, and tried to sound matter-of-fact.

"Dr. von Braun," I said, "we understand there's an extra Saturn V rocket left over from the Apollo program. We would like to use it for a citizen sponsored lunar mission, to get people involved. Do you think the rocket would be available? We could pay for it by a people's subscription, sale of moon rock, television and movie rights. It would be the first time individuals all over the world could do a transcendent act together."

For a moment he just looked at us in stunned silence. "Well, uh,

Mrs. Hubbard, I, uh, don't know why not." A funny half-smile formed on his face, as the rest of his jaw held rigid with novocaine. "Naturally, though, the Saturn V is technologically obsolete. Why not get the people interested in investing in Skylab B. They could grow big crystals in space."

I sighed. "Dr. von Braun, people don't want to grow crystals in space. They want to go to new worlds. Just to be part of that effort would stimulate millions; they'd buy subscriptions so their children might have a chance. We'd do experiments, testing the utility of the moon; searching for water; testing to see if things grow; installing a telescope to seek other life."

Von Braun nodded. "Maybe you're right. You know, I've spent my life trying to get to the moon. I can't see myself sitting here trying to persuade you not to try, too. I'll help."

He gave us a list of the top leaders of NASA and we went to see the space men of the age, one by one. Everywhere we went it was the same story, the same questions, the same response. Then we went to see Christopher Kraft, deputy to Dr. Gilruth, in Houston. He met us with a smile, his eyes gleaming with interest.

"Mrs. Hubbard, I've read your husband's book. This step into the universe is a religion and I'm a member of it."

I smiled back. "I know, and you're right. We're meant to be a universal species. The purpose of Harvest Moon is to give all those who feel this way the chance to say yes together. They'll instantly become a natural constituency for the future."

"I'll do whatever I can. Let me know."

We stopped at Dr. Gilruth's office next door and John and I told him the story.

He turned to an aide, almost tearfully: "Why isn't NASA doing something like this?"

At Homer Newell's office in Washington, we once again outlined our idea. Newell, too, was with us all the way. "Do you realize," he said, "the benefit from satellites if they become operational: education, medical care...."

"Dr. Newell, if we could initiate a people's mission, possibly we could break down some nationalistic barriers that prevent the benefits from being applied."

Newell agreed. "The benefits should be applied for all humankind. We are one people."

"I know."

"I'll do whatever I can," he promised.

I was deeply touched by the spiritual depth of the men of NASA. They, like I, saw the space program as an extension of human life. They were far from the cold engineers so often portrayed by those who do not know them.

Our next stop was on Fifth Avenue, Harry Winston, Inc., where one can find the most exquisite jewels in the United States. As we were carrying briefcases, suitcases, and papers, and looking slightly worn out, customers and salespeople stared at us on the way to some sequestered back showroom. We sat at a table covered with grey felt to show the jewels. A jeweler entered and looked at us quizzically.

"Would you be interested in purchasing lunar rock," I asked, "to turn into jewels? They would be on sale to sponsor a nonprofit citizens' mission to the moon."

He looked startled for a moment, then said, "You know, Harry Winston s son would be very interested in this. He won a prize building model rockets. Could you get stones in various sizes? What's the texture like? Are they beautiful?"

"They're not beautiful in the ordinary sense. They are a symbol. People stand in line for hours to see one. They put slivers of old rockets in their wallets. It would be a sign that humanity could touch worlds beyond earth. The mission could return several hundred pounds. Some would go to science, but most to people."

"Well, we would need the whole load. What would it cost?"

"A few hundred million," I said casually.

He did not even blink. "Comparing each lunar stone to a carat of medium-quality diamonds, that's a fair price."

From there we headed for UNICEF with Richard Nolte, former ambassador to the United Arab Republic and one of the founding members of The Committee for the Future. We had an appointment to meet with the director, M. Labouisse. John and I described Harvest Moon to him.

"Dr. Labouisse," I said, "if there's any profit beyond paying for the mission, we'd like to give it to UNICEF to benefit the children of the world. We want to make it absolutely clear that this mission is not for personal profit but for the good of the world."

Labouisse was poised, urbane, unruffled. "Very interesting, Mrs. Hubbard. But what would happen to our other sources of funding from the United Nations and our Christmas card sales? If you give us this money, how would it effect our next appropriation?"

I was annoyed. "That seems to be a rather narrow perspective to take on this great step for the children of the world."

We left Labouisse and located Congressman Olin "Tiger" Teague, Democrat from Texas, chairman of the Subcommittee on Manned Space Flight, the most powerful congressman for NASA's budget, and the third-ranking Democrat in the House of Representatives. He was sitting wearily at his desk, which was piled high with papers, mementoes everywhere. Teague was portly, red-faced, kindly.

He shook his head and rested his head in his hands. "I've never seen it so bad. What's wrong? I can't understand why Congress won't back the space program. I know the people want it. But I know they have to have a chance to get into it."

"Congressman Teague, we have a suggestion to help." I told him about Harvest Moon and suddenly he stood and took my hand.

"Barbara, you write a resolution asking Congress to request NASA to look at this idea and I'll introduce it into the House."

Without delay I called on my cousin Arthur Borden, a lawyer, in his Park Avenue office. "Arthur, would you write a resolution requesting Congress to ask NASA to cooperate with The Committee for the Future to consider the feasibility of a citizens' lunar mission?" He smiled with amazement, but he did it, and we sent it to Teague, who immediately introduced it into the Congress.

The Committee for the Future testified before Teague's subcommittee. We were a strangely incongruous group of citizens amidst the aerospace industry spokesman and NASA personnel. The purpose of the hearing was simply: the shuttle. General Bleymaier was wearing his Texas cowboy hat. Sister Mary Fidelia was there in her nun's habit. Richard Nolte was always the sophisticated intellectual, smoking his pipe. Lee Kaminsky was a long-haired, former Marxist-Christian turned video artist. Paul Congdon, academic dean of Springfield College, Massachusetts, was there. We all testified on our conviction that the space program is needed for the development of the human potential. After the hearing, one of the congressmen came over.

"Mrs. Hubbard, we're only the Subcommittee on Manned Space Flight. You're asking us to think about the whole world."

"Congressman, you can't discuss the importance of the step into space without discussing the development of the world. Why don't we have a meeting with the members of various committees concerned with different aspects of United States policy to examine the impact of a large space goal on the economy, welfare programs, international relations, education, taxes?"

He shook his head. "There's no way for us to do that. We have no way to get together. Why don't you call that meeting?"

My frustration was mounting rapidly. "But that would take me five years! I don't see how you can legislate, how you can make decisions, if you have no way to look at the impact of a major new option for the whole system."

"We can't," he said, looking helpless, and walked away.

Shortly thereafter, a reporter called us from Houston where he had overheard some astronauts talking about the project. The next day headlines around the world screamed: "Wealthy Group from East Plans Mission to Moon!" The NASA public relations people were queried, and without consulting us, they replied: "NASA cannot support a mission like this." Suddenly letters came from around the world, asking to subscribe to the mission. Then came an offer to appear on TV during Apollo 14, and we agreed to go. But just as the momentum rose to a new height, a letter from NASA's acting administrator, George Low, came, saying NASA could not permit the mission. John and I hastily arranged a meeting with him. When we arrived he was surrounded by aides, looking tense.

"Dr. Low," I said, "I realize that the mission might sound strange to you, but we wouldn't be going through all this backbreaking work if we didn't believe the space program is vital. Your program is being attacked. Funds are cut. Why not work with us to develop the concept? If it's not well-conceived, help us make it better." I told him some former astronauts had volunteered to fly on the mission.

"Mrs. Hubbard, I agree with you about the need. But the people would never tolerate an accident on a nonscientific mission."

"Dr. Low, we intend to perform scientific experiments that are life-oriented. The people would be hiring NASA to do the mission. Your safety standards would prevail. Of course we have to recognize that there will be accidents; no achievements were ever accomplished without some loss of life. NASA should face this. But I personally think it's *more* acceptable to risk lives on a people-sponsored scientific-cultural-social mission than on one doing pure scientific or military research alone."

Dr. Low listened, but shook his head. "You may be right. But another point, your cost figures are off."

"Well," I said. "we got them from the last director of Manned Space Flight. He said yours were unrealistic. You're loading all the research and development costs on the people. That's not fair."

Irritation crept across his face. "The fact is, even though I sympathize with you, you don't know what you're talking about!"

My heart contracted. The sadness of lack of understanding almost brought tears to my eyes, from sorrow that we could not work together. "Dr. Low, I admire the genius of the men of NASA more than almost anything else in the world. But I'm telling you from the bottom of my heart, it's a terrible mistake not to bring the people into the space program now. We are your constituency. If we are excluded, the space program will be cut back and turned over to the military. Please reconsider." He shook his head. I sensed his regret, his own entrapment as the head of a government agency. He knew, but he could not respond.

After the unsuccessful encounter with Low, Congressman Teague invited us to his office on July 19, 1971, to meet with Rocco Petrone, director of Apollo Project; Dale Myers of Manned Space Flight; and Mr. Grubb, NASA legislative liaison.

Teague surveyed our group collectively. "I don't want anyone to waste any more energy on this project. John and Barbara, I would like you to hear what Rocco has to say, and Rocco, I want you to listen to them. Anything you two can agree on, I'll support."

Rocco had a big, burly football-player's body, but a high voice. "Barbara, I never thought I'd have to say this, but we can't go to the moon after Apollo 17. The rocket teams are already being disbanded; the backup teams won't exist; industries are already shut down. It wouldn't be safe."

I tried to remain calm. "I appreciate that, Rocco, but if NASA had been willing to look at our proposal last year, when we first called on all the key people, it wouldn't be too late now."

However, expecting this response, we had an alternative plan prepared by space-scientist friends in Huntsville: we proposed a citizen-sponsored, near earth orbit mission, to be called "Humankind One." Its purpose would be to broadcast the benefits of the space program and the cultural unity in diversity of humankind. Both Myers and Petrone said they could "live with that."

Congressman Teague agreed. "Barbara, rewrite the resolution. If you can get NASA to agree with you, we're in business."

John and I rewrote the legislation, substituting "near-earth orbit" for the words "lunar mission," and resubmitted it to NASA. But they refused to respond. I called them from time to time, until my patience wore out. I reached the point once of saying, "The mothers of the world are going to unite! This is our children's future. You have no right to deny us access to our rockets. They belong to the people, not you!" They had no idea how to cope with me; I was becoming shrill. I was an annoyance to them.

Dealing with NASA was like working with a giant marshmallow: the further in you went, the more lost you became. They did not directly oppose you; they just absorbed you in their enormous inertia. I sensed the oppression of the faceless tyranny of bureaucracy. The corporate decision of NASA as a government agency was less responsive than the decision of any of the individual members.

We continued exploring the idea of Harvest Moon in spite of NASA's rejection. John and I took a trip to England, the Soviet Union, and Yugoslavia. I was invited to appear on Independent Television News in England during Apollo 16. ITN had heard of the Harvest Moon project. When we arrived at the studio, I was delighted to discover they had constructed a model of the experimental package called FIELD-1: the growing experiment, the search for water, with a telescope on the roof of the building.

I had about three minutes on television. Astronaut Gordon was with me and was asked very briefly about the Harvest Moon project. "We're in Britain to suggest a citizen-sponsored lunar expedition following the Apollo series. We want to know if anyone in England would like to subscribe to such a mission if it proves feasible." They showed the model of FIELD-1. Instantly the phone lines into the studio jammed. When I finished, members of the staff at the television station wanted to know how they could buy tickets.

I also was invited to be on a BBC interview. As I was waiting to go on the air, I encountered the ambassador from Bangladesh, a distinguished, urbane, elegantly dressed gentleman, who also was to be interviewed. I took the occasion to question him.

"We've been criticized for supporting the space program because people are starving in Bangladesh. Do you think it's right or wrong for us to be promoting an experiment for an internationally cooperative space program?"

With firmness and strength of conviction, he said, "We *must* support such a program. We, in Bangladesh, have no chance for survival in the old way. Our problems are too great. We have too many people; our resources are depleted. Unless there are new technologies, new methods, and new ventures, which we can eventually participate in, we are doomed in Bangladesh."

We went to the Soviet Union to speak with Ella Massevitch, one of the leading women scientists in the USSR Academy of Sciences, as well as with the editor of *Novotny Press*. The Soviet Union saddened me deeply. My heart went out to this great people whose struggle was unfulfilled. I knew that the *vision* of communism was for a quantum jump, a new humanity, a classless, stateless, society. "From each according to his ability, to each according to his need." I felt that the hunger which had motivated me all these years, for the next stage of evolution, was at the root of this society. But they had coerced holism, forced people to be a part of the whole. They had suppressed the creativity of the people. It was a tragedy.

We were required to stay at an Intourist hotel, a large, ugly building in a style they call "Stalinesque Gothic." It was jammed with visitors for the May Day celebration. John and I were in rooms across from each other. We were required to leave our keys with a concierge. When I called John in the morning, I was asked what I wanted to speak to him about. Furthermore, when we tried to make telephone calls to set appointments, we could not get through to the secretaries. We asked the help of the Intourist people. We made a call at 9:00 in the morning and were told to call back at noon; the secretary was out. We called back at noon and the secretary was still out; she would be back at 3:00. We called at 3:00 and the secretary was out again; she would be back at 5:00. We called at 5:00 and the office was closed. We had only three or four days in Moscow, and the frustration of being unable to contact anyone mounted. Then they assigned us an Intourist guide who said she would translate when we met these people.

I said, "Thank you very much but they speak perfect English and it won't be necessary to have a translator."

She said, "Yes, it will."

While we were waiting for our appointments, we took a drive through Moscow. Passing the giant University of Moscow, I asked her, "Is there any student unrest in Moscow?"

"No, none at all," she said. "If they have a problem, they go to their superior and get it solved."

"Well," I said, "the situation is entirely different in the United States. Almost everyone is restless, students are restless, and so are retired people and women and blacks, almost everyone."

She nodded. "It is unfortunate in the West, with your corrupt system, the drugs, the crime, the pornography. No wonder the people are restless."

"You're right, we have a serious breakdown. Tell me," I asked, "what's the goal of your society?"

She responded with the quickness of a rehearsed answer. "Better light industry, better consumer goods."

'Ah ha!' I thought, remembering, 'the toy culture!' "Wait till you get it. Then you will be faced with the same situation we are. Now you have a material goal, but when your society achieves it, as we have, even partially, you, too, will be seeking the next level. That's where we are, our society is breaking down because, once achieved, material sufficiency isn't adequate; you'll find that out soon."

She looked back at me, and said, "Well, we're not all that content."

She was intrigued by the idea that the discontent of the West was a prelude to something new. She forgot her role as spokesperson for Communist ideology, and we began to talk directly. I asked her what she thought about the cosmonauts and the space program. She had not given it much thought. I told her it was part of the emancipation of the human potential. I asked her for their vision of the good person. She spoke of the "Soviet man." I said, "Does this Soviet man represent a model for everyone?"

"No," she said, "we're superior and it probably can't come about until other people are changed, other cultures are destroyed."

"This Soviet man, does he recognize that we're all members of one body? Moving toward universal development?"

She shook her head. "I don't know."

We began to talk around this "I don't know." She told me afterwards that it was the most interesting conversation she had ever had. There was a real openness to discuss the future as soon as we got off ideological ground.

Later I had an unpleasant experience at the Intourist desk. I suspected that the Intourist people were lying to me about all these telephone calls. I was exhausted; throngs of visitors from North Vietnam, China, crowded around me. Suddenly I broke down, tears streaming down my cheeks. "I don't believe you, you're lying to me. I want to see these people and you're preventing it!" As I cried they stared at me with very cold eyes, except for one younger woman who gave me a handkerchief.

The next day I did get my appointment with the editor of *Novotny Press*. His first words were, "I understand you think we're liars." I had been reported on! I found the network of impossibility closing in. If I'd had to stay in that society, I would have become insane.

Ella Massevitch met us in her office at the USSR Academy of Science with two or three men. She was the major person there, an attractive woman, about my age. We told her of the Harvest Moon project, and she was immediately sympathetic, the first person I met in the Soviet Union of any high position with whom there was a personal rapport. She said, "If there's really an effort to do something for humanity and not for the United States to get ahead of the Soviet Union, I would like to support it." The men with her said the idea was unrealistic and not practical. But she was sympathetic, and, I believe, would have added her weight to it if we had been able to follow through with NASA.

We asked permission to postpone our departure one day to see the May Day celebrations. Even though there was free space in the hotel and passage on a flight the next day, the Intourist officials denied our request. Exasperated, I asked, "Why?"

"Because only a certain number of people are permitted in the Soviet Union from the outside at any one time."

When we arrived at the airport, we tried to change our tickets to a later flight to avoid a long delay in Frankfurt, Germany. Even though there were seats available on the more convenient flight, our request again was denied. No tickets were permitted to be changed in Moscow, they told me. The petty network of impossibilities closed in again. Suddenly I shouted at the woman, "You're acting like sheep; you call yourself free? Don't accept this!" No one would talk to me. I sensed a circle of fear; everyone backed away. I felt the way I had at the Museum of Modern Art. There, hope was being assassinated by those who had grown to love death; in the Soviet Union hope was being assassinated by the denial of individual personality and freedom. When confronted with denial of human development, whether the Western version of decadence, or the Soviet version of repression, I experienced a powerful driving force to break that bond.

As we pursued the Harvest Moon project back in the United States, it became clear that effort alone would not suffice. We were moving against the current bureaucratic system; they were stronger than we. Also, on college campuses, the climate of opinion was not congenial to any new hopeful option. I was failing to communicate. Earl, who was usually invited as our spokesman, would make an eloquent plea for new worlds, but although a few students would be interested, in general, there was hostility.

Furthermore, an unexpected reaction was occurring in me. I first felt it in South Carolina in October 1970. Henry Cauthen, manager of the Educational Television Station, had invited Earl to speak to a group of citizens in South Carolina for a whole day, presenting the ideas of new worlds. John had sought out Henry, who planned to produce a one-hour documentary from the day's conversation. I should have been delighted. Instead, misery. As Earl was rehearsing and John was busily making arrangements for him, I found my spirits sinking, falling down a well and nothing to hold on to.

During the day, a TV team and Earl went from location to location. Tears were running down my face and I stood behind trees, hiding in embarrassment. I felt faint. Without disturbing Earl, I went to our room, locked myself in the bathroom, and began to cry even harder. I could not handle this raging anger. I was shocked to discover that something inside me wanted to speak and would no longer remain silent for Earl. That feeling was tearing me apart.

When Earl returned, triumphant after a long day during which he had been well-received, he found me red-eyed and exhausted.

"Barbara, what in the world is wrong?" He tried to embrace me.

A frightful repulsion seared through my body. "I don't know, I don't know." I could not bring myself to tell him the truth. He had worked so hard. I felt so unfair. He thought he was pleasing me. He took me to dinner alone, holding my hand, mystified. "Earl, you did so well, so well." I said, and started to cry again.

Finally he understood it. Sighing deeply, he said, "I know what it is. You want to do it yourself. The more I succeed, the worse you're going to feel." He was really distressed, since I was literally his only contact with the world. He did not have a single friend otherwise, male or female.

"That's not true, not true," I said. "There's room for us both; there's room for everyone in this effort. But I can't be secondary to you anymore." It burst out. "I have to speak for myself."

All at once he turned against John and Harvest Moon. "You're a fool to be wasting your energy on ridiculous projects like that."

"Earl, I've spent twenty years on words and images. I believe in them with all my heart. But in this age, without the ability to act on them, they're inert, lifeless. We need a citizens' movement for the future." We really disagreed. I understood the necessity for his work, but he did not believe in the need for mine.

The combination of the need to speak, instead of being the person who was holding the microphone, and the desire for concrete action was leading to a major change in me. This change was made manifest one day in February 1971. John and I had an appointment to see Alexander Butterfield, President Nixon's special assistant at the White House, to inform the president about Harvest Moon. We were driving to the airport from Lakeville. We were late and I was irritable. We arrived at Bradley Field and missed the plane; the airport was fogged in. We missed our appointment at the White House and spent a great deal of time together at the airport.

John said, "It's been gradually dawning on me: Earl can't lead. If we continue to put him forward as the leader, this whole thing will fail. He's a brilliant artist, but he can't work with people. He's not the leader. You are. You're the one who's taking the risks, communicating, making things happen. I know we are going to fail unless you recognize yourself."

This was exceedingly hard for me to accept. During my whole life, I had tried to help someone else manifest the feelings I had inside me. Now John was saying I had to step forward and carry a primary responsibility. Deep in my heart, though, I wanted to do exactly that. So I accepted his vision.

At every step in the development of my new personhood it was necessary for someone to verify my own inner feeling to me. Seven years before, Jonas had made it possible for me to see myself as a useful part of the evolutionary process. Now, through John, I was able to see myself as a primary factor in the action.

I want to do this extraordinary thing.

The next major step occurred at Southern Illinois University, where we held a conference in May 1971: "Mankind in the Universe," the culmination of several small conferences we had in Lakeville with students from Southern Illinois University. John's son was in college there; many of the young people we knew were from SIU.

Earl was to address the student body in the Arena, which was like a prize-fighting ring with thousands of seats around it. He gave one of his set speeches, which he had asked me to edit for him from our morning dialogues. Elegantly dressed in a dark blue suit, white shirt and red tie, he was totally out of phase with the style of the students and faculty in blue jeans, the casual garb of protest. His speech did not go over. It was a call for pure heroism in the age of the anti-hero. He had his own form of courage: to stand, completely different, and expose himself to the hostility of those he would serve without accommodating one iota.

Subsequently we had several small meetings in which I spoke to classes. On one occasion, I proposed the idea that there was a new way to meet the hierarchy of human needs. I was trying to shape the humanistic argument to include the space program. My vision was that the combination of holistic consciousness and high technology joined for the evolution of the human race would allow the natural transformation to occur. However, this was the time of the radical rejection of human society by certain elements of our culture. I was attacked by students.

One of the students asked me, "Why do you want us to continue 25,000 years of failure?"

An older man, a professor, rose in towering wrath directed at this question. "You would have kept us in the caves! You wouldn't even have dared step into the light."

I went on to say, in a gentle way, that man had not failed, that we are a young species at a point of transition. Now it is possible, for the first time, to overcome those terrible lacks such as poverty, disease, and ignorance that had forced us into destructive behavior. Our new tools might transform the species on earth as well as liberate it for new life in the universe. Each one of us is needed, valuable, precious. I heard one student snicker at me. I took courage, stared him in the eye, and said, "Did I hear you snicker?" The long-haired, blue-jeaned, twenty-five year old, perennial-student type sank in his seat.

"How dare you snicker at humankind! How dare you condemn the effort of the past! Do you have any idea of the struggle that went into the development of the human species? The suffering, the anguish of the people working day in and day out to eat, to survive, to keep their children alive? You are sitting in this heated building in an affluent society, snickering at the past!" I felt a strange love for this person. I spoke like a mother defending her family, yet he was one of the family, too. I was trying to attract him towards hope, but to no avail.

I felt myself rising to defend humanity against this arrogance of pessimism. The nights in Lakeville, listening to Beethoven, looking at the paintings, meditating joyfully on the goodness of the human struggle, strengthened me to speak in total love. But I left the platform feeling a failure, defeated. My desire had been to create consensus and affirmation. Instead I had instigated dissension. Earl's speech was out of context in its purity, and my efforts had aroused heated argument, rather than affirmation.

The next morning Professor Tom Turner, director of special projects for Buckminster Fuller, asked John and me to sit with him on the stage. In the audience were several hundred people who had attended the various seminars and activities of the "Mankind in the Universe" conference. Earl was there, too. Tom looked like a soft, comfortable dolphin: round, gentle, and sweet, a very intelligent man. He started out mildly by saying that Buckminster Fuller had been talking for some time about the importance of women's leadership for the new age.

"Therefore," said Tom, "we would like to make a recommendation: that Barbara Marx Hubbard run for the nomination for the presidency of the United States on the Democratic ticket. Her role would be to carry the options for the future into the public arena. She can state the alternatives and new possibilities better than any other candidate." He called on the assembled group to pass a resolution from SIU.

I was stunned. The surprising thing was that I felt that it was a good idea. The conviction of the rightness of "new worlds on earth, new worlds in space, new worlds in the human mind" was so deep inside me that when Tom said it, I stood without hesitating and made an acceptance speech. "It's true women do have a new role to play. As we lessen our role in reproducing the species, we must strengthen our role in the maturing of the species; love, cooperation, and nurturing qualities, combined with intellect are needed." Suddenly I noticed Earl's face staring at me. He was in anguish. I avoided his eyes; I did not want to be stopped. By the time I finished, the hunger was tremendously excited by the possibility of large-scale, mainstream action. Unaccountably, I wanted to do this extraordinary, unprecedented thing.

Many people got up to second the nomination. Various constructive suggestions were made: it would provide new international initiatives and a new, trans-political approach to the future. The last person to speak was Earl. He was sitting along the aisle and began to pace up and down like a prisoner. "I think this is a very bad recommendation," he said. "The idea must not be associated with one person, certainly not with my wife! It could be ruined. What we need is for Southern Illinois University to take it on. You people, professors and students, should develop the ideas and bring them into the political arena."

He tried to make a case for the university to undertake this goal, which was totally unrealistic, since large state institutions do not advocate new socio-political goals. I understood his anguish, and felt it with him. Still, I was angry that he would cut me down like that.

We broke for lunch. The resolution was written and read as soon as we reconvened. It said: "We propose that Barbara Marx Hubbard carry the positive options for the future into the public arena, seeking the Democratic nomination for president of the United States." The vote occurred, everyone was affirmative, except for two: Earl Hubbard and a young man brought by Sister Fidelia.

Later that afternoon I received a message that Buckminster Fuller wanted to see me. Naturally Earl came along. Bucky was sitting in his office, surrounded by his books, plaques, pictures - memorabilia of a lifetime. I sensed the tremendous contribution he had made to humanity. The first thing he said was, "Well, young lady, I hear you've been nominated for the presidency."

He spoke laughingly and I laughingly said, "Yes." I wanted to discuss it with him, but I was not given the chance to say a word. Earl broke in, asserting his vision of the importance of space. Fuller became irritated and asked Earl whether he had read his books. Earl said no, he had not read them. "You know," Fuller said, "the ideas you're promoting I've been writing about for years." Fuller became outraged, and said, in essence, "How dare you set foot on my campus if you haven't even read my books!"

I felt caught between my attraction for Bucky, my desire to really hear what he thought I should do, and my pain at his angry words to Earl. Earl and Bucky were locked in a masculine ego-driven encounter. I felt I had lost my opportunity to establish a relationship with this man who was one of my mentors and guides in this world.

Later that night, in our bedroom, Earl couldn't sleep. He was pacing the floor in the middle of the night and woke me. "Barbara, I beg you not to accept this nomination, it would destroy me. I could never hold my head up again with my children. I could never hold my head up again with my family, or with my peers."

I weighed my decision carefully. My innermost desire was thrilled and wanted to try. The voice that guided me intuitively from time to time urged me onward. But my reason asserted it was an incredible act that might do what Earl said: diminish the viability of the new worlds' goals. For me the main question was whether it was right to hurt Earl to satisfy what might be merely an ego need of mine. Dare I risk his well-being because I wanted to do this extraordinary thing? I meditated for hours and he paced the floor. We did not speak. Finally, I made my decision. I could not hurt him to satisfy myself. My signal on running for the presidency was not authoritative or clear enough to risk mortally wounding him.

"Earl," I said softly, breaking the tense silence, "I promise not to run for the presidency." It sounded strange. The sentence hung in the air like a sound I had never heard before.

He stopped pacing; his body relaxed. "Thank you, Barbara. Do you promise never to run?"

"No, Earl, I can't promise that."

Although I had acquiesced in order to save his pride, something inside me shifted definitively. I resented his need to dominate me and be "the one" to speak. I knew that I would have to stand up for myself. Yet my heart was broken because I loved him.

The following morning I had to face John. He wanted me to do it. He thought we had a chance to gather the energy of discontent and disenfranchisement: those who liked neither Nixon nor the familiar Democrats. "John, I've decided not to do it. We have very little chance, and it would hurt Earl."

He shook his head. "You're wrong, Barbara. You've made the wrong decision. It could make all the difference." He walked away from me, still shaking his head.

A few days later I joined my father for lunch, stopping first in his office on Fifth Avenue. He sat behind his desk, puffing the familiar cigar, leaning back in his large chair, beaming at me. "Well, Barbara, how are you? What's been going on?"

"Dad, I've been asked to run for the nomination for the presidency on the Democratic ticket." I pulled the SIU resolution out of my purse and handed it to him across the desk.

He read slowly, looked up, and said matter-of-factly, "You ought to do it. It's a good idea. Run on both tickets, like Eisenhower did. You're not a politician. Call it the Unity party."

Strategies started to crop up in his mind like daisies in spring. I was amazed at his acceptance of this idea. But it has been consistent with my father: when a great concept took root in me, such as the citizen-sponsored space mission, and running for the presidency, he, of all my family, instantly understood it and wanted to support it.

My total commitment had been triggered by the dissension and self-disgust after the 1969 lunar landing. In 1972 nothing had improved. Groups did not trust each other; no one really knew what anyone else thought; communities, disciplines, generations, races, religions were fragmented. The problem was attitudes. There was no method, no process for people to find out what others thought. Society had separated us from each other unnaturally. The result was disintegration, social disease. Politics was polarizing people unnecessarily accentuating the adversarial mode. There had to be something else. The Unity party - it echoed in my ears. Certainly something was needed, a new way to bring people together.

*I am beginning one of the most
fascinating journeys of my life.*

One day John was pondering the idea of new worlds on earth, new worlds in space, new worlds in the human mind. Whenever we had discussed this idea with a businessman, he would say, "I get this, but labor never will." A labor union executive would say, "I get it, but you'll never get the politicians to buy it." Then a politician would say, "Of course, I believe in it, but the people will never vote for it."

In a flash of insight, John decided to put all the apparently opposed forces into one wheel to actually experience one another directly. He put all the functional areas of any social body in the inner circle of the wheel like pieces of a pie facing each other. There were sections for production, environment, technology, social needs, other regions of the world, government, with a coordinating hub in the center where each sector could match needs and resources and compare each other's goals. He added a satellite at the growing edge of the circle called nature of humankind. The new potentials were also put at the "growing edge" of the wheel. These were the biological revolution, new powers in the physical sciences, new capacities in the information sciences, the psychologies of growth, extraterrestrial development, political-economic theory. The arts were represented by a dotted line, the skin around the wheel; they were the synthesizers and motivators. Without the arts, people cannot see themselves struggling to be whole, cannot visualize where they want to be. Finally, there was a far-out satellite, unexplained phenomena: the intuitive, mystical, psychic experiences of the human race. Seeing the first picture of it, I thought it looked just like a cell, a social cell!

John said there should be television in every section, a reality factor and a security blanket, with a central, open "mission control" where anyone could see everything at once. "Just like you did for the space program," I said. "We'll be able to see ourselves in all our separate parts as one organism, that's great!" It looked as though we had a social process to bring the body together as a whole.

"Yes! We can broadcast live and have people call in," John added.

"My God!" I said. "You're giving us a social nervous system!" I was thrilled. I knew it was right. We decided to use the wheel format for the next conference at SIU, May 1972.

John and I then hit the road for one of the most fascinating journeys of my life. Our purpose was to get the broadest possible cross section of people to form task forces in each sector and ask them to look at their own needs in light of the growing capacities of society as a whole. During the process they would have the chance to merge gradually with corollary but apparently conflicting groups, such as environmentalists with technologists, to check for common goals, and to match the needs of one functional group with the resources of another. Finally, we would remove all the "walls" and the groups would meet as one body. The growing edge of new capacities would report on the social body's new opportunities, and the conflicts would be discussed in the open, seeking a win-win situation. The attempt would be to solve one group's needs without hurting someone else. It was a new game, with new rules: how can everyone benefit?

The timing was right. Almost everyone we invited said yes. Labor had reached the point where, if it demanded more benefits, it would seriously jeopardize the industry and the economy upon which it was dependent. Business could not continue to maximize profits at the expense of an environment of which it was a part. Environmentalists were advocating stringent controls, which were affecting the economy upon which people were dependent for survival. Technologists could not continue to advocate solutions that damaged the biosphere. Human services recognized that after thirty years of welfare and an estimated trillion dollars' expenditure, there was still no success in providing genuine well-being to those who are excluded. Everyone had a vested interest in a cooperative solution to fulfill their own goals. An expanded self-interest was possible.

We wrote an article for *The Futurist* and as a joke named the process SYNCON, an acronym for synergistic convergence. It meant the coming together of all vital elements of the social body to discover their functional relationships to each other and to the whole. Together the whole is greater than the sum of its parts; therefore, each participating member becomes "greater" through inclusion in the whole. Building the SYNCON was a vital experience for me. I learned to communicate with every part of the social body.

One incident stood out vividly. My job, that particular day, was to invite Joe Berney, the head of a major union to the SYNCON. I walked into his office and saw a gruff, unsmiling face. I jumped in, describing the SYNCON process and inviting him to participate.

"You're so dumb, you must be rich." His response was like a slap in the face.

I stiffened. "Yes, I am rich," I said, "And I'm spending my money to do something to bring us together. What's wrong with that?"

"What'ya want me to do...?" he smiled.

"I just want you to come to the SYNCON with some members of your union, to state your goals, and see if there is some way of achieving them through cooperation with others, through matching your needs with other people's resources. There will be people from business, environmentalists, scientists..."

Suddenly, he broke in, "I've always known there is a better way. Ever since I stood on those damn picket lines, I knew we had to learn to do this without destroying one another. But I was afraid of losing the support of my men, afraid of being called a communist. I'll be there, and I'll bring the best people I've got," he said.

He had turned on a dime, literally, from negative to positive, when a new, non-adversarial option was offered in a non-threatening way.

I came to believe that a substantial portion of the violent opposition of one sector against the other was due to a lack of a process of communication. We needed a new game with win-win rules, rather than the traditional win-lose.

The year of the first SYNCON, 1972, was the beginning of the end of my past family life. In 1970-71, although I travelled a good deal, my home base was definitely Lakeville. But with the SIU SYNCON my physical base shifted to constant travel, so that 1972 was the year the family fabric ripped apart. Suzanne and Stephanie were away at school. They sympathized with me. As much as they loved and admired their father, they knew I had to be free to grow: they wanted to do just that themselves.

I had a long phone conversation with Suzanne. "Mummy, we're with you all the way," she said. "You're right to do what you're doing. You must!" She gave me enormous moral courage.

Fortunately, Alexandra, Wade and Lloyd led a normal, happy life with Mademoiselle Baldet. She was able to act as a living link between them and me. They trusted her deeply. She loved both me and them; spiritually, she joined me in my task while physically, day by day, she cared for them. I telephoned them almost daily, to find out what was going on in their lives. Once I could get beyond the "fine, thank you" stage of the conversation, they reported the major events: seeing deer, the movies, skiing. We never lost connection with each other. With Earl, though, it was far more painful. His personality demanded total dedication from me and he required to be on center stage with others. His pain broke my heart, but there was nothing I could do. For even as he awed people with his brilliance, he pushed them away with his demand for perfection. We couldn't get anything started with him at the core.

SYNCON eve, John was already at Southern Illinois University. I was to fly there the next day with the participants from New York. About 250 people were expected.

When I arrived at SIU I found John in the student ballroom. I was thrilled, the students had built a cosmic wheel! It looked like a space craft, a flying saucer. In the center was the coordinating hub, with a little spiral staircase that went up to a balcony, where anyone could look down upon the body as a whole. The stage was being set for a new experience of wholeness and transcendence that had urged me forward and tantalized me from the very beginning. In each sector of the wheel was a TV camera and a monitor so participants could both see what was happening in the other sectors and be recorded themselves. The internal nervous system was ready operate.

The task forces worked all that first day until the afternoon of the second, preparing their first summaries of goals, needs, and resources. Occasionally John, who produced the event, would flash a focus item over the internal television system, such as Lazar Mojsov, United Nations ambassador from Yugoslavia, addressing the need for cooperative technological exchange between the developing and developed worlds. Each of these talks was given from the site of the functional task forces, to symbolize that there was no audience, no speaker and that everyone was a participant, each sector was vital to the whole. We were all members of one body! John had recreated the cosmic birth experience so others could feel it, too.

Every evening before dinner we presented the "New Worlds Evening News," a newscast in a format like "CBS Evening News," taking the highlights of the day's SYNCON activities, adding news highlights of the outside world. The contrast was obvious: most of the news from the mass media was of catastrophe, breakdown, and disagreement. The news from the SYNCON was of the struggle to find linkages and to match needs and resources. There were arguments, but they tended toward seeking agreement, rather than stressing differences. These evening newscasts were played during the cocktail hour; people wanted to see them over and over again.

On Saturday morning the walls came down. Participants gathered in the wheel, in their merged groups. Questions went around the wheel, each group trying to gain the assistance of the other in handling some problem. I could feel the social body adjusting and coordinating itself as one, each element trying to avoid injuring another. It was the same feeling when I sensed myself part of the planetary body trying to coordinate on the hill in Lakeville. There were experts in each part, but no experts in integrating a planetary system. Thus we experienced a new kind of equality. We were, in that instant, a microcosm of the macrocosm; we were all in it together, learning something new.

People felt increasingly united by some bond deeper than words could express. A psychological field of force was drawing them closer and closer. They did not want the "SYNCONing" to stop. People of enormous diversity had grown attached to each other. John Yardley, the space scientist, Carl Madden, the establishment economist, and Wayne Woodman, the radical evolutionary, drove away in a convertible, with Wayne's long hair whipping into Carl Madden's face. There was a desire to "do it again"; some wanted to hold one where they lived. As the body of people were forced to separate, they wanted to hold the links together in some way.

For the hunger of Eve, this was a feast, a social manifestation of the birth experience of oneness. We had created a model of social relations that represented humankind as a whole, with its functional systems present, with a process for each group to discover how it could best fit and grow in the whole. I felt we had invented a new social form which we called synergistic or cooperative democracy. It was the politics of the whole in embryo, beyond win-lose, right-left, toward wholeness. The use of television to dramatize convergence heralded the maturation of our mass media to become the nervous system of ourselves as a living system.

John's capacity in creating the SYNCON attracted me deeply. Together we were joining our genius to create something new. My love for him was solidified, while my relationship with Earl grew distant. I realized that although I believed in fidelity, to stay together when the creativity had stopped is in itself a form of immorality, the immorality of suppressing growth.

After the SYNCON, on June 14, we met Astronaut Edgar Mitchell at the Gotham Hotel, where we had taken a small suite. He had been a SYNCON participant. It was Saturday morning. John had gone to park the car, and I was alone in the apartment when Ed rang the doorbell. As he entered the room, trailing clouds of glory of his experience, I began to laugh. "Ed, what in the world brings a former housewife from Lakeville and a former astronaut together at the Gotham Hotel to talk about the unity of humankind?"

Ed said, "Barbara, all I know is that I'm operating under orders.

I've lost all fear. I've come to believe that there are no accidents. Just when I think all is lost, I put my foot down over what seems to be an abyss, and something comes up to hit it, just in time."

John returned, and Ed described to us his plans for The Institute of Noetic Sciences. Its purpose would be to demonstrate that psychic phenomena: the mind force, healing, telepathy, clairvoyance, psychokinesis, astral travel, consciousness itself, were "real" phenomena and could be studied scientifically. I asked him how this happened to him, a trained physicist. He'd had an experience similar to mine. "When I was on the moon," he said, "I looked at earth, I could feel its anguish, its struggle, and I fell in love with humanity as a whole."

We established a linkage on a deep level. I sensed a new element fitting perfectly into my own being, enlarging me by the extent of his being, and hopefully, my being enlarging his.

But in spite of these cases of individual empathy, it became apparent that even at the highest level of development, various sectors of the body of humankind had not recognized the validity of the other sectors.

When we met biologist Dr. Ben Schloss and were discussing the study of the aging process, I asked him what he thought about psychic phenomena. He said, "It doesn't exist."

"How can you be so dogmatic?" I asked. "Throughout history there have been reports of healing, of telepathy, of intuitive experiences, beyond the ordinary."

He shook his head, dismissing it. "I can prove that it doesn't exist."

When I asked Ed Mitchell what he thought about physical immortality, he said, "It's of no significance. Our consciousness will live on without our bodies."

"How do you know that?" I asked. He had no more proof of that than Schloss had that there were no psychic phenomena.

Edgar Mitchell, the physicist, and Ben Schloss, the biologist, both breaking frontiers, had views that excluded the other. It was as if the young humankind had developed an allergy to its various parts. One side of the body got hives at the thought of the other. The cosmic child had colic! The fact was, brilliant as any individual might be, no one knows *all* the laws of the universe. It was arrogant for a young species like humankind, barely gaining access to knowledge and to self-awareness, to make dogmatic pronouncements on the nature of the universe.

Furthermore, although I always tried to bring leaders together to align with one another, I began to suspect that it would not be such leaders who would recognize each other. It would be the general public, the people, who would see the whole, rather than the leaders who had vested interests in the different parts.

I was totally absorbed in this new action, but I kept returning to Lakeville for the weekends to be with the children. I do not know when it dawned on me that I had separated from Earl. It was not a conscious act; it was simply that I was involved totally in a new life.

For many months I had not written in my journal. It represented to me the quest. Now that the emphasis was on realization through action, the need to write lessened. It wasn't until 1973 that I wrote:

> Since I last really wrote in my journal, Earl and I have separated. I can only explain it in terms of different "karma" or destiny. I am literally commanded to go forth. John Whiteside, the first man who has really loved me for what I want to become, helped me to see that my role is not to remain a secondary function to serve the liberation of Earl's potential. Earl adamantly and steadfastly remains true to his own destiny, which is to conceive in word and image the next step of the creative intention. He wants me to serve him in his purpose, and I simply no longer can. Every fiber of my being is calling out for independent action.

John, in one of his intuitive flashes that I was growing to trust more and more, decided we should have a meeting in Tucson directly after the SYNCON with Paul Henshaw, the biologist, as our host. We invited Krafft Ehricke, space scientist; John Yardley, vice-president of McDonnell Douglas; and Florence Hetzler, philosopher. We met in John Yardley's motel room.

When Krafft arrived I asked him about his concept: the "Extraterrestrial Imperative," the technological-industrial basis for the next step in evolution. He's a silver-haired German, one of the original rocket-building Penemunde group that left Germany, one of the greatest, little-known geniuses on planet earth. Sitting on the foot of the bed, his cheeks flushed, his eyes alive, his hands gesturing, he talked about the entire process of creation. He felt it, like I did, and I loved him.

He spoke of how during the first crisis the single cells, having depleted the organic compounds synthesized during the formation of earth, responded with the "biotechnical accomplishment of photosynthesis," gaining extraterrestrial sources of energy. However, the process of photosynthesis produced a "waste": oxygen, which was poisonous to single-celled life. In response, multicellular organisms emerged, and they could metabolize and use the oxygen.

Now, facing the second great crisis of limited fossil fuels and the danger of increased industrialization to the fragile biosphere, we needed to build the "androsphere," humanity's sphere, creating an integrated, indivisible environment of earth and space. Weightlessness, vacuum, continuous solar energy, lunar and asteroidal materials, and the lack of a biosphere make outer space a better place than earth for certain elements of the next phase of industry. He told us the second great crisis was actually another evolutionary driver, pressing us forward to develop an "open-world" system, the material basis for the next step in human development, a step that will also provide the basis for immeasurable development of the human mind and spirit. This discussion was one of the most exciting of my life. Krafft was describing the technology of humankind's birth into the universe! He was to me the Darwin of technology.

As John Whiteside went to the flip chart on the headboard of the bed, everyone suddenly burst out laughing at the incongruity of our seriousness and the setting. After we settled down he laid out a strategy, first outlined in the "Green Book," for achieving a public mandate to call for the goals of "new worlds on earth, new worlds in space," or the building of the "androsphere." We planned to act out the philosophy Krafft had abstractly presented. We were responding to evolutionary drivers. We were evolving as we sat in the motel!

Conversation flowed rapidly from person to person. We were gaining access to each other's minds, knowledge, and very being. We were fusing! Every nerve and cell in my body awakened, and I had to leave the group, I was so infused with energy. I rushed out to the patio near the pool and began to do some yoga exercises to release the pressure. In fact, I was standing on my head when John Yardley joined me, and in that comic position we conversed about our personal intuition of universal life.

He wanted to record our conversations and had brought four different tape recorders; each malfunctioned. They speeded up or went dead. He was mystified. I had experienced the same curious phenomenon while I was dictating one of my first books. This phenomenon was not unheard of, however. Puharich wrote in his book on Uri Geller that when the voices of a group, which they called "Spectrum" and experienced as extraterrestrials, were recorded on their tape, it erased mysteriously. Similarly, Laurens van der Post, in his biography of Carl Jung, reported that he was preparing to interview Jung for the BBC, when Jung said, "I warn you, things of this sort hate me. You might think they are inanimate but in my regard I tell you they're highly animate and even active and hostile..." We speculated that if it was true that the extended nervous system of the body of humankind is its media, perhaps the media is literally blocking out signals of the new voices; their vibrations may overload the existing electronic system.

Throughout the meeting at Tucson, I developed the feeling of parts of the body awakening, linking, "turning on and tuning in" to each other until the whole earth became alive. In my thoughts, I could sense the earth recognizing itself as one and a feeling of love of our larger self, the body of humankind. In those instants I knew myself to be both parent and child. I loved the whole body from the perspective of a mature, parental culture. I could forgives us our sins, much as a mother forgives the infantile behavior of the newborn child. From the cosmic perspective, we were infantile, unable to coordinate, fighting ourselves, unaware of who we are, where we came from, or what we may grow up to be. We were "dangerous," capable of causing our own destruction, perhaps even affecting our portion of the universe. Like that of a newborn child, our condition was serious, but the potential for survival was there. On the other hand, I felt myself to be part of the body, an infant, too, with the same irritability, self-centeredness, and faults. I could forgive myself and have compassion upon myself as well as all others.

After the meeting, John Yardley drew a most interesting diagram. He said that his experience of fusion with the five of us in Tucson, as we joined together for a transcendent purpose beyond our individual egos or agendas, had given him a clue as to how extraterrestrial contact will be made.

"We are like component parts of a radio," he said. "We need a certain number of parts to be able to receive and hear radio waves. So with us, we need a certain number of people to be united in resonance, as we were, to be able to receive and understand signals from higher intelligence. I think three is too few, seven or nine is too many. Five seems like the right number."

He drew a picture of earth filled with little clusters of core groups of five people. These cores acted as receiving sets for contact, drawing to earth corresponding clusters flocking toward us in outer space. This reinforced my intuition that it is our own experience of union which will bring us in contact with other life.

My experience at Tucson was the closest I had ever came to touching the Tree of Life, of participating consciously in the evolutionary process. It felt normal, once again affirming that the hunger could be satisfied by real action to evolve our species.

We are already cooperating ...
we are one.

John was developing the concept of the "new media." The use of television at the SIU SYNCON was a first prototype. He was applying what he had learned through live coverage of the space program to the live coverage of human interaction and development. He became convinced with almost inexplicable certainty that we should purchase our own television system especially designed to make a new model for the communication of human convergence, creation, agreement, and synergy. I would never have conceived of this myself. I was acting under sheer faith in his ability to envision a new communication system. I did know, from experience, that the media, as it was operating, was one of the blocks to evolution. Therefore, I decided to invest a substantial sum to purchase a specially designed television system.

I always had felt the money I inherited should have some purpose other than making myself and my children comfortable. My father was opposed to my using the money he had given me for my own work. He thought of what I was doing as a charity. From his perspective, I was like a young lion cub giving away the hunt that had been brought in by the father lion. I was squandering the material security he had so laboriously built up. From my point of view it was an investment in the future, which might benefit all children. I understood his perspective. But I thought it was proper to use some of my inheritance to develop a model for a new communications system that might have a chance of furthering humanity toward universal life.

Once, during this process, I was inspired to talk to my father about using his entrepreneurial skills for our projects. I was deeply moved by a movie, "The Poseidon Adventure," in which a man had led people to life upward, from the bowels of a sinking ship. I identified the ship with humankind, and felt motivated by the force of life itself to ask my father's help. I was nervous.

"Dad, I have something important to ask you."

"What's that, honey?"

"Dad, I want you to be my partner. I have the sense of direction, you have the business genius. Together, we could really do something magnificent for the world."

Without even a moment's hesitation, he said, "You fool! You think I would do that? Don't kid yourself." He was harsh, almost abusive, and derisive.

My heart sank. He got it in flashes, but never associated it with his own endeavor or life.

So we ordered the new equipment: "SYNCONsole," which is a central board very much like mission control at Houston, where you can see all the sectors at once. Television cameras and monitors for every sector of the wheel were purchased. I thought it might help the interconnecting of people, so we could share the experience.

We tested the SYNCON in a variety of places to see if the SIU event was a lucky accident or if the process was repeatable. We tried it twice in Los Angeles, once with brilliant leaders like Ray Bradbury, Jean Houston and Mayor Yorty, once in the inner-city Watts area with black and Mexican-American gang leaders as the major participants, also in Huntsville, Alabama, Knoxville, Tennessee, and in Washington, D.C. during the Watergate crisis. It worked every time. People connected.

Six

The Evolutionary Way

Greystone! One of the great mansions of Washington. The Chinese and the East Germans offered fortunes for it as their embassy, but my sister Jacqueline refused to sell. Someone in the family might want it.

John and I had decided we needed a "center," and he suggested I ask Jacqueline about Greystone. It was being used by various friends since she, her husband Wayne, and five children were in California, where Wayne was teaching law at Stanford University. I called Jacqueline and asked whether she would lend us Greystone.

My brother and sisters and, of course, my father, had been the most tremendous support to me, even when they did not fully understand or sympathize with what I was doing. Their willingness to help, their unqualified love, regardless of specifics, was one of the great strengths of my life. Jacqueline led an entirely different life than I. Her husband was a brilliant lawyer; he clerked for Supreme Court Justice Harlan; he worked for Archibald Cox in the solicitor-general's office, and argued government cases before the Supreme Court before moving on to teach at Stanford. Jacqueline dedicated herself totally to the development of her children and husband. Her growth potential had fulfilled itself in the creation of her family. She did not go through the traumatic break, rebirth, and new life that my hunger drove me to.

Jacqueline asked how I was going to manage, what I was planning to do. She said I sounded very tired, was I really able to undertake a venture to develop an educational center? Did I have the resources? My family had obviously grown concerned about me, with my television purchase, the SYNCONs, and the financial and emotional burden involved. They started to question my sense of reality. It is true I was driven to experiment with the process and the media in a way that was causing me to sacrifice my own substance; there was no question about it. But I really didn't look on it as sacrifice. I saw it as a necessary expenditure, even though I knew at some point this mode of operation would have to change. I operated on faith that the goodness of this effort would manifest itself in new forms that would be viable in society and become self-supporting.

I persuaded Jacqueline I was completely rational, and she agreed to lend us the house. John chose the date of September 15 for opening the center. This seemed utterly impossible in May. We were overburdened; we were doing the work of ten; we did not have enough money; our organizational problems were pressing; the evolutionary mode of organization had not emerged yet. However, we announced to our friends in our newsletter that we were opening The New World Center in September 1973, and we did.

Hidden in Rock Creek Park off Connecticut Avenue, Greystone was truly Shangri-la. As you drove up the bumpy driveway (the gravel has long since washed away) you could see on your left an old carriage house of stone being renovated with Buckminster Fuller-inspired hexagonal structures nestled in the high grass. On your right was a tennis court. Farther on was a grape arbor, thick with untended vines, lined with years of old daffodil greens, and the outlines of a stately walk. Then at the top of the hill you could see the house: a bosomy, loving, Georgian, motherly house with white pillars, peeling paint, four stories: cozy, yet grand.

Inside was a lovely stairway, very few chairs, exquisite antique tables and a fantasy of TV equipment. It was a decorator's disaster area. The SYNCON-sole, our social mission control, was in the foyer. TV cameras, hulking dinosaurs lurking in corners, stared at startled visitors with ugly lens eyes. Rows of kleig lights lined the living room ceiling for video-taping "seminars" with friends.

We were a pioneering outpost on new territory. We built our evening fire to keep warm and hailed every pioneering stranger: "Come! Tell us what you have found! What is it like out there? What have you seen? What do you know?" We absorbed information like all pioneers. We did it for life's sake.

Then there were the "residents." 'Who in God's name were they? What were they doing?' visitors wondered, as they were being led through the house by me (who still looked like a Lakeville matron who smiled a lot).

Mike Coffey, the towering, former Black Panther leader from Los Angeles, could be found eating in the kitchen; Jerry Glenn, a doctoral candidate in futurism from the University of Massachusetts, in pinstriped grey, was often sitting behind his desk on the phone; Marilyn Joy from SIU, four-foot-ten inches, with long hair and a tiny face, whom John chose as our "Walter Cronkite," was rereading scripts for the "TV Evening News"; Phil Kryst, a twenty-one-year-old "Polish genius" to whom John taught TV direction, fixed the maze of wires under the SYNCONsole. Susan Bell, a warm-hearted, organic food enthusiast, watered the plants. Bill Adler worked on renovations projects.

Each resident was self-selected. We had met most of them doing SYNCONs. I encountered Mike Coffey while building participation in the Inner-City SYNCON in Los Angeles. We had met in a small room with a Mexican-American gang leader and an American Indian who had been in prison for outbreaks of violence.

"What's the difference between you and the rest of the do-gooders?" Mike asked me.

I looked at their intense faces. I was frightened, yet deeply drawn by the combined power of so much suppressed anger. Something gave me the courage to tell the straight truth, because they were so tough and straight in their language. "The difference," I said, "is they're working for better living conditions, but we're working for humanity to become one and to move forward toward universal life. Our goal includes food, shelter, and education, but goes beyond."

The American Indian smiled. "That's what my people think. We're a cosmic people." The Mexican-American talked about his people's visions, he had heard something like this before. They smiled. We relaxed and became co-conspirators to create something new.

Mike decided to join the committee. Later I told him he looked like an African prince; his bearing, his dignity, his sheer physical beauty, were splendid to behold.

One night Carl Madden, chief economist of the U.S. Chamber of Commerce, came to dinner and spent most of the night talking to Mike. They were in essence cosmic poets, the Black Panther and the chief economist. But only at a place like Greystone would they be likely to let each other know who they are.

Carl told me the house had a magic about it. I believed it was the sense of expectation that something extraordinary was about to happen because of each person who entered the house. It really had an influence on people. Attraction to the future pervaded the atmosphere. No one came in order to create a more comfortable way of life. Each came because he or she wanted to build something new. We felt it our first dinner together at Greystone. Everyone had been dressing very casually, to put it mildly. Suddenly, without saying anything, Jerry Glenn went and put on his tuxedo. We unearthed our best clothes from the bottoms of drawers and trunks. They were wrinkled, but the militant garb of protest had disappeared; the style of the sixties was symbolically transformed. We ate together and toasted this effort to start a new community for the future.

There were about fifteen people in residence at Greystone. We did not have enough money to pay anyone, and no one had enough money to pay us, so everyone moved in, until all the rooms in the house were filled with volunteers. The only ones on salary were Jerry Glenn and a secretary. Everyone there shared the vision of the importance of cooperation on earth and the desire to develop both mind potential and extraterrestrial capabilities. There was quite a difference of opinion on the spiritual aspects of the movement, however. For example, Jerry Glenn had a revulsion against religion and the word God. To him it symbolized passivity and irresponsibility. To others, the spiritual aspects were primary; the process of evolution appeared to be representative of God's will.

The beauty of the effort was that it did not matter whether a person had a secular or a religious orientation. The activity was the same, and the feeling became the same. The monasteries at the time of the fall of Rome offered oasis of learning to preserve the knowledge of the past. We saw communities such as ours as new places of communal effort where we would learn how to share resources and build new worlds together.

We soon developed some course material. Jerry gave a couple of talks on epistemology, the science that investigates the nature and origin of knowledge. He asked people's concept of the nature of reality, how they knew what they knew, bringing out a philosophical perception to most of the residents who hadn't thought in those terms. I gave a course on the evolutionary perspective: how to see reality as a process; on the birth image (the concept that we are being born as one body); on the evolutionary spiral (the history of humanity with a vision of the future when all our capacities are up and working.) I presented what I called "Shift Papers" that analyzed how every functional system in society (environmental, economic, political, etc.) is shifting from earth-only to universal/global life. I also spoke on the meaning of synergistic processes, such as SYN-CONS, as the next stage of self-governance. We invited friends to these lectures, and televised some of them.

To study the new options, we invited key people at the growing edge to spend a Saturday with us, describing their activities; Robert Hieronymous, who founded the first accredited school for occult sciences: AUM in Baltimore; Christopher Byrd, who published *The*

Secret Life of Plants; F.M. Esfandiary, author of *Up-Wingers* and *Optimism One*; Eliot Bernstein of ABC News; and several others. Each, except for Eliot, who was in a current profession, was pioneering in a new field. Winifred Babcock gave an all-day seminar on *The Shining Stranger* and the thoughts of Preston Harold. Beth Robinson did a video documentary called "The Voice of Harold," based on the seminar that Winifred had given; this was one of the first television products that TCFF produced.

One day, shortly after the center opened, Jonas called. "I'll be in town next Wednesday. Could I see you?"

"Fine, I would love to see you," I said. "Why don't you come here as soon as you are finished with your appointments?"

He sounded doubtful. "I may not be available until late."

"That's all right; we'll be up." I grinned to myself.

I assigned his book *Survival of the Wisest* to the residents, and each reported on a section during dinner. Marilyn Joy summarized the essence: "Human society is undergoing a shift from 'Epoch A' to 'Epoch B,' implying not only the limitations of population growth, but a profound shift in values from competition to coalescence, requiring a double win rather than win-lose or, at least, nontotal loss by either element. Something must be gained by both elements of the complementarity even if it is only continued existence, or continued survival in the evolutionary scheme of things."

I pointed out that this coalescence and all-win approach is the essence of the SYNCON process. We were primed for his visit!

Wednesday night, I put on a long dress and a little mascara. As I went to answer the door, the scene ten years before in Lakeville flashed through my mind. What years! I had come through alive and was at the beginning of a new life. The bright light of joy was turned up all the way as I opened the door. "Jonas, how nice to see you!" He looked around in surprise. I waited in silence while it sank in.

"Barbara! What have you here?"

"A launching pad, Jonas! We're educating ourselves. Let's talk a few minutes before you meet everyone." I took him into the small, intimate library. "You see, Jonas, a new thing has to begin a new way. People can't coalesce attached to hierarchical, dying institutions; there is too much negative energy. We're groping toward a new form of organization and education for this age. It's not clear yet, but it's based on attraction to the future and what we call sapiential authority. When you know, you lead, and when you don't know, you follow. There's no boss, no employer. The evolutionary process is in charge; it's up to us to try to understand it and also understand how the forces of change really work, and then work with them."

He nodded, saying, "That's right, that's right."

"We had better join the others," I said, and led him into the living room, introducing him to the residents. "Jonas, would you mind if we televised your talk?" He was surprised, but agreed. However, when they turned on the terribly bright lights I couldn't stand it. I was afraid it would distract him too much, so I made them turn the whole TV system off. John was furious with me, but I told him we had to learn not to let the media destroy spontaneity.

Jonas explained his theory and very kindly offered to spend more time with the residents, to teach them in depth so they could have a deeper intellectual base for their work with the committee.

One evening, during cocktails and dinner, another of the country's leading thinkers dropped in: Willis Harman of the Stanford Research Institute in Palo Alto, California. We crowded into the study during cocktails, probing him for his vision of the future.

"Catastrophe!" was the word. Willis said he had come to feel the needed changes could not occur until there had been a major breakdown in our economic-social system. Society would probably have to feel deep pain before the shift of behavior from competitive to cooperative could occur.

"Willis," I said, "there must be *some* way to avoid this. We can't just sit here waiting for Armageddon."

He agreed. "It's true, Barbara, we have to do everything we can to avoid it, but I really don't think we can. The bureaucracies, the inertia, the patterns of selfish behavior, are so ingrained."

"How do you feel about this, Willis?"

He looked very composed. "Well," he said, "the success of humanity isn't inevitable; maybe a better species will come along. We're not indispensable to the universe, you know."

The residents protested. They kept asking again and again: "What are our best chances of going into the next phase without disaster?" But he seemed to have accepted a Buddhist-like approach: somewhat detached. Willis later became president of the Institute of Noetic Sciences and has changed his own mind to see a world that can be changed by the shift in our perception of it.

We have sold the big house in Lakeville and must be out by March. Earl is moving his studio to the hill beside the apple orchard. My beloved "thinking chair" and apple tree still stand, a memorial to the decade of my silent, search for purpose, while living amidst the beauty of the Berkshire Hills. I hover on the brink of deeper contact with universal consciousness.

It was the Christmas season 1973, as usual a time of deep reappraisal for me. It was to be my last Christmas at Lakeville. Earl and I had separated. I had asked him for a divorce. He agreed, full of regret. The process of separation had been so long and finally so definitive that the formal dissolution of our marriage was a recognition of what had already happened. I felt a wrenching sadness that we had not been able to expand our relationship to include my growth as an independent being. I was married in the old pattern and was not able to transform the pattern. I had to free myself from it. Yet my love and admiration for Earl remained intact. I felt deep compassion for him. I was the one who was growing on. He was the one being left. I shared his pain.

Lloyd was going to live with us full time at Greystone. Wade was to go to Taft: a boy's preparatory school in Connecticut. Stephanie and Suzanne would use Greystone as a home base during holidays. Alexandra had called me recently from Milton, where she was a junior. She was a very independent, strong-willed girl and had been thinking of running away. Her best friend had said, "Call your mother; she will understand." Thank God, she did call.

Alex said she was "dying at Milton," unable to do the work that interested her. She wanted to perform certain experiments with animals but was not permitted to; her independent work simply was not of interest to the faculty. She found no kindred spirit, and did not like the attitudes of the teachers or students. Most of the students spent their time trying to break the rules in petty ways and most of the teachers had to spend their time reacting, trying to enforce the rules in petty ways. She asked if she could come to Washington, live with us and "study at the Smithsonian."

I immediately sympathized with her, remembering my own experiences at Rye Country Day School and Bryn Mawr. I thought school may be one of the most difficult places in the world to learn anything in this age. Having no vision of the future, they cannot give meaning to the past or the present. "You come to Washington," I said, "and we'll work it out. I'll explain it to the headmistress. But you're only a junior in high school, so you should have some kind of academic connection. And you need to leave Milton with a good relationship. But I understand, let's find out what to do."

We all gathered after that: Alex, Suzanne, Stephanie, Wade, and Lloyd, with Earl and me, for the last time in Lakeville, Connecticut. My life had already transformed totally; I had disconnected from my past. It was a strange feeling to walk through the house, the apple orchard, the garden, looking at those sites and symbols of the past, where I had sat for hours searching for meaning, praying for guidance, hoping for a new life. Now that the new life had come, it had swept me along with it.

I felt deep compassion for Earl, but no attachment to my past with him. I felt as if the house had never been mine. In a curious way, I have always experienced the sense of not belonging permanently anywhere. I was not nostalgic, sentimental, or unhappy. Actually, I felt relief that I no longer possessed the mansion for, in reality, it had possessed me. I was beginning to throw off desire for material possessions. They had burdened me all those years of taking care of them, but they had never truly gave me joy or security.

My sense of security came through dynamic action, rather than possession, whether of a house or a husband or even children. Still, financial matters loomed large in my life.

A short time before, my brother and father had moved to protect me from the excesses of my own evolutionary hunger by refusing to let me have further access to my inheritance. Nonetheless, as always in times of desperate need, I knew I could count on my family.

I went to New York with Stephanie to have lunch with my father at the Twenty One Club. Almost everyone you see there has accomplished something, is beautiful, or famous. Stephanie was a very pretty girl. Her grandfather was proud of her and called over his old friends and introduce me as his crazy daughter who wants to go to the moon and Stephanie as the smartest girl in the family. My father lectured Stephanie that the most important things in life are health and money, and women should behave like "puppy dogs." Stephanie told him she thought Americans were obnoxious, greedy, and materialistic, but she practically swooned when Aristotle Onassis arrived at the table next to ours. My mind was elsewhere. I was in a state of panic because we were in debt; I had been spending my own money to finance the SYNCONs since we had not been able to raise the money needed to cover costs.

After lunch I hurried to Louis' office. He calmly asked me what I needed, what the problem was. When I said I needed a $100,000 loan, he nodded. "I can help you on that," he said, and called in his secretary. "Make out a check for $100,000," he told her, and shortly handed it to me. I practically fainted. He told me he had no way of evaluating what I was doing, but I'd had a normal life, had raised five good children, and had coped with reality. Now I was developing this idea and he would like to help me. I was flooded with happiness. There was hope! Somehow, I was given the resources to continue the experiment.

Earl had been invited to speak somewhere after Christmas, so I took the children, at Stephanie's suggestion, for a week's vacation in Jamaica. Stephanie had a deep need for security and for the family to be a secure entity. It was difficult for her, this separation. So I took them all on holiday. We rented a little cottage by the sea where the children could enjoy themselves. But I suffered as usual; I never liked vacations. For me, they produced a feeling of emptiness. All the old anxieties came flooding in. I never felt that way with John, though, even when we were not working. Every now and then he would force me to stop working and fretting, tease me about my P.W.E. (Protestant Work Ethic), and make me stay out until two in the morning listening to music, dancing, talking. I loved that because with him the evolutionary reality never stopped. To remain stable it seemed necessary to be acting together with at least one person you love who was committed totally to the same goal.

I am literally dying to get back into action. I struggle to maintain a sense of evolutionary reality in an environment that in no way acknowledges it. It must have been a comparable experience to be early scientific observers in a monastery where action was thought to spring from the unknowable mind of God.

Neither mystical nor secular forms of consciousness expect to transcend the human condition through real-time conscious action commensurate with the processes of the universe.

I personally feel close to some great understanding. I suppose it will come forth through the dream realized, through the synergizing earth when the whole world experiences our oneness.

Our plan, now called SYNCON '76, is to generate a SYNCON in every state from 1974 to 1975, then to encourage their replication through 1975-76 in as many congressional districts as possible, aiming at a national-global bicentennial SYNCON from June through August 1976 via communication satellite, to be held at Kennedy Space Center. Shirley Patterson, head of the Horizon's section of the American Revolution Bicentennial Commission, has said she will staff and present our SYNCON proposal as one of the nationally approved bicentennial programs. She described her meeting with John, Warren Avis and me as a "religious experience." Dad has said he will sponsor a dinner in New York to initiate the national program. I see the dinner as a celebration of genuine hope in every field of the SYNCON wheel and a kick-off for the "politics of transcendence," the actions necessary to obtain the new options for humanity now.

With the coming of 1974, the action we had initiated was underway. It was halting, a little uncertain in its form, but the SYNCON process, the new media, the networking, the outreaches of various kinds, began to have a dynamism of their own.

With a new year upon us, I renewed my desire to bring together the pieces of experience in an intellectual context. Ideas began to coalesce in my head very rapidly. In Jamaica, I had sketched a book, *The Politics of Transcendence: A Platform for the Future.* I wanted to write the book, but John kept saying it was not time, because when I write I become academic and lose the joy and reality of the evolutionary purpose. I forget the "the story."

Along with the need to provide the conceptual whole in a communicable form, my motivation for empathy and contact with the force that was motivating me grew. I began to sense myself increasingly as a vehicle that had no personal desire for anything other than the fulfillment of this larger effort. I had become so totally identified with the process that I had lost the need for identification with anything personal. You might say I had no personal life, only evolutionary life.

To me this state was exciting, natural. I was maturing to a level, however, where I wanted to be free from some of the organizational burdens of how to organize SYNCONs, how to handle the various residents, what to have for dinner, who would clean floors; yet I could not escape those requirements. We had been developing an evolutionary life-style at the center, and even though I was ready to move to a conceptual, evolutionary state of consciousness, I was still confronted with the day-in, day-out maintenance of human life.

We had established a system for running our operation that bordered on an evolutionary organization. Menial tasks were shared. Authority emerged through knowledge in specific fields. I felt strongly that we should not develop a mandarin class. I began to think about Mao Tse-Tung's revolution and the natural tendency of certain people to think they are superior to others in all ways and to want others to serve them. So we developed a rather inefficient system: each week one person, by alphabet, was kitchen manager; everyone took turns cooking by alphabet; we tried to share the shopping; and we were supposed to share the cleaning. The result was a messy house and an occasional slip-up at dinner! But the deeper reward was that we were learning to trust one another in a new way. We learned that the sign of leadership was a willingness to accept responsibility and act responsively. The group was taking shape on the basis of a person's willingness to accept responsibility for the whole action, not just for his or her specific part in it.

The horrible anxiety of debt and financial crisis was gradually being overcome by the work of this evolutionary team. We were generating a "positive cash trickle," as John called it. People were asking us to do SYNCONs, from the Federal Energy Administration, to the General Federation of Women's Clubs, to the American Society of Information Sciences; even the White House wanted to engage us to consult on a national youth conference. The young people became expert video camera people. We paid our monthly mortgage on the cameras and televised the president, football games, anything and everything, to earn our living, in order to be free to initiate our own projects. All that I had accepted as a child, affluence earned by others, I now was forced to learn to do myself, I had to earn my own way. And what a joy! I found nothing would be left out of the learning process if I was ready to grow. I began to honor money as energy to work for humankind.

We often questioned ourselves about the rewards: "Why are we here?" The answer was not always clear. One evening we asked each other what we would do personally if The Committee for the Future should earn a lot of money, either through an enormous grant or through contracts. How would each person spend a personal income over and above committee work?

Many could not think of anything except the opportunity to develop themselves through the work. They wanted better television equipment, more access to the media, a chance to do TV productions we could not do because we did not have the money. Those things we wanted to spend our personal money on were minimal in importance compared to the greater desire for self-development through action.

A new reward system clearly was emerging, or people would not have felt that way. They would not have been there because every one could get a job; some might be able to earn a good deal. Of course, they were learning skills with us in media, process, futures, that would suit them for many jobs, but they were building no security, career, position, required for survival in the current world.

Even though we were learning to cooperate, I continued to have difficulty bringing evolutionary leaders together for cooperative action. Early in my life, when I met Jonas, he spoke of the mutants and the "invisible college" forming around the world. We met at that time as individuals. There was excitement, empathy, joy, but when each of us set out to build new institutions and actions in society, we went through a phase of differentiation and difficulty in cooperating. Maybe it is because each of us was so burdened with the effort to establish a foothold, that no one had the excess energy to share it with anyone else. The funding sources were limited, too, and the bureaucratic structure did not respond. The number of human beings willing to dedicate their lives to evolutionary action as opposed to revolutionary action was a tiny minority. It was one thing to empathize personally; it was another to develop organizational activities that could synergize. Many of us were using as much energy as possible to establish the new beachhead.

Even though intellectually I understood the difficulty of cooperation at this stage, the hunger for empathy, deep communication, and working together remained. I could not overcome it, it was so real. I learned when the hunger is real, its satisfiable. The hunger of Eve that drove me from one pattern to another had proved to be right, satisfiable, natural, normal, good, thrilling, at each step. Whether it was for community, for action, for thought, for a new way of life, in a seed-like form at this stage, every aspect of that hunger was realistic. The idea that the desire for deeper meaning was unpragmatic was proving to be incorrect. Just look at the so-called pragmatists running the institutions, the cities, and the bureaucracy, failing to meet their own needs and those of their fellow humans. They were not pragmatic. The hunger was pragmatic; the food was real. I believed that a stage was coming wherein the empathy would flower rapidly; I felt it intuitively. Humanity would have a stage in which the capacity for empathetic organization would manifest. I intended to do whatever I could to help make that happen.

Ever since I wrote, "I'm a magnet feeling the attractive power of another magnet," I had been drawn by a real force toward this new life. From the awakening of the hunger in Scarsdale to the confusion in material life with my husband, children, and home, to the first nourishment of the hunger through contact with evolutionary people, to the epiphany of the oneness of humankind and our birth toward universal life, to the totality of commitment to an evolutionary way of being, I had followed the pull at the core of my solar plexus. Each phase grew naturally from the next, never denying the past but rather fulfilling it.

My children were imbued with a strong motivation to grow also. The girls became artists. Suzanne went to Sweden to study the art of weaving. Stephanie strove to put her loving spirit into images. Alexandra matured at Greystone, skipping her senior year of high school, passing through her freshman and sophomore years at American University's Learning Center with straight A's, while doing all the graphics for New Worlds Video and getting a job at ABC-TV News in Washington. She did graphics for their evening news show. Eventually she decided to take a year away from school and drove across country in her little Toyota with a friend to Los Angeles. She wanted to try her abilities in the competitive world of television. She earned her own living, working with Dr. John Lilly in his study of communication with dolphins. She found him by herself.

Wade left Taft. He and Lloyd moved to Greystone and went to Georgetown Day School. At sixteen Wade was a philosophical businessman, earning money painting houses and setting up the New World Sandwich Service at G.D.S. He was accused of being a capitalist the first day of business which forced him to sort out the morality of capitalism versus socialism. He would talk with me for hours about the evolutionary entrepreneurship we were developing at the center based on motivation to facilitate the next phase of evolution, our own and humankind's. Lloyd, at thirteen, decided on something quite different. He wanted to be a pro-football player and go to U.C.L.A. He saved his allowance to buy weights and every afternoon we would jog together, I in a half-hearted attempt to stay in shape, he with visions of glory dancing in his head. He would run ahead, jogging in place, waiting for me.

Earl continued to be devoted to painting and writing. The children would visit him and say he was radiant, the tensions gone. There was no doubt I was a burden on his soul. He wanted to make me happy while I yearned for total involvement in life, and found it. Earl and I had joined to pro-create five beautiful children; and we had joined to co-create a philosophy of hope. Our marriage was not a failure. It was a success. I learned that separations can be as natural as unions. I determined to honor the best of our relationship and forgive any pain I may have inflicted or received.

John and I were now evolutionary partners in a co-creative relationship. Instead of vowing to remain faithful till death do us part, we pledged ourselves to give all we had to help humankind toward universal life.

My father, Louis, Jacqueline, and Patricia were all flourishing. Dad sold Louis Marx and Company to Quaker Oats. Until the day he died he presided over his children and grandchildren like a patriarch, judging everyone, yet loving us. He wished I had more status, a job, some recognizable position. He would say, "My God, Barbara, you've been at this for years, you ought to have something to show for it!" When he took me to lunch at the Twenty One Club, there was no snappy way to introduce me to those aging friends of his who wave and blow kisses at you as you come in. It used to be, "This is the daughter who speaks French." Then, "She's the one who wants to go to the moon." But now...? I think he knew my hunger was related to the drive that brought his own mother across the sea at sixteen, and to the drive he had as a boy in Brooklyn: the aspiration to work toward the highest level of freedom and growth he could imagine. I was lucky to be born at the time when the energies of past civilizations gathered into a concentrated force to break through into the first age of conscious evolution.

At times of high excitement, my thoughts are
irresistibly drawn to politics.

We submitted the proposal for SYNCON '76 to the American Revolution Bicentennial Administration (ARBA), but did not hear from them. They were constantly being reorganized; anyone we made contact with usually retired immediately or was moved to some other position. We decided that, with or without the approval of ARBA, we would organize SYNCON '76, raise the funds and find a way on our own. However, late in 1974 we finally received national recognition from them. The vision of the International SYNCON was that people from different cultures and regions and functions of the world would meet at the Kennedy Space Center in light of the growing capacities of humankind as a whole to identify common goals for the future based on the broadest horizon of choices. Television would link people globally for a shared experience of oneness, a step toward the synergizing earth.

Meanwhile, the theme of a politics of the whole, to bring together the various parts of the body to realize the potential of the whole was pounding in my head.

Then a critical event occurred. I was invited by the Church Women United to their international conference in Memphis, Tennessee, in October 1974. The theme was "The Journey to Wholeness." Margaret Shannon, executive director, had asked me to serve as responder and synergizer, to help bring the conclusions of the various task forces into some holistic perspective.

My turn came at 11:30 P.M. Exhausted myself, and recognizing the exhaustion of everyone else, I raced through my statement to the hundreds of women from all over the world: "The journey to wholeness requires holistic action. We must go beyond adversary politics toward a 'politics of the whole.' The diverse parts of the body must aim at a solution to their own needs that does not hurt other sections of the body, that ideally enhances every section's development. A 'Platform of the Whole' should be developed out of the politics of the whole. The Church Women United should take the leadership in both the politics and the platform of the whole. Anyone interested in 'Assemblies of the Whole,' please meet with me directly afterwards."

I do not know exactly how many women congregated, but I estimate that as many as a hundred wanted to meet, even though it was 11:45 p.m. Our place of meeting was not even certain; some waited in the lounge until 2:00 a.m. Their receptivity triggered in me a profound desire for a more overt role of activation. I was charged with excitement. The cells in my body seemed to have more electrical energy as I got nearer to the incorporation of action into the whole body.

I left the women in Memphis with my heart full of love. Immediately upon landing at National Airport in Washington, I took a taxi to rejoin our New Worlds Video crew who were video-taping a motorcycle race at Rosecroft Racetrack (one of our efforts to earn our daily bread). When I asked the taxi driver to take me there, he looked at me askance. I did not strike him as the type who usually attends motorcycle races, and I think I was still wearing my Church Women United badge. When I arrived I plunged into a totally different atmosphere, one of competition, disorder, dust, noise, screeching young people, men hawking flags, popcorn, and other tawdry items. Alexandra was operating a camera on the grandstand. Lloyd was pulling cable in the pit. Everyone was covered with dirt.

I stepped gingerly toward the racetrack, having a horror of the needless risk of life. I forced myself closer to watch the young men going ninety miles an hour, risking their lives at every turn. One pebble could cause death. All at once this willingness to risk life for the sake of breaking a limit, combined with the profound love of wholeness expressed by the Church Women United, caused a chemical reaction in me. Wholeness and risk-taking fused. Suddenly I had a powerful inner commandment: 'You must take a risk to create a more holistic world.' It threw me into a state of great agitation and contemplation. I felt disoriented.

Rushing over to John, I said urgently, "I *have* to talk with you. We have to leave, now. Let's go to dinner, alone, so we can talk." We drove directly to a restaurant.

"Something's happened to me," I said. "I know I have to do something, but I'm not sure what. The fact that the women responded so quickly to the suggestion of Assemblies of the Whole makes me believe the social body is ready. What can I do, what act, to offer the option of wholeness-in-action to the body? The motor-cycle races made me realize that risk-taking is part of it. I can't trigger this act, whatever it is, without taking some risk. It's inherent in the body of humankind to take risks; that's as much a part of our nature as love." I kept repeating to John, "I *have* to do something; I feel it's there to be done; I know it can be done; I have to do something about it." John listened receptively. My thoughts were irresistibly drawn to politics, because politics seemed the best way to translate ideas into action.

It came over me with a wave of certainty from within that I should run for the presidency of the United States in 1976. Although the idea had been suggested to me several times in the past, this was the first time the idea came from within me. I knew there was a potential within people that could be called forth to action to build a humane community. The act of running for president appeared in my mind as a sacred act. It had nothing to do with ordinary power; it had nothing to do with wanting to be president; it had nothing to do with wanting to become a Republican or Democrat. It had everything to do with wanting to help trigger the action. We returned to the center in a state of awed contemplation.

The next morning I was too restless to get dressed and was sitting in my robe in the kitchen, before our usual 9:30 meeting in the basement. It was about 9:15 when I said to everyone, "I want to tell you something." I explained what happened in Memphis, and my experience at the racetrack. "I believe we should launch a candidacy for the presidency of the United States." My heart was pounding.

I looked for some reaction in their faces. I think it was Marilyn Joy who first said: "Far out! Great!" One after the other expressed his feelings. Some were instantly positive; some were cautious; Jack Frost was concerned about which party I would run on and how it would be organized; Bernie Kraska was excited; Bill Adler was ready to go; Jerry Glenn was perched on the last shelf in the back, looking upset, saying nothing; I do not know what he thought. Alexandra just looked amazed. So we left the discussion open, and I spent the next few days telephoning other people to see what they thought.

Among those I telephoned was Margaret Shannon. "I want to meet with you as soon as possible. I have something very important to discuss." John and I went to see her at Riverside Church Center. She brought Margaret Sonnenday, the next president of the Church Women United. We went at mid-morning to the large, empty cafeteria downstairs, where I had a cup of coffee and an apple. Margaret was probably expecting me to discuss the Assemblies of the Whole. But when I told her, "I've decided to run for the presidency of the United States!" she was delighted. "Wonderful! This is what we need. I'm going to retire in March, and this is something I would be willing to work on. We need a woman willing to speak about a new way of action for the future."

I called Al Rosenfeld. "I was wondering how long it would take you to decide to do this," he said. But Carl Madden did not think it was a good idea; neither did Herman Kahn. "You can't change the rules of the game," Herman said. "You would have to play the old game; you would have to join one of the parties." He gave me a quick, pragmatic analysis. "I feel your best chance would be to run as a Republican."

"I can't become a Republican," I said. "I can't become a Democrat, Herman. The point is to create a politics of the whole."

"Barbara," he repeated, "you can't change the rules of the game."

"We have to change the rules." I said, though I didn't know how.

I called Norman Cousins and asked if he would have lunch. John and I met him at his usual restaurant, The Barbary Room, next to his offices at *Saturday Review/World*. The room's wooden panels, soft lights and attentive waiters gave me a sense of comfort and security. Once again, I took a deep breath: "Norman, I've decided to run for the presidency of the United States." I looked deeply into his eyes, drawn to his wisdom and sense of inner authority.

He took my hand, smiled, and said, "Barbara, I believe that of all the candidates, you're the most pragmatic. You understand better than any of them the new age of interdependence and future orientation. But you lack credibility. What's needed is a major announcement over national television, a twelve-minute statement in which you announce your candidacy, state the case, reveal the supporters and backing you have, at least intellectually and socially; that would be the way it would have to be done. But," he added, "you know what you'll be subjected to personally. I hate to see you expose yourself to something so horrendously destructive and difficult. You would become the target of so many negative forces. Why would you want to expose yourself to such a terrible onslaught of negativity?" His concern was touching, yet I felt a constriction in my heart. He did not have quite the same evolutionary drive.

"I'm really not thinking of myself," I replied. "I'm not even sure I would be considered seriously for the presidency, much less win it. I don't think I would. But the courage to do it, if the idea is right, would change history. What better thing is there to get destroyed for than that? I could get killed by a car, walking out on the street after lunch. I don't mind if I'm destroyed as long as I feel it does some good. I don't seek death, and I don't seek destruction; I seek life. Exposing myself to negativity doesn't worry me. The only thing that worries me is that I would make this act insignificant by my own inadequacies. Can I make a difference?"

He gave me his blessing but remained separate from my actions.

As time went on I spoke with about thirty people. Almost everyone thought it was a good idea at first. But as I plotted and strategized with John and others as to the steps required to make it a reality, I became increasingly distressed. I found myself becoming self-promoting. A friend asked, "What about Jimmy Carter? He looks like a good man," and I found myself saying I was better than Jimmy Carter. That was the last thing in the world I wanted to do: to proclaim myself better than Jimmy Carter! I was different from him; we weren't in competition. But I saw I would have to be in competition with him and everyone else in the field. I found myself becoming self-promoting in the adversary mode, concerned about the organizational aspects of the move, the funding, the institutional interface. My energy level started to drain out of me. My strength was in the motivation to do something new, but the act of doing it was requiring me to do all the old things.

I could not figure a way out of that bind. So I postponed my campaign, never quite putting it out of my mind, feeling that the idea had come to me as a signal that there had to be a trigger act, that the act was connected with the presidency, that I would play some role in that trigger, but I would have to wait and see how and where and why. This type of faith is one I have learned painfully. There was such a desire for immediacy when a powerful commandment comes from within, but that impatience was immature. It was childish to think I could do something of that magnitude so fast.

In that same month, during the arduous effort to build participation and to fund the First International SYNCON, we were invited through the good offices of John Yardley, who had become director of Manned Space Flight for NASA, to testify before the Outlook for Space Committee. NASA had finally decided to invite citizens and scientists to express their views on long-range goals for space.

We had planned for some time to form a "Choiceful Future" research group of active colleagues to develop a new worlds program based on emerging potential in all fields. The NASA invitation was an incentive to develop the Choiceful Future proposals in time to enter the arena of public discussion by 1976. Instead of running for president, I decided to put together the elements of a platform that anyone could run on: a platform for the future. There was a real vacuum of direction there. Traditional politicians weren't articulating new directions, and the futurists who had gained public attention were limited in number and scope.

At that time, there were two major world views contending for support of the futurist-political scene, both partially true but neither, it seemed to me, sufficient. Either, if pursued to its fullest, would lessen humanity's chances for an open future. One was the Club of Rome's Limits to Growth, which considered earth a finite system with fixed resources and counselled us to adapt to the current limitations, or even to "return" to a simpler stage of life as proposed by the deep ecologists. There was much that was positive and right about this perspective: restoration of the environment, decentralization, self-sufficiency, re-localization of industry, energy efficiency, non-money economies, the barter system, cooperatives and the rebuilding of community. However, many of its advocates denied even the possibility of a concurrent and complementary, and equally natural, development of a new environment beyond our biosphere.

I had met Aurelio Peccei, head of the club, in Bucharest in 1972 at a Futurist World Congress. I asked him if he had examined Krafft Ehricke's "extraterrestrial imperative." "Dr. Peccei, it seems as though the future isn't limited if you consider the universe," I said.

"Madam," he replied, "we've looked at the universe and consider it irrelevant."

I was almost speechless. "Dr. Peccei, that's impossible!"

"There is no time to develop the universal frontier, it's already too late. We don't have the resources to do it," he said flatly.

I felt as though he was closing the lid on human evolution. I discovered that there was a deep, metaphysical bias in many environmentalists against technology and the building of new worlds.

The second world view, called Post Industrial Society, was advocated by Herman Kahn, founder of the Hudson Institute, and others. Herman believed that by carefully developing science and technology, taking into account the new needs for conservation, pollution, and population controls, it would be possible to provide more of the same for everyone on earth, aiming toward a wealthy world somewhat in the mode of the West. He believed in the "trickle-down" theory and said things were better now than ever before. He viewed the future as a static, humanistic culture, with emphasis on sensual pleasures, cultism, interest in gourmet food, aesthetics, and such "exotic adventures as space travel."

Herman told me this while we were relaxing together at Michael Michaelis' swimming pool in Washington. He was sitting on the diving board wearing gargantuan bathing trunks that encircled his enormous girth. He always spoke rapidly and mumbled a stream of ideas and facts with extraordinary brilliance.

"Herman," I said, "to me that view is shortsighted, uninteresting, and blind to real changes. You're not taking into account that we're moving forward in the universe, that the potential of the mind is immeasurable. By the middle of the next century this world could be a global society with interconnecting, interfeeling awareness of its members. We could be living and working in outer space and could have made contact with extraterrestrial life. There will be new social models from the communities of people living in space, as well as those who live on earth."

"Barbara, you're not stating a likely forecast but an intuitive desire" (which was true) "but then I've never been able to have a 'peak experience'," he said. "What's real for you isn't real for me."

"I understand that, Herman," I nodded, feeling sympathy for that lack, "but there's nothing I'm saying that's not technologically feasible. We must take into account motivation as part of the energy that creates the future. Your view of human nature is basically materialistic. But there is a far longer history of the primary urge to grow beyond material comfort toward greater awareness and transformation. Every time a group of people achieved comfort, some became restless and began to break the walls down, moving forward to overcome some new limitation. That's human nature. It is the nature of nature to transform." I came to the same impasse with him as with many others. He did not see what I saw ahead; he had not felt the experience or the magnet.

We had a surprising conversation at the Knoxville, Tennessee, SYNCON. He spent two days with us, starring in the "New Worlds Morning News," working the SYNCONsole with John, surrounded constantly by a group of avid listeners, like a wise uncle. He was seated next to me at dinner one night when I received a note that Joanna Leary, wife of the imprisoned Timothy Leary, had telephoned and wanted to come to Knoxville to present their ideas.

I turned to Herman. "Would you like to hear Joanna Leary?"

"What does she think?" he asked, although I'm sure he knew.

I explained what I understood of their vision. "She and Tim believe earth has undergone its larval stage and is now in the process of metamorphosis toward universal life. The religions were intimations in the cocoon of our destiny. They were signals from real higher beings. Tim and Joanna are developing a sort of myth about building a starship to begin a galactic voyage with those who want ready."

Herman said, "Well, that's basically what I believe."

"Herman! Is that true? How come you never say it?"

"Barbara, I'm a plumber. My job is to fix things, basic things. You and I are members of the same religion, different church."

An alternative to Herman's Post Industrial Society and to the Club of Rome's Limits to Growth was being developed by The Committee for the Future and others; we called it "Choiceful Future." This view synthesized elements of the other two and added a third: the development of inner and outer space. Choiceful Future took the evolutionary perspective, viewing the world as undergoing a natural transformation from its earth-only to its global/universal phase of growth. It accepted the Limits to Growth position of the necessity for conservation of nonrenewable resources, for decentralization, diversity, self-sufficiency, use of appropriate technology, and respect for nature, the environment and all people as members of our own body. It shared the goal of planetary consciousness and equitable distribution of wealth. It fostered inner growth, spiritual development and community. It also accepted Herman Kahn's position that where industrialization can be developed while sustaining minor or no damage to the environment, it should continue; that through sustainable development the basic needs of most people on the planet could be met while preserving the environment. It also shared his buoyant faith that human intelligence is equal to human problems and that we, as a species, have been steadily improving in our capacity to care for others.

Choiceful Future transcended the other views by the expectation of new options. It suggested, as did Buckminster Fuller, that through the "emphemeralization of technology" - doing more with less, and the "design science revolution," everyone on earth will have enough energy without pollution and without the spread of nuclear power plants. It also accepted the ideas of Abraham Maslow, Margaret Mead and countless others that held that the mind's potential has barely been tapped and can be emancipated to reach levels of creativity heretofore considered the prerogative of genius. It viewed humankind as a transitional species, a link in a vast evolutionary chain, and the essence of human nature as a self-transcendence, stimulated to continual growth in a new spirit of holism.

The Choiceful Future research group met twice, and Professor Gerard K. O'Neill of Princeton University came to our second session at Greystone. He was a scientist of international reputation, working in the field of high energy physics. I first read about his activities in the *New York Times* and called him immediately. We had a superb talk. He arrived at Greystone toward the end of the afternoon with his young and attractive wife. He was a handsome man, with just a hint of the strange perfection of Mr. Spock of "Star Trek." He had wanted to be an astronaut, and has that sense of bearing, precision, and physical discipline.

Gerry gave a slide presentation on the concept of building communities at the L5 Libration, a point equidistant between the moon and the earth. He believed space habitats could be built at L5. The communities would pay for themselves by producing inexpensive solar energy from space. Evidently the "islands in space" could be designed to be aesthetic with varied climates and new architectural forms. Gravity would be simulated by rotation. The center of the habitat would have no gravity. People could experience weightlessness there. The first of these habitats could be ready in 1990, in our lifetime! He showed artists' renderings of beautiful earth-like cylinders, with trees, animals, clouds.

"We *can* inhabit space," he said, "and do it without robbing or harming anyone and without polluting anything. If work starts soon, some of our industrial activity could be moved away from earth's fragile biosphere within less than a century. The technical imperatives of this kind of migration are likely to encourage self-sufficiency, small-scale governmental units, cultural diversity, and a high degree of independence. The ultimate size limit for the human race on this new frontier is at least 20,000 times its present value."

The amorphous hunger of Eve found itself in the presence of a scientist providing a way to develop physical universal life that corresponded with my intuitive sense of the future. As we become one body of humanity on this planet, it is natural that we reach outward into space for new life. However, if we had gone out when Gerry wanted us to, we would have carried our unconscious infantile behavior to the moon. It appeared necessary for the human race to change its consciousness before it travelled too far from home base.

The idea of space colonization created a remarkable polarization in the future-oriented community. Some were violently opposed to it while others were passionately for it. I discovered the meaning of this polarization with my dear friend Hazel Henderson. We had been invited to debate before the Congressional Clearinghouse on the Future. The subject was "Space Colonies - Pro or Con."

Hazel was a co-worker with E.F. Schumacher's *Small Is Beautiful* concept and had been quoted as saying space colonies were a crazy manifestation of "the testosterone factor gone berserk!"

Her friends hoped she would defeat me, and others felt Hazel was a "neo-luddite," a know-nothing, who should be brought publicly to her knees before Congress so we could go "per astral."

We decided not to debate each other, but rather we would discover each other's metaphysical pictures and share that before Congress.

Byron Kennard, a friend of Hazel's, hosted us one long and fascinating evening. Hazel and I explored everything. A rare combination of powerful intellect and Earth Mother, Hazel was a lanky, handsome blonde. She loved to converse brilliantly about the new economics while planting shrubs and painting her house in Florida, where she lived with her former husband Carter. An author and lecturer, he had been the front page editor for *The Wall Street Journal* and had worked for IBM.

Hazel emphasized the immediate necessities for environmental and economic change with specific policy changes needed by "Mother Gaia," while I was expressing the requirement for global link-ups, inner transformation, space exploration and "new worlds."

We discussed our childhoods and our relationship with our fathers.

Both sometimes acted tyrannically. Mine, while terrifying, was generous and loving, and could be placated, hers would not be. Hazel learned to hate power; I learned to placate it. But then came the deeper revelation. We were exploring why I wanted to go into space and she did not.

"Hazel," I began, "I expect something new to happen. I want to be there personally."

"Barbara, I'm not interested in being in some tin can hurtling through the void. I'm part of the Big Mind. I'm here as a little mind, too, but I always am it *All*. I do not seek what you do."

"Hazel, do you mean you don't want to go on, personally, with a continuation of consciousness, as yourself, beyond this life?"

"No, I don't. I'll be glad to get rid of this body when it's time."

"I want to go on, personally. I want to have a new body. I want to become a universal being. I have work to do. I don't want to return to the All. I want to evolve as a new being!" I said.

We both laughed. We had different "metaphysical preferences." It was not that one was right and the other wrong. It was not right or wrong to want to return to the All or be an immortal universal being. It simply may be a matter of a choice! I realized that the people who were for space colonies wanted to go personally and evolve into universal beings. Those opposed to this initiative chose to remain in the current human mode, joining the universe in the spiritual rather that the physical dimension.

Hazel and I joined at a very deep level, far beyond the need to persuade or agree with each other. We honored the differences and tempered our policy persuasions with respect for the others preferences. Perhaps there is an "ecology of souls" to complement the ecology of nature. Perhaps all types are needed to keep the balance, from the deep ecologists to the passionate engineers.

The Choiceful Future scenario went undeveloped, a seed planted that had not yet grown. Perhaps it was ahead of its time, a synthesis that was premature given the immediacy of human needs, the environmental crisis and the persistence of the militaristic mentality.

I do not yet have a transitional language to make a link between pragmatic men and new action.

In the summer of 1975, Harris Wofford, a refined, sensitive, imposing man, the president of Bryn Mawr, came to the New Worlds Center. Literally, the first words he said were, "Sargent Shriver is going to run for president on *Building the Earth* by Teilhard de Chardin." He handed me the book.

It was Shriver's own copy, dog-eared, underlined, starred, obviously a much-loved text. Harris told me he had spent the previous day with Shriver (whom he had worked with when Shriver was director of the Peace Corps). Shriver had told him not to sleep that night until he had read the book.

I was amazed and telephoned Shriver right away to say I had heard he was going to run on Teilhard de Chardin and that I thought it was just terrific. "Where are you?" he asked. "Let's meet." I was surprised at such openness from a man getting ready to run for president. "Believe it or not," he said, "I'm at the Watergate, overlooking Kennedy Center. How soon can you come?"

About two hours later John and I went to his large offices on the tenth floor, the law firm of which Shriver is a member. He was being interviewed by the *New York Times*. His son, a student at Yale, came out and apologized for the delay. He was a tall, ruggedly attractive young man, with the natural charm I associate with all the Kennedy's. Finally we were escorted in. The phone rang constantly. In between calls Shriver managed to turn to us.

"I'm amazed at your interest in Teilhard, because we have the same motivation," I said. "I've always felt the presidency should be guided by these principles."

"I would like to run a campaign using television-in-the-round," he said, "asking people to participate in building the platform with me. I don't want to stand up at rallies and wave my arms. I'm looking for a way of bringing people forward to build the earth."

I must have been beaming. "This is amazing, because it's exactly what The Committee for the Future is planning to do." I opened my briefcase and got out the plan for developing SYNCONs throughout the United States. I told him we had been using television-in-the-round with the SYNCONs, and that we were developing the outline of a Platform for the Future to be built by the people through SYNCON-like meetings.

"This is spooky," he said. He called in one of his intellectual aides, Dave, who did not seem to have any of the same feelings, certainly not about Teilhard de Chardin, or interactive media.

I laughed. "I can see, Dave, you're a liberal, somewhat skeptical of the evolutionary potential in humanity."

He smiled and said he was hired to be that way; he had to try to "keep our feet on the ground."

Eunice Shriver called while we were in the office. She remembered me because my father had given toys to her charities at Christmas. Sarge said, "Barbara Marx Hubbard is here and she loves Teilhard, too. Here, tell her about Teilhard." Eunice has a voice something like Katharine Hepburn's. She quoted Teilhard to me for five minutes.

I shook my head. "I can't believe it. This is great!"

Shriver, John, and I began to talk about his strategy for the presidency." I once thought of running myself," I said, "to bring the synergistic process and Teilhardian thoughts to political action. I think it's wonderful that you're going to do it." We developed a rapid empathy that had nothing to do with the realities of his position or mine. "I imagine you're going to have a woman for your vice-president," I said, in all seriousness. He looked shocked; apparently it had not occurred to him. His aide looked even more shocked. I said, "It's a shame for two men to run. You really have to have a woman for vice-president. How about me?"

I spoke only half in jest, and Shriver was getting worried. On the other hand, he knew in his heart we were on the same wavelength. In fact, he promptly asked me to join his national committee, and we left with good feelings toward each other.

As John and I thought more about it, we became interested and decided to call on him again to see if the meeting had been real and how deeply he felt about the concept of building the earth. We also wanted to ask him what he thought about space. We had decided if he really intended to do what he said, that we should go all the way with him. We were ready to put our media, our fortunes, our lives, and our sacred honor at stake for his candidacy.

I called him again. "Sarge, when would you be free to see us?"

"Barbara, I'm always here. You come whenever you want."

That afternoon John and I were at his office again. We waited quite awhile as he was making phone calls, trying to get support from various political figures. The man's humility and openness were most impressive. But my heart sank that Teilhard's vision of building the earth seemed impossible to communicate in those telephone calls. He said, "I'm trying to figure out how to translate Teilhard into the rhetoric of politics."

I told him I had the same desire and handed him a speech I had made at the Choiceful Future SYNCON, called "The Politics of the Whole." He read through it and asked who wrote it. I said, "I did."

"This is fantastic!" he said. "These are precisely the ideas that I have!" He expounded on the concept of a new process for the presidency where people would be invited to interact and discuss on television. Then I pulled out a paper in which I had described that very idea. "I wonder if you'd do something for me," he said. "We're meeting tonight at 7:30 at Timberlawn with some of my closest aides to draft my announcement of candidacy. Could you be there?"

"Of course!" A chill ran down my spine. From the earliest days our goal had been that a presidential candidate would carry the message of new worlds on earth and in space in 1976. Maybe this was it!

Before we left I asked his views on the space program. He said, "I haven't given it much thought; I think it's a good thing, but there's no way in this current political climate that we could overtly promote it. We have to have a low profile on the space program, even though I agree with you that it's important."

I tried to persuade him that, if properly put, it could be shown to be a new hope, a new transcendence, a new start for the world. But he did not agree.

As we were walking briskly out together, talking about Teilhard's "Omega point," I said, "You know, Sarge, there's something beyond the Omega point — the beginning of our life in the universe." He looked at me with astonishment, and his aides, who already thought Teilhard was far out, looked even more startled. (Although Teilhard himself had pointed out that once we experienced our oneness as humanity, we would begin to notice our aloneness in the universe and seek out other life.)

That night John and I drove to Timberlawn. It was a Kennedy-like estate. We saw pictures of such settings many times during Jack Kennedy's era: sprawling lawns, big white houses, swimming pools, young men from Yale and Harvard jogging and playing touch football. Eunice and the children were away. People were clustered in different nooks and crannies of the house, working on various projects. No one greeted us, and Shriver had not yet arrived.

We wandered through the house and onto the lawn where I saw a table set for dinner with six or seven men sitting at it. I walked over: "Are you people writing the announcement for the candidate?" They nodded, and John and I sat down. No one paid the slightest attention to us. They were talking low-level politics: what Kissinger had said to someone; who's getting whose hide today. There were two Catholic priests, a man from Brookings Institute, a Harvard lawyer, a press secretary, and other professionals of that kind. Then Shriver arrived around 8:00 p.m. We had a cook-out dinner served by his son in an informal atmosphere that reminded me of the center. It was quite charming and wonderful.

Shriver said he would like to make his announcement in the form of the Declaration of Independence: first the vision, then the grievances, then the statement of action. There was a superficial discussion of possible grievances. People were searching for an issue that could be as specific as the Vietnam issue; they thought it was economics; "break up the oil companies" was the favorite theme. Many suggestions were thrown back and forth and discarded. Finally I broke in. I was an outsider and the only woman present. "What's the vision of this campaign?" Dead silence.

Shriver looked at me. "You say what you think it is, Barbara."

I restated his own vision. "This is a time when every man, woman, and child is needed to build the earth. This campaign will call on the people to work with the candidate to build a platform of direction for the future. Together people can build a new world." Dead silence again. No one picked it up. The meeting went on.

Later Shriver asked his press secretary to get in touch with John to help set up the television process for the announcement of the candidacy and the campaign. This seemed to be a specific that we could work on. But the phone call never came. I wrote a letter by hand to him, trying to reinforce his own vision by affirmation. "If you'll carry out the campaign theme, 'building the earth,' and truly invite the people to build a platform with you, you can do more good than any leader in the world at this time. For such a campaign, John and I would dedicate our entire efforts." We signed it, pledging our lives, our fortunes, everything.

I received a note back sometime later saying, "Thank you for the endorsement." The Sargent Shriver I had met was gone for the moment, lost in the back-breaking effort of his campaign. We did have some sympathetic conversations with his community program developer who responded to the idea of using the synergistic process and television. He invited me to "slip into" New Hampshire, without any official authorization from the candidate or the staff or anyone, to try a few SYNCONs with Shriver people and other citizens to see how it would work. I had always longed to try a SYNCON in a political context. But because there wasn't any response from the candidate or his staff, we decided it would be misusing the process, which had a chance of spreading in a transpolitical mode through the country in the Bicentennial year. We might lose our chance of doing it by being identified with one specific candidate.

We were not invited to help Shriver design his television campaign or his process. However, on their own initiative, the young people of the New World Center brought our mobile television van and cameras to televise his announcement at the Mayflower Hotel in Washington. It was done up in traditional style. The press corps was sitting in the center of the crowded ballroom. Supporters and friends, numbering at least a thousand, were jammed in the room. Shriver made a traditional opening statement that had no bearing on the Declaration of Independence, building the earth, or television-in-the-round. His main point was that he represented the Kennedy legacy. It was an old "New Deal" approach.

When asked by the press, "How are you going to involve the people in your campaign?" Shriver gave an traditional answer, saying that he and his staff were always interested in people's ideas.

I was deeply disappointed that his opportunity had been lost, but I also knew the old game of politics had forced him to be silent about his true vision. He had said to his press secretary, when we were discussing television-in-the-round for his announcement, "I want to get to the people. Maybe John and Barbara can help me." The press secretary had said, *"The New York Times* will have Johnny Apple and Scotty Reston there. They might think it was a gimmick and make fun of it. We would be ruined at your first statement." Shriver had said, "I don't give a goddamn about Johnny Apple and Scotty Reston; I want to get to the people." But the fact was, he did not try the new approach.

This experience with Sargent Shriver, along with my own experience in contemplating running for the presidency, gave me a new sense of inner authority. I believed the next step was going to be taken by nonpolitical people who had a whole picture in their heads. I used to be distressed by the refusal of the men of America to take initiative. But I was beginning to feel it was in the interest of humanity that the existing structures not lead the way.

Those who were taking overt initiative in the development of both inner and outer space were usually working not against but outside the current system and large institutions. It appeared the initiative was coming from people who had no vested interest in current growth patterns. Perhaps once again the mammals will eat the dinosaur eggs rather than confront the prevailing giants directly.

An example of this "mammalian initiative" occurred in Acapulco in January 1975. One of our active colleagues, Orville Freeman, was president of Business International, an organization that serves and informs the largest multinational corporations in the world. Orville was secretary of agriculture under Kennedy. He was a man of great ability and integrity, with a kind, gentle face. A pragmatic idealist, he was attempting to bring social coherence to this great worldwide force of development. But he had never thought about new worlds, just as most persons in positions of high power had not. I had asked if I could address his executive conference of eighty-six chief executives: "Doing Business in a Resource-short World." I wanted to present the Choiceful Future scenario.

When I described the potential for manufacturing and building habitats in space, he said, "Barbara, you blow my mind! I would like to get you to the conference. But these are the heads of the most important corporations in the world. What would you say to them?"

"I would tell them we are entering the universal age, becoming interdependent on earth and opening immeasurable horizons in the universe, that we have new limits on this planet and completely new areas of development in the universe, but that the development must be done in a cooperative, synergistic manner, or it will fail."

He said if he could "package" me correctly, so I wouldn't look too different from the rest of them, I could speak. My theme was to be "Beyond the Limits to Growth."

Warren Avis picked up John and me at the airport and took us to his beautiful home in Acapulco where we stayed during the conference, which was being held at the Princess Hotel.

The meeting began at 8:30 a.m. every day. Long tables were lined in an enormous ballroom and at each chair was a plaque with the name of the chief executive of an international corporation: Olivetti, General Foods, TRW, Mercke, Nippon Steel and The Committee for the Future. Also present were some resource people. I was the only woman, except for the wives who were seated at the side of the room, several hundred feet from the long table, on chairs in rows. I felt totally out of place. I would rather have been with a group of flaming radicals, because at least they are for social change.

I did not know what to say to any of them, and they did not know what to say to me. We went to a few painful cocktail parties, but usually John and I rushed back to Warren's house when the meetings were over. We swam in the ocean, and we talked for hours in the starlight about the future. I became convinced of the need for people like us to become financially independent of existing sources of funding to initiate new worlds' projects.

When the time came for my speech, Dr. Knoppers, a member of

the Club of Rome, introduced me as a "historical discontinuity who was going to give them a new insight." There was a bit of guffawing (I was a historical discontinuity simply by being a woman).

I said, "Yes, I'm speaking of a historical discontinuity, gentlemen. Our world is going through an evolutionary shift from the earth-only to the global-universal phase. I'm speaking to you from my experience as a mother." This was not very well received as a background, but I continued on, "Motherhood is the greatest experience a woman can have to develop concern for the future."

Then I described the three world views. I told them that the Choiceful Future offered the best system for nonexploitive development and the most realistic, enduring incentive for their own development, if they would work together to build the next platform for human development. I also said there are processes of citizen involvement that are liberating the greatest potential on earth: human energy. The hierarchical structures within which people are operating in the large corporations and institutions are suppressing potential. I asked for their initiative in opening their structures to more consensual participation in decision making.

I read from Ted Taylor's article (which he had written in the *Saturday Review* about The Committee for the Future). He listed resources that could be mined on the moon. The chief executive of the Nippon Steel Company, who had given a talk about the limitation of resources, saying the last remaining resources available were in the ocean beds, looked at me with surprise and wrote down verbatim the minerals to be found on the moon. I spoke of the low cost possibility of solar energy from space and the feasibility of manufacturing in zero gravity with no fragile biosphere to damage. I mentioned O'Neill's concept of communities in space. I called for a decade of "open worlds development," to initiate the "benign industrial revolution," as Krafft Ehricke called it. I suggested that the multinationals participate in a concerted effort to identify new options, to formulate and assess action, and to outline strategies to pursue lines of development consistent with their business objectives and their objectives as members of humankind-in-transition.

After I sat down, Dr. Knoppers asked, "Are there any questions?" There weren't; I think they were stunned. However, later, when Orville Freeman was making his concluding statement, one man stood up: Sy Ramo, chairman of the board of TRW, one of the largest corporations in the world. He said, "Mrs. Hubbard told us something I believe we should listen to. She told us we are not thinking ahead, that we are limited to the present. I want to support her and call upon us to examine these new options for the future."

When it was over I stood there awkwardly, feeling inadequate, wondering if I had done any good at all. Several chief executives came up, somewhat shyly, and expressed interest. But I lacked the power to make anything happen directly; my "reality factor" was low.

This was one of the agonies of my particular role. I did not yet have a transitional language to make a link between pragmatic men and new action. I spoke with Sy Ramo later at a party, and thanked him for his comments. "Why are so few of those brilliant men thinking about the obvious new horizons?" I asked. "There's nothing that I have said that isn't fully known. It isn't like Einstein explaining $E=MC^2$ for the first time. We have been to the moon; we have examined the resources; we know the earth is finite. We know we have a responsibility to the environment. These executives are more aware of all of this than I."

Ramo agreed, but said, "The pressures of their work, the competition, the enormity of the organizational task, the significance of every little fluctuation of the stock market, the complexities of the Common Market, working in different nations, are all so great they literally can't lift their heads and survive unless they give everything to the present. I'm the same way. I have no time. I can't think."

We clearly were up against an interesting barrier. The best people in power positions have been prevented from taking initiative to do what they believe should be done by the structures they successfully maintained. Success in the old system seemed to be a barrier to enabling the birth of the new.

I am reaching for the Tree of Life.

Visionaries, such as Paolo Solari, were attempting to birth the new through creating new forms and systems independent of the old. I saw this firsthand when the United Methodist Global Ministries Research and Development Board invited me to be a "resource futurist" to meet with their board and others, including the theologian John Cobb, to view the Arcology being built by Paolo Solari with amateur volunteer help in the desert near Scottsdale, Arizona. A chapel to Teilhard de Chardin was to be its focal point. The question we were asked was, "What are the future religious implications of Arcology and how should the United Methodist Church relate to it?"

Paolo had told us he looked upon the evolutionary process as the urbanization of matter, from macromolecule to single cells to multicells to humans to cities and now to the next phase of synthesis of complexity, the Arcology. It's a prototype for a new, human, architectural ecology, inviting hundreds of thousands of people to live in close communication with each other, eliminating urban degradation and suburban sprawl, waste of energy in transportation, and misuses of land, and creating a pattern wherein individuals can grow more humane.

John Cobb spoke to the ministers the day after we arrived. He told them "Christian realism" had become insufficient, that "Christianity had to become future-oriented again." He was addressing the criticism of ministers working on the front lines of urban suffering, concerned daily for people living in poverty and disease. The ministers shook their heads in disapproval. They did not want to give up the care of the suffering. It made them angry even to consider the "diversion" of funds to something that might not work.

"But how well is the Church working in Harlem?" John asked. "Is all the charity of the churches of the world and all the charity of the welfare state sufficient to create a better society?"

Paolo, who was sitting quietly at John's side, said, "Charity on this scale has become naive."

"We can't happily choose to let anyone suffer," John said, "but I'm beginning to feel we have to build something new rather than just try to stop the collapse of the old."

Someone asked Paolo if he was sure the Arcology would work. He shook his head. "No. In biology, most mutations aren't viable. The same is true of social inventions. The Arcology is a conscious mutation. It may not work, though I personally believe it will. How will we know, though, if we don't try?"

I was hanging onto every word. "You're in the midst of a quantum leap here," I said, glancing at the ministers. "Paolo Solari is making that leap."

"What's a quantum leap?" someone asked.

"In evolution, there's a seeming discontinuity from one mutation to another, such as from non-life to life. Something does occur, but it's subtle and hidden. You are in on an evolutionary secret here, listening to Paolo. He's showing you a change that's almost imperceptible now, happening in the midst of the desert, with volunteers. He's experimenting with the next level of cooperative habitation for the evolution of humanity. If you miss it, the Church will miss being part of it, but that's all, because it'll happen anyway. We need a theology of the quantum leap, how to get from here to there." Heads began to nod in understanding.

"We can take the quantum leap *and* minister to suffering during the transition," I said. "Society still has enough energy to do both. There *are* people willing to help where help can be given, and there are those eagerly trying to work on the quantum leaps. We must not divert the geniuses willing to risk their lives for evolutionary change and condemn them as uncharitable just because they aren't working on immediate suffering. We should understand the great morality and compassion of the people building arcologies, planning space communities, people trying to understand the aging process, people building laser information technologies and educational satellites. We are excluding our own genius! They need spiritual blessing as much as someone assuaging the suffering of the dying on the streets of the world. They're not far out, they're far *in!*"

As I was talking I caught the eye of one of the ministers. I could see he was weighing my remarks skeptically. I continued. "We have the tools for either global catastrophe or transformation. We know we have a larger purpose than to eat, sleep, reproduce, and die. The fact that our tools are developed through our mind's capacity to understand and work with the laws of the universe means our new powers are natural. It is natural to understand the potential of our own minds. It is natural that we can build rockets and leave earth alive. It is natural to understand our own genetic codes as we approach new environments in space. It is natural that we understand nuclear energy, the power at the heart of matter, as we launch toward the thousands of suns of the galaxies. It is natural to build the "androsphere," just as it was for the cells to build the biosphere. It is natural to be born into universal life."

For forty-six years, I had carried the hunger and been motivated by it with a mysterious persistence. It had guided me to peaks of human experience. Each of these peaks acted as a compass of joy leading me through the labyrinth of life to the mountain top of a new normalcy, a fuller humanness, until I became that which was pulling me. I became the magnet. I became the evolutionary drive. I knew that something radically new was both coming and needed.

Louis and Rene Marx, Barbara's parents, 1930's.

Barbara and her mother, 1930.

Barbara, Patricia, Louis and Jacqueline, 1937.

Barbara and her dad, 1951.

Barbara, age 16.

Earl, 1945.

Barbara, Stephanie, Suzanne and Earl at the Lime Rock house, 1958.

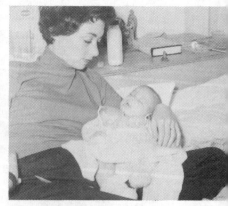

Barbara and daughter Suzanne, 1952.

Standing: Gen. Omar Bradley and Gen. Emmett "Rosie" O'Donnell.
From left: Emmett Dwight, Pres. Dwight D. Eisenhower, Spencer Bedell, Walter Bedell Smith, Gen. George C. Marshall and Bradley Marshall.

At left: Ike, Idella and Louis Marx

Below from top:
Louis, Idella, Barbara
Emmett Dwight, Spencer Bedell, Bradley Marshall
Suzanne, Curtis Jeffery, Woodleigh

Top Right:
Barbara, John Whiteside and Ray
Bradbury at the Los Angeles
SYNCON, 1972.

Below: Barbara explaining the
Evolutionary Spiral, 1983.

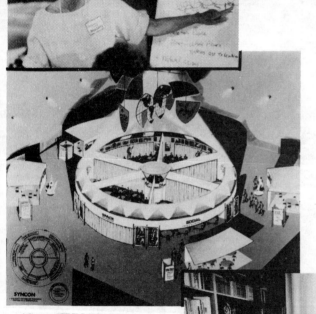

Lancelot Law Whyte

Above: SYNCON Diagram

Right: Barbara and Patricia
in Moscow at the home of
Yevgeny Velikhov in 1987.

Top Right: At the far left is
Rama Vernon, at the
Soviet Peace Committee.

[M]ichelle Nichols (Lt. Uhura of
[St]ar Trek) at Los Angeles
[S]YNCON.

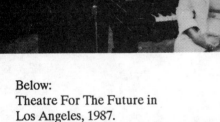

Below:
Theatre For The Future in
Los Angeles, 1987.

Swami Satchidananda blessing
Barbara at the Soviet American
Citizens Summit, Alexandria,
Virginia, 1988.

Above: Wade Hubbard and daughter, Danielle.

Top Right: Daughters Suzanne and Woodleigh with Barbara in Boulder, Colorado.

Below: Lloyd and his wife, Laura.

Louis, Jr. and Louis, Sr. at Jacqueline's wedding, 1956.

Barbara, Gale Whipple, Danielle's mother and Danielle Hubbard

Alexandra Hubbard Morton at Echo Bay, British Columbia

Below: Earl and grandson Peter

Above: Patricia and Dan Ellsberg

Below: Jaqueline and husband Wayne Barnett

Jarret Morton and friend.

Above left: Barbara with Tovi Daly of Island Pacific NW

Above right: A few of the people who helped with her book, from left: Michael and D.K. Shumway, Claude Golden, Tovi and Greag Daly with Barbara seated.

Center right: Barbara after completing ropes course at Gold Lake Ranch, Boulder, Colorado, 1988.

Above: Barbara warming her hands on cool spring day, Orcas Island

Painting by Earl Hubbard "Mankind in the Universe", 1964.

Seven

The Joy Of Union

In the mid-seventies, I experienced some confusion and exhaustion after the joy of discovery and freedom that had forever transformed my life. I had been given a vocation: tell the story of the birth of humankind as one body. But what to do daily was a question.

The SYNCONs had been magnificent experiences. They were seeds of cooperative self-government, ready to flower when the season was right. But they were too complex and expensive to self-replicate. The International SYNCON for the Bicentennial had been a small event in Washington, D.C. because the large funding needed never came through. John and I did not have the organizational or entrepreneurial skills to make a business out of the SYNCONs. Nor did we have the inclination. He was a soldier on a mission, and I was a missionary with a vision.

A depression crept in and marred my enthusiasm for life. I felt I had failed. We had misjudged the timing. I worried that I was suffering from grandiosity. How dare I envision new worlds on earth, new worlds in space, when I had trouble organizing my own house! I felt empty within.

I agonized over the presidential election in the Bicentennial Year. Our future-oriented efforts to look at the next 200 years barely made an impression. All emphasis was on the past and present. Jimmy Carter called upon us to be as good as we once were.

Meanwhile I had written a letter to NASA offering myself as a payload on the shuttle. At that time they were thinking of picking a citizen to fly. A reporter from the Washington Post called me and said he had seen NASA's files of volunteers: people like Walter Cronkite, Hugh Downs, Zsa Zsa Gabor, Jerry Brown, and myself. Beside my name he said there was a handwritten note: "Get Barbara up in the shuttle...J.Y." My heart leapt. I thought it was John Yardley, the man who was in charge of NASA's manned space flight, a key architect of our shuttle program, and our dear friend from SYNCON days. He understood my purpose.

The reporter said he was asking all these people why they wanted to go. When he asked me the question, I answered, "Because I believe that when a person such as myself is in space, connected to billions of people on earth in a moment of shared attention and awareness of our oneness, there will be an experience that will unify humanity. We will become aware that together we have the capacity to meet all our needs on earth and to reach out into the universe for new energy, new resources, new knowledge, new life."

I told him I proposed that the first citizen in space be the occasion of a planetary celebration of human creativity and compassion. I was, once again, attempting to act upon the cosmic birth experience to provide a point of focus beyond the planet to assist in the experience of our integration.

The reporter said, as far as he was concerned, this was the best reason any one had given. He was rooting for me, he said. But it did not happen.

John and I went through a difficult time. To support ourselves we had to do TV shoots. The residents were not being paid a living wage. We were losing our joy and I was depleted financially, since I was the sole financial source. Whenever there was a deficit, I paid it. I began to resent my role.

John wanted to expand our work and build Futures Network, as a for-profit company. This was the beginning of a long arduous effort to create a media vehicle for the on-going story of the "new" news of who we *really* are as an evolving species. We began discussions with Gene Roddenberry, the creator of Star Trek.

We moved all our gear from Greystone to a large basement at the Sheraton Hotel. John assembled the residents and Buddy Nadler, a Hollywood producer, to develop Futures Network radio. They looked to me to fund it, but I had lost faith that we could do it successfully. One grim, rainy, snowy day, the basement roof fell in, and many years of accumulated pigeon droppings literally fell on our heads, covering valuable papers and equipment. It seemed as though we were pushing a rock uphill that continued to fall upon our heads, like Sisyphus in Greek mythology.

I felt that I had to radically alter my life. I did not want to be disloyal. Yet the deeper in we went to sustain ourselves in the material world, the further away we got from the vision. Finally, I broke down and asked people to leave. I could no longer maintain the situation. The residents, now highly trained, were able to find excellent jobs. We gave the TV equipment to the Southern Baptist

Church. My heart was filled with sadness. I felt like a total failure.

I called my sister Patricia, whose love has always sustained me. "Patricia, I'm upset. I don't know what to do next. Could I come to California to visit you? I would like to meet everyone you love."

Without hesitation Patricia welcomed me into the warm bosom of northern California. She introduced me to several extraordinary women of the human potential and transpersonal movements. I met Leni Schwartz and Frances Vaughn, both leaders in the Association for Humanistic Psychology, Virginia Satir, founder of the family therapy movement; Joan Halifax, a practicing Buddhist; Diane Pike, wife of Bishop James Pike, and Judith Skutch who published *A Course in Miracles*. These women were a new phenomenon, embodying the feminine co-creator. They were powerful, loving, independent world changers. They were models for me. Within a few days I felt restored and reinvigorated. This reemphasized to me the importance of associating with peers who affirm human potential.

But my attraction to the holistic/global/spiritual people put a severe strain on my relationship with John. He felt I was deserting him, seduced by "the bells and feathers people," as he called them. He refused to join me in this spiritual odyssey. He was a soldier and a Southern Baptist. He saw himself as a servant of God, not an heir of God or a co-creator with God. It was all right for me to speak of these matters to him, in fact he loved it and understood me well. But he felt I could not "go public" with it or associate with others who believed in these spiritual realities if I wanted to be effective in the world. And it seemed to be true. I became a partial misfit everywhere. My space colleagues thought I was being taken over by a fringe element. And, the human potentialists in general reacted violently against high technology and the space program.

*I am coping with the relationship between
the possible and the infinite.*

In 1979 I went to Findhorn, a small community in northern Scotland, that had been founded by Peter Caddy, a British Air Force officer, Eileen, his wife, and Dorothy McLean, a nature sensitive. Eileen received guidance, an inner voice that gave specific instructions regarding humankind's relationship with nature. Peter followed the guidance. Night after night, in their little trailer, Eileen would go into the bathroom and listen, writing down what she heard, transcribing the instructions on what to do. For example, to Dorothy a pea plant might 'speak' its needs, "Plant me deeper than the package says to, and give me much more water."

Following instructions, Peter built gardens in the sandy soil where almost nothing would grow according to conventional wisdom and common sense. The results were amazing. Sixty pound cabbages and enormous flowers grew where before, nothing had grown. The British Soil Society was astounded. People came from all over the world to see the "miracles."

Soon the Findhorn group realized they were not only growing vegetables and flowers, they were growing people! The process of attunement, holding hands and "tuning in" to the deeper harmony that guides and binds us all, was encouraging both natural and human growth, harmony and joy. Thousands flocked to Findhorn, flooding the tiny nearby Scottish town of Forres with visitors.

While at Findhorn, I decided to do the job I most disliked, kitchen duty, to see if the magic of Findhorn really worked. My group's task that day was to set the table for lunch, three hundred places in the baronial dining hall at Cluny Hill, overlooking the Scottish fields.

We were told to stand in a circle, hold hands, and feel love for each other. This lasted for a few minutes. I felt a warm glow rise in my whole being. Then we were instructed that with the placement of every fork, knife, and spoon we were to consciously infuse love in each utensil, thinking with love of the person who would sit there. After placing hundreds of utensils, I myself was in a state of overwhelming joy. (I vowed to remember this experience at all future kitchen duties!)

By the time I visited Findhorn, Eileen had received guidance *not* to receive any more guidance. Rather than depend on Eileen for direction, residents were requested to tune in to their own guidance. They formed "core groups" to do the work. Leadership came to mean the characteristic of being able to tune in and represent the whole community. It was self-selected. Decision-making included listening for guidance, and sharing the guidance until the whole group agreed on the action. Findhorn was a first experiment in the next stage of self-government. What we had experienced in the SYNCONs during intense three-day events, and what I had experienced as a single flash of union during the cosmic birth experience, they had normalized as an ongoing sustainable process of spirit translated into action. I realized that the reason we were surrounded by oppressive bureaucracies is that we were not self-governing. We kill, cheat, steal and destroy ourselves. 'Only when we become self-governing,' I thought, 'will the giant state systems wither away.' The next phase is not world government, but *self* government.

On my way back from Findhorn, I stopped in to see Baron and Baroness di Pauli in London. They are aristocrats in the finest sense of the word, totally dedicated to improving the world. Through their "Centre Link" program they brought together networks of educators, healers, scientists, and business people who were interested in the new paradigm: seeing the world as an interrelated whole.

They drove me to Stanley Hall, their beautiful estate in Essex. It was a magnificent old, stone house, with English gardens, a pond, daffodils and mists rising from verdant lawns. Generals of the Second World War had spent time there in secret strategy meetings. Churchill had been there. I had a feeling of deja vu, of deep nostalgia, as though I had been there before at a high point of my life. Many years ago, someone asked me who I most admired in history. I was surprised when a string of powerful male generals and political leaders arose in my thoughts: Pericles of Greece who stopped the Persians at the famous battle of Marathon, Abraham Lincoln, Winston Churchill, John F. Kennedy. Here at Stanley Hall I remembered the presence of these shining knights of the past. With some obvious incongruity, I felt myself to be related to them by purpose.

They took me to a little round church, one of the oldest in the country, dating from Roman times. The three of us entered the church and stood beneath a round sky light, alone, praying silently, holding hands in a small circle.

The idea occurred clearly to me that the torch of freedom has been passed to our generation. I felt we must work for the transformation of the American Presidency. I thought to call Thomas Paine, Adlai Stevenson and Norman Cousins.

I told Edmee and Kili di Pauli of this idea, and we all bowed our heads in prayer for the emergence of a transformed American Presidency that would take leadership to co-create a global society beyond the Cold War in which so much of our resources, technology and genius are now imprisoned.

Upon my return to the States I called Tom Paine and invited him out to dinner in Washington, feeling somewhat ridiculous and nervous. We met at Romeo and Juliette's, an elegant D.C. restaurant. Tom represents to me the cosmic engineer. He is a descendent of the Tom Paine, one of the heroes of the American Revolution. He carries within him the far-seeing, all-knowing awareness of evolutionary capacity. He knew what humanity could do, and what's more, he knew how to do it. He was administrator of NASA during the Apollo Program, and had encouraged us during the Harvest Moon Project. He has those same extraterrestrial eyes that I saw in John, in Chris Kraft, and other men-of-the-universe.

I was in awe of Tom because he combined the capacity for vision and action, which I so longed to be able to do, but was never quite able to achieve.

Dinner was almost over. I had not dared bring up my mission. Over coffee I finally said, "Tom, there's something I want to ask of you."

"What's that...." his eyes looked in to mine.

"Tom, I wouldn't ask this on my own, but I feel guided."

"What is it, Barbara?" he asked patiently.

"Tom, I want you to run for President of the United States..."

The extraterrestrial eyes opened in amazement, "You're kidding," he said, rapidly swallowing his hot coffee.

"No, I'm not kidding. Isn't it true that you would know what to do to start us on a new worlds approach?"

His eyes narrowed. "Well, yes, we could do that. The first thing I would do is create a new state for all refugees of the world, we could work with Canada on that...." The ideas began to stream out.... For a moment I thought he might actually be interested.

But suddenly he closed down and became quite formal. "Barbara, there is no way I could do this. I don't want to... but I'll help you. You do it. I'll be one of your consultants."

"Tom, what has happened to the men of America? Why is it that those with vision are so unwilling to act, and those who manipulate and control are so well organized and effective? I'm disappointed."

He was too. He did not want to let me down, but this mission was not his.

I went to Norman Cousins. He gently counselled I should do it. As he had before, he warned me of the negative reactions I would receive. "But," he said, "you would be the most pragmatic candidate because you know the direction of the future." He advised that if I wanted to do it, it would be necessary to arrange a television special, with key colleagues stating the themes.

Once again, I was confused and unsure. I retreated from this impetus. I could not find my partners, a team of peers. Yet, surely, something new was being born.

As we entered the decade of the 80's, the dichotomy between the rising strands of positive action and the falling strands of destructive action deepened. Ronald Reagan entered the presidency, holding a strange mixed picture of reality: he had faith in people, belief in the free enterprise system and in the mystical destiny of the United States. But he also intended to build the largest peace-time military state in the history of the world. Anti-communism became the battle-cry to rationalize extraordinary military expenditures to control and maintain an economic power in the name of "defense." It was a "slow-motion coup d'etat," as Hazel Henderson said.

In general, the global thinkers and activists expressed no shared vision, no dream, no hope, and above all, no process of cooperation to counter this power in the political arena. It seemed to me that Reagan was holding the fort for the new wave of leaders to show up. Not liberal Democrats and the welfare state, but transfor-mationalists, people in tune with the pulse of evolution who would unify and restore the earth and liberate human creativity. Yet our folks were not even in the dialogue. We were mysteriously inef-fective. We had no strategy. Maybe we simply were not ready. Perhaps our political obscurity was a natural protection until the movement could mature.

By the end of 1979 I was experiencing intense changes, both on the external level, through my attraction to evolutionary action, and on the inner level, through personal impulses to transform. It was as though the hunger was compelling me to grow beyond my limits.

I had been doing a "Theatre for the Future," a multi-media story of creation with music and images, which John had designed. I stood upon a stage, with gorgeous slides of the universe behind me, saying "Imagine the universe, billions and billions of galaxies, multitudes of solar systems, some that may have life comparable to our own. Imagine ourselves as a more mature species."

The Theatre concluded with a cosmic birth experience. An artist created an image of thousands of points of light connecting throughout the earth, until the whole planet glowed. Light ascended from within us and descended upon us. We became a "haloed earth." I described the evolution of the human race, beyond planet-boundedness, beyond self-centered consciousness, beyond degeneration. Pachelbel's Canon in D played. The audience and I became one, as we imaged ourselves into the future!

After each performance, my body was throbbing with energy. I seemed to be activating my own nervous system. I remembered Willis Harman describing how a caterpillar turns itself into a butterfly through an "imaginal cell," that holds the picture of the new being, and actually transforms the caterpillar into a butterfly.

This experience of inner activation propelled me toward a deep spiritual experience.

I was so filled with these ideas that I decided to go away quietly to see if I could write a book about the next stage of evolution; to get this powerful surge of emotional ideas out of my system. I rented a small house in Santa Barbara for three months, the first time I had ever been alone, without a man or a family, in my whole life. I left John in Washington.

But I had a writer's block. The ideas were dammed up. I had no frame of reference or belief system through which to express them. One day I surrendered and stopped trying. I called my sister Jacqueline, who lived in Palo Alto, California, and asked her to come and visit me. I would take a few days off.

When she arrived we decided to go for a walk in the Botanical Gardens. We drove up the mountains outside of Santa Barbara toward Cold Canyon. The day was intoxicatingly pure, brilliant, clean, light and glowing. The vegetation was alive after ten days of rain.

We followed a winding road up the mountain. On the left was the sea, glittering and shimmering in the sun. On our right were the mountains, framed by the utter ultrablue sky. The air felt like heavy sweet water upon the face. We drove up and up. Suddenly I saw a little wooden sign: "Mt. Calvary Monastery."

"Let's go and see it," I said to Jacqueline. She was still an agnostic, as our father had been.

"Why?" she asked.

My answer came quickly, "Because I feel something is going to happen to me there."

We began an even steeper climb. Excitement rose within me. I began to feel both an inner radiation and a type of electric field which seemed to surround my body. It felt like the light surrounding the earth during the cosmic birth experience, when all humankind smiled the planetary smile.

We arrived at the exquisite little monastery and got out of the car. I sat upon a stone wall, looking out at the great arc of the shining sea and upward toward the mountainous earth when something in space caught my eye. Mystically, magically, miraculously, sky divers, hang gliders appeared. They were human butterflies, jumping off a higher mountain, floating above Mt. Calvary Monastery in an ecstasy of freedom and weightlessness.

The symbols were revelatory to me. Mt. Calvary was the place of the crucifixion, the death of the old. The hang-gliders represented the resurrected multitude, the birth of the new humans, the metamorphosis of the butterflies out of the caterpillars. 'Behold, I show you a mystery, we shall not all sleep, we shall all be changed,' echoed in the deep recesses of my memory, reawakening the cosmic birth experience.

Suddenly, as I sat upon the stone wall, the light surrounding me intensified. It became the all-pervading living presence of Christ. My attention was magnetized. I turned my inner eyes to face the light and made direct contact.

I was electrified. He was real! He was alive! My heart was flooded with love. And in that flood of love I seemed to be receiving a stream of ideas, a direct knowingness; 'Whenever you feel the rush of warm joy in your heart, it is I - open your heart to the joy.'

I became acutely sensitive, every cell in my being poised to receive this presence, this relationship with a living being, a full embodiment of God. The stream of ideas continued:

'My resurrection was a signal for all of humanity's. Why do you suppose I submitted to the calumny of Calvary but to demonstrate that the physical body can and must be transformed....

'The resurrection was an early-attraction signal to the human race of what can be done through love of each person as a member of one's own body and of God, above all else. The intensity of that love, the power of that connectedness, is the key to the resurrection which is now known as the transformation.... The resurrection was a future forecast of an approaching new norm.... The transformation of Homo sapiens to Homo universalis is the acting out of that forecast by the human species. What I did alone, all can now do who choose to love God above all else and your neighbor as yourself... That great commandment of pure love combined with the knowledge of God's processes of creation gained by science in the past two thousand years is the formula for victory....'

I remained there in silence for what seemed to be an eternity. In that instant the hunger of Eve was fulfilled. I bowed my head in overwhelming gratitude.

Jacqueline had been standing watching me. She looked at me questioningly, with her deep, motherly gentleness and unconditional love. Silently, I embraced her as the hang gliders glistened and danced freely in the wind above our heads.

Several days later I returned to the monastery for a visit. I was guided to the New Testament once again to read the "predictive passages," to study the Bible as I had studied the story of creation as gleaned by science from the Book of Nature. Each passage of scripture opened the floodgates of my mind. Everything I had ever read, heard or imagined at the growing edge of personal or scientific capacities, Jesus had done, thereby setting a pattern for our own radical transformation "in the fullness of time."

When Jesus spoke in the Bible, I felt it was the voice of evolution, the very pulse of creation guiding us to become our potential self, the fully human human being. I received deep guidance and personal instruction how to become a demonstration of my potential self.

I wrote for six months, sixteen hundred pages of journal entries. The most extraordinary insight I received was that there is now a new dispensation on earth due to the rapid rise of consciousness in so many millions of ordinary people. The violent scenario is not necessary. An alternative to Armageddon is a "Planetary Pentecost," a time on earth when every one who so choses would hear from within, in their own language, the mighty words of God. It would be a shared mystical experience for the whole human race, similar to what happened to the disciples in the upper room at the time of the first Pentecost, just after Jesus' resurrection. Each person would be empowered to be a co-creator expressing both their own and God's potential. The illusion of separateness would be over. The next stage of evolution would begin.

I realized that the cosmic birth experience was a pre-cognitive flash of just that event. It seemed to me to be a genuine possibility and that Christ was our partner, if we chose to join with one another in the "upper room" of our awareness on a planetary scale.

> *My life has shifted from within. There has been set in motion a process of personal transformation that matches the planetary transformation. The presence of Christ has become my living partner.*

I wanted to share this tremendous experience with Buckminster Fuller. Somehow I knew he would understand. So I sent him excerpts from my journal.

One evening we were both scheduled to be speakers at the Annenburg School of Communications in Los Angeles. At the very last minute it was announced that Bucky would not be down to speak, he was reading something! This seemed very strange. So I was the only speaker that evening. Toward the end of my speech, I saw him standing outside the door leading to a garden, at the back of the auditorium, his bald head and glasses glinting in the light as he beckoned urgently for me to come.

Someone came up and whispered in my ear, "Dr. Fuller wants to see you, *alone*." I was led hurriedly past the people who wanted to talk with me, to Bucky, who took my hand, and sat me down opposite him, at a table in the dimly lit garden.

"Darlin'," he said. "I have just read your journal. I know it is true, because the same thing happened to me. It was in February, 1928, that I had this real and extraordinary experience, the only one in my life that was utterly mystical. I was walking on Michigan Avenue in Chicago when suddenly I found myself seemingly floating along at the center of a sparkling sphere. Then I heard a deep, loud and clear voice, such as I had never heard before, saying, 'From now on you need never await temporal attestation to your thought. You think the truth.' I was directed to the New Testament and began to write, just as you did, almost precisely the same words. But I hid it under my bed. No one has ever seen it."

He stood up and embraced me. "Darlin', there's nothing but God, there's only God."

We stood there in the garden for some time, hugging one another. I felt I was absorbing his knowledge by osmosis. He understood the design of creation that will empower humans to become "continuous humans" in an ever-regenerating universe. He comprehended the technology of transformation. He used to get angry when people said they did not like technology. "Do you like your thumb?" he would ask irritatedly. There is a technological aspect to all things.

I called David Smith and asked him if he could arrange for Bucky and me to do a video tape together. David set it up at Xavier University. Michael Toms of "New Dimensions" was the host. Bucky and I discussed together "Our Spiritual Experience" before an audience of students. But he never mentioned the words Christ or God on tape. He told me later that they were too divisive.

It seemed our deepest and most passionate spiritual experiences often had to be watered down or hidden because the associations people have with these words preclude them from hearing what we are truly saying, and cause polarization.

I thought that what sexuality was to the Victorian Age, mystical experience is to ours. Almost everyone experiences it, but almost no one dares to speak about it. We have been dominated by a scientific, materialistic culture which has made us feel embarrassed about our natural spiritual natures. Yet we read that sixty percent of the American people have had mystical experiences. We are a nation of repressed mystics! Clearly some synthesis of our inner life and our outer action is needed.

I communicated my Christ experience to John, reading him excerpts from my journal writings. As a Baptist he already believed in Christ. He was joyful at my experience of this relationship with Christ.

But something was wrong, he was ailing. He had lost his focus. One evening as we were dining in New York, he turned to me and said, "Barbara, I don't know what's wrong with me. I'm depressed, I've lost my energy, my drive...." He complained of pain in his chest. He was a three pack-a-day smoker. I urged him to have a checkup.

We went to see a doctor. He found a lesion, diagnosing it as caused by John's years as a coal miner. But the pain grew worse. We were not sure what to do next.

In June of 1981 John complained that he could not use his left hand. We went to the Air Force Medical Center where they did a CAT scan. We went together for the verdict. It came all too soon.

"You have inoperable cancer. It started in your lung and has metastasized to your brain. You have less than one year to live. All we can do is make you more comfortable."

It was incredible, unbearable. I could not believe it. Everything had always been able to be changed, improved. This was terminal. I suggested alternative therapies. But John became suddenly angelic, peaceful, almost blissful. He trusted the Air Force medics, he said.

He gradually lost the ability to move, and his mind degenerated. Often he did not recognize me, yet he continued to smoke and drink. Every day I bathed and cared for him. One night as I was tucking him into bed he smiled radiantly at me.

"Sweetheart, why are you smiling?" I asked.

"Sunshine, I know humankind is born into this universe, I know we will build new worlds. I know you will carry on the mission." His eyes fluttered shut, leaving me helpless to save him, and alone.

On the night of December 24, 1981, he was unable to function. He had been placed in a crib in his room. J.P., his son, and I stood by him and decided to call an ambulance. They lifted him onto a stretcher. He seemed as small as a child. I knew it was the end. He died that night in the hospital. I returned early the next morning and they took me to see him.

I had never seen a dead body. It was as unbelievable as birth. Where was he? I touched his lifeless hand, and his lips, already hardening and cold beneath my fingertips.

I stood by him in the hospital on Christmas morn, praying, asking to reach his spirit. My heart felt like a painful weight in my chest. Tears blurred my sight. "Why did you die?" I asked.

I heard the words, "I died to set you free. I have work to do to prepare for what's coming. We will rendezvous again. Over and out." I nodded. He was a great soldier. He would never abandon his mission. My love for him became secured. Memories of our problems faded. As I stood by his dead body, I truly believed that he was connected to the planetary event, revealed to me as the Planetary Pentecost, which would finally link humanity together as one body.

After his funeral, which drew people who loved him from all over the country, I took a retreat alone at the Madonna House, a small Catholic retreat in Washington D.C. where they serve you bread and water. I was in deep depression. I could hardly lift my head. I felt the full load of our mission upon my shoulders. I missed John, his love, his companionship, his humor, his joy.

I groped for guidance. I heard the words, "Will you accept full responsibility for your mission?" I felt myself poised at the edge of an abyss. I did not know how to do the work without John. My partner was gone. If I said yes, I would step into the abyss of the unknown. If I had said no, I would remain on the threshold and die. I said, "Yes, I accept full responsibility for my work," and stepped consciously into the emptiness. Fear gripped my heart as I felt myself falling into the dark.

Suddenly, brilliant light surrounded me, the same brilliant light that enveloped the earth and permeated my being on the hill at Mt. Calvary. I was totally supported in the light. The words arose, "When you accept total responsibility, the angels of creation are with you, you shall never be alone."

I had only begun to regain my inner strength when two months later, in February of 1982, my father died at the age of 86. I was giving a lecture at Antioch West in Seattle. Someone passed me a note in the middle of my talk. I stopped and began to cry. When I shared the news the whole class embraced me. We talked of our fathers for the rest of the time.

I described how he challenged me to do my best and supported my quest, even though he did not understand or approve of it. I had wanted to give him a sign of my love, but toward the end of his life he had become irascible, irritated at everyone. I barely could reach him. He lived with fourteen dogs and nurses alone at Scarsdale. His second family had been a terrible strain on him. His five new sons rebelled against his authority. They experimented with drugs and went to Esalen, the growth center at Big Sur, California where they explored various personal growth techniques. Yet, their godfathers were the generals of World War II: Eisenhower, Omar Bradley, George C. Marshall, Rosie O'Donnell, Walter Bedell Smith, Hunter Harris and Prince Bernhard of the Netherlands, (included because my father ran out of five-star generals!)

My father and the generals who had fought the war had been able to communicate directly with my generation, but the generation of the sixties had mutated. They were different. They were born in the nuclear and the space age. My father's anger at his sons echoed across the generational abyss, he could not reach them. It ruined the last years of his life.

The two men closest to me in the world had died within a few months of each other. I was alone for the first time in my life. In some sense I was an inexperienced child, having stepped directly from college to motherhood, to my life with John, without ever entering the professional world. I felt inadequate, weak, defeated, and miserable. However, it was my sense of mission and purpose that lifted me out of my despair toward a new stage of my life.

Eight

Toward A Politics
Of The Whole

I was deeply inspired by my experience of Christ as a living presence guiding us toward a planetary awakening, if we so desired. I deeply wanted to communicate this possibility to help replace the widely held idea of inevitable violence with a positive idea of a gentle birth and a desirable future. But it was not to be. I took another path.

One evening in 1983 my friend Ward Phillips of Orcas Island arrived at Greystone. He was an imposing, successful real estate developer who had been studying higher consciousness for the past eight years. Having seen "The Theatre for the Future" in the late 70's, he told me it was, in his opinion, the best description of the "story," that he had ever seen. We went into the library and lit a fire. I told him of all my projects. He listened impassively and asked, "Barbara, why aren't you using the one vehicle available that can get your message out: the presidency? Why isn't anyone who knows running for president. I will back you all the way."

I argued against it.

Ward said: "You're not running to win. You're running on principle. You are a master. There is no one in the country or world who can do what you can. If you tell the story of what this country can do and be, it will affect civilization."

I groaned. It awakened in me the ten years of frustration around the idea of the "transformation of the American presidency."

I discussed the idea with many different friends, including Jack Baldwin, who served on the Democratic Platform Committee and was active in California Democratic politics. He laid out a very strong case for me to run for the vice presidency. He said it was the Year of the Woman for vice president. It was also 1984, the year when George Orwell had predicted we would be taken over by Big Brother. I was a well-known futurist. I could carry the ideas for a positive future into the political arena as well as anyone.

The deciding factor for me was a discussion with my sister Patricia. She described in detail our foreign policy with its nuclear weapons build-up. I realized this policy was not simply wrong. It was insane.

It was claiming to protect us by threatening global genocide. I realized, that as Willis Harman said, "It is necessary, at such times as these, to delegitimize authority which rests on such belief systems." We did it with the divine right of kings. We did it with slavery and women's rights. Now we should do it again with nuclear war and the attitudes that support this thinking.

A subtle shift occurred. I always had assumed that, although I bore some responsibility for the world, others, superior to me, were in authority. I moved from feeling responsible to assuming the mantle of authority. I delegitimitized any authority that threatened the world with nuclear war, and assumed that we, who believe the world is one sacred, interdependent whole, are the authorities. I decided to commit to running to be selected as the vice presidency candidate by whomever was nominated as the presidential candidate.

I announced my decision at a sixtieth birthday party for Bill Thetford, who had typed *A Course in Miracles* from Helen Schucman's handwritten notes. It was held at Judith Skutch and Bill Whitson beautiful mansion in Tiburon, California.

I said that evening, "We are the children of the discontent of the whole world, descendants of the ones who wouldn't put up with something in the old world. We are made up of the people of all cultures who were attracted to the future. The roots of our vision go back to the ancient knowledge of the human race. Our founding fathers gave us a dream that is not the dream of a nation, but the combined aspiration of the peoples of the world.

"We are launching a campaign for the future in every field: environment, health, education defense, economics. We will request from people models of their success. There are examples of solutions and innovations, social and technological, in every field. We will build a platform for the future, beyond liberal or conservative. It will be a pragmatic synthesis of "what works." We shall act locally and think globally.

"We will approach the genius of the military-industrial complex to design the framework for a thirty year process to apply the full spectrum of our potentials to meet the full range of human needs. We are not facing a missile gap but a *vision gap*. That's the gap we commit to fill! We will introduce massive exchanges of people to people throughout the world. We believe the American political system is one of the most precious human resources on earth. It is a system which is open to change, which holds within it the process of change...."

Jack said the Campaign would speak to Democratic groups throughout the country, and to all other groups who were interested. We would ask people, first of all, to commit to building a positive future in their own lives, and second, to become delegates to both parties, to petition that Barbara Marx Hubbard be the vice presidential nominee to carry the Campaign for A Positive Future to the presidential level.

The event was a great success. People committed to support the Campaign, and promised to help get speaking engagements for me.

Then began the most interesting journey of my life. I sent out word through friends and colleagues throughout the country that I was running an idea campaign to bring our positive options for the future into the political arena. This had been the original purpose of the Committee for the Future. I asked my associates to set up occasions for me to speak. Rallies were organized all over the country, in church basements, school auditoriums, living rooms, mostly involving people who had been a-political or anti-political. I began to develop the main theme of the campaign: Humanity is at an evolutionary crossroads. We have the power to destroy civilization as we know it or build a future of immeasurable possibilities. The nuclear and environmental crises are evolutionary drivers forcing us at last to become aware that we are all interconnected with each other and the earth. All our problems and opportunities are long-range and interrelated. They cannot be successfully approached in separation. Our generation must change its behavior from violence and separation to cooperation and unity, or die.

> *I know there is a need for a new social function as important as the jury or the vote was at the beginning of the invention of the institutions of freedom. When the idea of freedom finally found its political expression in the Declaration of Independence, it let loose a tide of creativity. The world was never the same again for humanity.*
>
> *Now, two hundred years later, I am witnessing a comparable end and a beginning. What is ending is the idea that we are separate, that one part of society can win at the expense of another, that one nation has the right to war against another, that one race has the right to dominate another, that one sex has superiority over another, that one species can dominate and destroy other species and nature herself. We are at the beginning of the age of the whole. We are becoming an interdependent*

world. What is being born is the idea of holism. The whole
person, the whole community, the whole world. What freedom
was to the 18th century, holism is to the 20th century. It is a
new concept. When it achieves its political expression, it will be
as big a step forward as the institutionalization of freedom.

I described a new social function that would liberate human creativity and move us toward a new "process of the whole, by the whole and for the whole." This new function was to be called the Office for the Future and the Peace Room, under the supervision of the vice president in the White House.

I proposed that the Peace Room should eventually become as sophisticated as the War Room, where they track every possible danger and strategize how to defeat it. In our Peace Room we would track every innovation, solution and breakthrough. The "generals in the forces of creativity" would gather in the Peace Room around the maps of emerging breakthroughs. We would discover the pattern and connections among those breakthroughs, understanding the design of what is now working. Out of this design, we would see the "Critical Path," as Buckminster Fuller called it: How to get from where we are to where we choose to go. The social agenda for a positive future would emerge out of the pragmatic prototypes and models of success in every field. We would all be working toward one common goal — a sustainable future for life on earth. Our environments, our economies, our defense systems, all could be integrated in response to the organic acceleration of interconnectedness in the planetary body.

In the Peace Room, we would strategize our victories over our common enemies of hunger, disease, injustice and war itself.

I also proposed that the vice president work with our ambassadors and embassies to establish Peace Rooms in every country with which we had diplomatic ties.

Such Peace Rooms, or "convergence zones," would be the exact opposite of war zones. They would be places where that which is rising in our society would converge, cooperate, and be empowered.

This idea caught hold everywhere. As I talked about it, it took on an ever greater reality for me. I realized I was not so much an idea candidate as a process candidate. I wished I could actually do this, not merely talk about it.

We made the formal announcement in Lawrence, Kansas, in recognition of the significance of the movie "The Day After" which portrayed the world after a nuclear war. A panel of experts had followed the prime time television movie, including key architects of the current situation, such as Robert McNamara and Henry Kissinger. They confessed they did not see how the arms race could be stopped much less reversed. We seemed caught in an insane belief system requiring us to prepare for Armageddon, as if there were a perverted theological concept driving us to fulfill the prophecy in the Revelation. I remember expressing my opposition to Star Wars to one of Reagan's arms negotiators in Geneva. He told me, "Barbara, don't worry about it. All people who believe in Christ will be saved." I was stunned.

The announcement of my candidacy had all the trappings of a real political event. We rented a hotel press conference room in Lawrence. Our team gathered in full force. Members of the local press were gathered, complete with television cameras. It felt to me like a rehearsal of something to come.

I started my announcement statement with the idea that the Campaign for a Positive Future proposed to change the game by pointing to the new reality of an interdependent world in the nuclear age. We would convert the military-industrial complex to real "defensive defense," which protects but does not threaten. And we would actively participate in developing mutual global security, including environmental restoration and a cooperative space program.

In conclusion, I said, "Let's imagine it is July 1984. We've reached millions of people and we have persuaded two hundred delegates to be for us. My name is placed in nomination at the convention, and we have a chance to speak of this opportunity. Our theme is Open Your Heart, America! We will say with Gandhi, 'We must be the change we wish to see in the world.' We will extend Thomas Jefferson to say, We hold these truths to be self-evident, all people are born creative, endowed with the inalienable right to express that creative capacity. We call forth Buckminster Fuller, and acknowledge, with him, that humanity can be a 100% physical success. We join Martin Luther King by saying, *we have a dream*. We are going to the mountain top together and will see the glory untold of the human race as a more mature species, using its full capacities harmoniously, restoring this earth, freeing all people from poverty, releasing our magnificent creativity to explore the further reaches of the human spirit and outer space...."

Willis Harman and Virginia Satir also spoke. Virginia, one of the world's great family therapists, likened our situation globally to a family problem and proposed psychological approaches. In fact, after the announcement, she made the whole Campaign team "family" sit together in a circle and act out their resentments against each other and me! It turned out that there had been many grievances, none of which were shared, which were causing friction in the system. I realized then, that if we could model the change in our work, we thereby could contribute toward changing the world. We vowed to continue the process of communication and trust-building ourselves.

The announcement and following news conference were very exciting to me. At such moments, the Campaign took on an air of reality. The press, while attentive, seemed stunned, unable to think of questions, unsure how to take this. We were a "political paranormal experience." The political pros did not expect to see such a thing, therefore, they did not see it! We got good local coverage, but no national media whatsoever.

One writer in Kansas, assigned to write a feature story, called and said, "Barbara, it's too positive, they won't let me print it. Give me some negatives, who and what you are against."

"That's not the purpose of the Campaign," I said, my level of frustration rising with my voice.

As the Campaign continued, I began to speak of a powerful idea for another campaign-to-come and presented it to standing ovations throughout the country. The idea was that we should develop a team presidency. It was ridiculous to assume one person could lead a whole nation. The presidency is a team anyway. The voters should have a chance to see who was really going to run the country. The presidential and vice presidential candidates (hopefully a man and a woman) should bring together their whole cabinet before the campaign becomes public. This group should take time, before the heat of an election, to develop an integrated set of policies based on the broadest horizon of choices: new worlds on earth, in space, and in the human mind. They should develop trust and unity among themselves. They should then announce as a team, from a live and functioning Peace Room, in a dramatic television special that would demonstrate to the public what their new options really are, in terms of actual programs and projects and people successfully at work. "If you elect me president, here is what you will actually get," the presidential candidate would say.

After their announcement, they would run a new kind of campaign, taking their Positive Futures Platform to the people in a series of regional SYNCON-like town meetings. They would invite all sectors and political persuasions of a region to meet, looking for common goals, matching needs and resources by function: environment, business, social needs, and so forth.

The presidential team would not only present its ideas, it would listen to the people at those regional events, asking them to activate their own creativity to solve problems and to inform the presidential team of their solutions, so they could be communicated to others, and empowered by the campaign. They would look for what is already working, and how to strengthen it.

> *I am realizing that our campaign, if amplified by the media, would act as a transformational catalyst on the traditional Republican and Democratic campaigns. It would change the political conversation. It would open up the political dialogue to include the options for the future. It would attract people to positive goals that would stimulate social creativity. It would result in the transformation of the American Presidency, either by winning or more likely, by changing the perspective of both parties and the voters on what is possible.*
>
> *I have found most people don't know they can make a difference, or that a truly open, choiceful future is possible. Once an idea is lodged in the public mind, they act on it, just as when Columbus proved the earth was round, not flat, people rushed to explore new worlds. This campaign can go beyond liberal or conservative to help us become a whole society.*

As I saw Jesse Jackson campaigning, rousing people with his magnificent oratory, I thought that at the end of his speeches he should ask people not simply to vote for him, but also to help each other, and see what they could do together by way of joint projects and cooperative action to meet problems and realize new potentials. He needed a process of linking people with one another at his rallies. This would have been a genuine creative revolution, drawing on the psychological surplus, that unused creative energy in millions of people that desires to play a more meaningful role in the life of their families and communities. He already did this in his Operation P.U.S.H. (People United to Save Humanity) in Chicago. He never thought to apply that process to his own campaign.

One of the highlights of my campaign was my visit to Operation P.U.S.H. Jan St. John, head of the Chicago Positive Future Center invited me to speak at one of their Saturday morning rallies to celebrate local heroes and heroines. She dropped every name she could, finally putting forth our most precious ally. "Barbara is supported by Bucky Fuller," she said proudly. "Who?" they asked. They had never heard of any of my supporters. Finally, they just let me come because I was running for vice president.

Each honoree, sitting upon a crowded stage, had three minutes to speak. The hall was crowded with blacks, as many as a thousand. A band played upbeat music. I was led to the stage by Jesse's team: lean, handsome, graceful men exuding disciplined power. The moment I walked in and up to that stage I felt at home. The enthusiasm, the warmth, the joy of the black, spiritual community lifted my soul!

Jesse was not there, but his spirit pervaded the scene. The speakers were rousingly cheered: a local fireman, a teacher, a mother who took care of neighborhood kids after school, each introduced with flowery language of praise. Then came my turn. I was introduced as a brave white woman, bucking the system to bring a Peace Room to the White House.

Wild cheering greeted me. I was amazed, and began in praise of Jesse. Then I told them there is another large self-disenfranchised group out there: whites who do not vote, especially those, like myself, who are working for peace, environment, women's rights, human potential and spiritual growth, who did not feel we could make a difference. If our twenty percent joined with Jesse's twenty percent, we could win!

Cheers and stomping. I ended by saying I felt so at home there, "I think I have the soul of a black preacher and the mind of an extraterrestrial . . . and this place is home!"

The master of ceremonies hugged Jan and me, and took us back stage to plan strategy with members of Jesse's team. Would he be interested in meeting with me and seeing how to join forces?

The answer, in the end, was no. We never caught his attention.

Several weeks later Bucky and I appeared on the same platform at an event in Los Angeles. I was there to publicly make the discovery and fulfillment of his "Critical Path" the purpose of my candidacy for the vice presidency. After the talks, we had a brief conversation.

"Bucky, I would like to meet with you to know your best analysis of the Critical Path. What are the major trim-tab acts we should be for? (A trim-tab is the tip of a rudder, which when turned slightly, turns the whole ship.) Is there anyone else who really knows your work, that I should be speaking to?"

"No, darlin', you should talk with me."

We made a date for several weeks hence.

Over the fourth of July weekend, I took some time off at my friend Helane Jeffreys' house to write a campaign book on the Philosophy of A Positive Future. Helane gently interrupted me to tell me that both Bucky and his wife Anne had just died. (He had always said he did not want to live without her.) She was ill and in the hospital. He had come to visit her. Sitting by her bedside, holding her hand, he died. She died a few hours later.

It was a great loss. One of the few men on earth who truly seemed to understand it all was gone. He had passed his legacy to thousands of us, who would now take up the work "to fulfill the dream"... the design science revolution to make humanity a 100% physical success. I felt an amazing shift within myself after his death. I wrote:

I have experienced myself in authority. I am overcoming the feminine dependent personality that is afraid of power for fear of loss of love. Somehow Bucky has passed on to us his faith in what the ordinary individual of integrity can do.

An unexpected but interesting aspect of the Campaign was the formation of Positive Future Centers. Clearly, I was issuing a particular type of bird call, and a particular type of bird was responding! They were mainly people who were spiritually-based, human-potential oriented, what the Stanford Research Institutes's VALS (Values and Lifestyle Study) called "inner directeds." In fact, Marie Spengler, one of the key architects of VALS was very active in the Campaign. Most of my supporters were apolitical, non-political or even anti-political. For some it was the first time in their life they had taken an interest in politics. I had to explain what the word "caucus" meant. I felt a little like Jesse Jackson, who for years has been registering blacks who never before felt they could make a difference. I was involving another part of the large non-voting constituency in the United States. (But we were way behind Jesse's organization in political sophistication.)

I remember one disheartening visit to the National Democratic Committee early in the Campaign. They associated me with the human potential movement. Their attitude was condescending, "Those people only care about themselves...they are too self-centered to be interested in the issues we care about, such as women's rights, poverty and social justice." I argued with them that they were ignoring a vital constituency. But they, as traditional, liberal

Democrats did not see it. This large segment of upward rising, spiritually motivated innovative people were as left out of the political mainstream as the very poor.

What actually happened is that after just about every speech some people would come up excitedly and say, "I want to form a center for *this*, for *it*... whatever it is." I probed for the mysterious it.

I asked: "What do you mean by 'center?' What do you really want to do? What is *it*?"

I gradually discovered that the center people were craving was not an institution, a physical place nor an organization. It was not a leader nor a philosophy. It was the center within themselves, felt, touched, amplified and shared with others, center to center, heart to heart, in a core of "resonance," or harmony, that could support each member in both their personal growth and social action.

After a meeting I would sit and talk with these people, sometimes far into the night. People shared their life's passions and purposes, and discussed their visions for the future. Most important, they wanted to work in this environment, to express their vocations and creativity. All sorts of projects arose: in education, health, business, the arts, and media, to bring positive options and people together.

I returned to many of the centers during the Campaign and noticed a certain consistent set of practices, disciplines, and rituals. It was the emergence of a new social life form, a unit that was transforming its members from self-centered to whole-centered consciousness and action. The centers had elements and practices of the sacred circles of the Native Americans, the early church, and of support and self-help groups everywhere.

They were turned outward into the world for social action from an inner core of love, or "resonance" whose Latin root "resonantia," means echo. The centers' experience of resonance was literally that of resounding with one another, vibrating on the same wave length, experiencing a harmonic that seems to produce a field of energy which bonded people together in a feeling of union.

The inner work of personal growth and outer work of social action was combined in these groups. I could see that the real political transformation was happening through people who were willing to transform themselves, their relationships and how they work in the world, by modelling the change they would like to see. I realized that for twenty years we had been focusing on personal growth. Now the focus was on social growth. How do we cooperate? How do we achieve alignment and co-creation among ourselves?

Over and over again, during the Campaign, as we visited Positive Future Centers, we went through sessions where people were learning to trust each other, to share power, to respect each other's uniqueness. Sometimes the sessions seemed laborious. However, wherever it worked, we felt the joy of union, of home, of love.

I was uplifted by the people I met. I discovered the way of life I had always craved, felt at SYNCONs, in flashes, and seen as sustained at Findhorn, the community in Northern Scotland. Now we were seeding the life pattern through a political campaign. I began to see that we were not so much involved in changing the system as in changing ourselves!

A core group of people connected at the heart doing work for the world is an arena in which to practice higher self-government. As cores, by whatever name they are called, stabilize, replicate, and connect, I think we will become elements of a new infrastructure of the next stage of social evolution. It will not be a world government made up of nation states but a world organism made up of living members and social cells, connected in vast organic networks of federated functions, resonant with the implicate evolutionary pattern or design of nature. Just as each cell in our body has the same DNA and a unique function, so each person on earth is motivated by the same evolutionary pattern and has a unique and natural function in the whole, a place where the genius is drawn forth in self-actualizing work.

Positive Future Centers began to create new social activities, usually called projects. They spawned these projects very much like young-marrieds spawn progeny! Some of the projects survived, many did not, but the energy that motivated people seemed to me to be the same force that draws atoms to atoms, molecules to molecules and cells to cells. That force was now drawing us together, humans with humans, in non-bureaucratic, non-hierarchical, partnership models, that hold the seeds of new social life forms - "islands of the future," as Ken Carey called them in *Starseed Transmissions* and as Riane Eisler describes in *The Chalice and the Blade*.

Everywhere people were struggling to become entrepreneurs. For who was going to hire us to do our vocations of destiny, our life purposes? We had to learn to become self-employed, self-supporting, and to develop cooperative, chosen family businesses. There appeared to be no other way to be free to live our vocations as our life's work, but to learn business skills applied to cooperative social purposes. Just as the earlier pioneers set up family farms and businesses at the physical frontiers, so we social pioneers were learning to be entrepreneurs at the social frontier. The familiar free enterprise system applied to social good, appeared to be one of the basic economic models of the future.

As I travelled from center to center, I frequently drew a map of all these various practices which I observed people doing, and called them the "Rings of Empowerment." As in earlier days when I had drawn the Evolutionary Spiral and the SYNCON wheel on the back of napkins in restaurants, so now I drew the core model. Even as I was campaigning I began to teach the model to Positive Future Centers. My dream of an activity that would integrate spiritual and material, inner and outer, began to take shape through these centers.

One of the most dynamic Positive Future Centers was created in Palo Alto by Carolyn and Sanford Anderson, a business couple, and Jeff Daly, a lawyer. They produced "commitment events" and a ritual called "Rings of Power" in which people lit candles and expressed their life purpose within the growing community of friends committed to a positive future. Soon I asked them to take over the management of the Campaign and eventually I moved to Palo Alto to work with them.

I found that I was leaving Greystone psychologically. It was too much for me to manage at a distance, too great an expense to maintain. I was $50,000 in debt in the Campaign. Jacqueline was most generously lending the house to me free of charge (to her own detriment financially; Louis was urging her to sell it.) Finally, with real regret, I called Jacqueline and said I would return Greystone to her, and move to the Bay Area, to be near the Campaign headquarters. She said she was sorry. Her kindness to me had been an amazing grace.

I had no idea at the time what a loss this would be, and still is, to me. I had always lived in large houses filled with people. However, at the time, I was so busy I did not even notice that I was homeless. I had become a traveling campaigner. I put all my things in storage, cleared out the immense amount of papers and memorabilia in the Greystone basement. As I had left Lakeville, I now left Greystone, walking forward without looking back. A new leaf in life was opening up and I did not know what it would be.

As I was traveling from center to center, I felt that I lived everywhere and nowhere, my life was motivated from within. I experienced a certain sober exhilaration from knowing, at last, that the strength I depended upon was within me, rather than in some external masculine support. I was becoming a whole person.

It was only a few more weeks until the convention. Everyone who knew anything at all about political conventions advised us not to go to San Francisco. Someone told me I would be lucky to get one delegate's vote, if she were my mother! We had no money, no media, and no passes to the convention floor. I was exhausted and in debt. I could not ask my brother for help on this one. He thought I was crazy, and was embarrassed by his sister when he was with his powerful Kennedy and Rockefeller friends.

I remember one afternoon we had to make the decision whether or not to go to the convention. We had very little money. It would cost at least $20,000. We listed pro's on one side of the blackboard and con's on the other. In the pro column, there was only one reason to go: we had committed to do it. I quoted Churchill's phrase, "never give in, never, never, to nothing large or small... except to honor and good sense."

Was it honorable and good sense to stop now? Ultimately it was up to me. No one else could make the decision.

We became silent. I heard a strong, clear signal from within. "You have not yet completed your mission. Go to San Francisco."

I announced my decision. Every one rallied. We raised $20,000 on a "Connect-a-thon," a telephone link-up with Positive Future Centers nationwide. I was stationed at a rally in Santa Fe organized by Mary Lou Cooke. Each Positive Future Center announced its commitment over the phone. It was exhilarating.

And so this tiny band of brave souls headed to San Francisco, to stay in a small apartment in Palo Alto and attempt the impossible. We decided to practice every spiritual discipline we had learned. Our job was to get 200 delegates to place my name in nomination.

We visualized me giving the speech. We practiced love and forgiveness with each other. We began to operate as one body, flowing gracefully almost without rest or food or overt management.

We spoke to delegates in lobbies, bars, bathrooms and at early morning caucuses. I learned to make a 30 second presentation work. "My name is Barbara Marx Hubbard. I ask you to place my name in nomination for the vice presidency so I can propose an Office for the Future and a Peace Room in the White House under the direction of the vice president, which will track innovations, breakthroughs, projects that work and strategize our victories over hunger, disease, injustice and war." Then our group mingled among the delegates, getting signatures. We would call the day before... South Dakota, North Dakota, Alabama and ask for 30 seconds at a 6:00 a.m. caucus. Dottie Lamm, wife of Governor Lamm of Colorado, my one 'inside supporter,' invited me to address the Colorado delegation. Gary Hart promised to set up an Office for the Future in the White House!

The delegates were preoccupied, inattentive, tired and totally disinterested in hearing me speak. They were sophisticated, and in many cases, professional politicians who take conventions very seriously indeed. This was the year of Geraldine Ferraro. She was the one person everyone agreed on. Furthermore, highly sophisticated political groups, such as Mayor Harold Washington's of Chicago, and well-organized and funded peace and environmental groups were trying to get their spokespeople nominated for the vice president, to be given the valuable and coveted opportunity to address the world from the Convention podium.

The first day we had one hundred signatures. The second day we had two hundred, and on the third day we were heading up to three hundred signatures on the petition placing my name in nomination for the vice presidency. Each delegate was a new stranger to make contact with, build trust and persuade to sign. It is my belief that our transcendent purpose - the Peace Room in the White House - and our strong, inspired experience of being part of one organism, for that brief period of time, gave us an element of attraction that somehow penetrated the harsh veneer to the hearts of the delegates who said yes, spontaneously, surprising even themselves.

Faye Beuby, our campaign manager, who had been an executive officer of The Club of Rome, took the petitions to the Democratic Party headquarters at the Convention. Faye was very pretty, chic and professional looking. She put on her best, most formal suit, and headed to meet them. They were amazed, and I assumed, horrified. How had a grass roots candidate slipped through this web and done the impossible? To their credit, for they surely could have disqualified me on some technicality, they verified two hundred and two signatures. There would be two names placed in nomination for the vice presidency: Geraldine Ferraro and myself.

Faye was told that I was to speak first. Dick Celsi, the Chair of the Oregon Democratic Party, had agreed to place my name in nomination (in the highly unlikely event that this should occur.)

We were astonished, exalted, amazed and thankful, and rushed to find Dick so he could make the nomination.

I went to the little Palo Alto office to write my acceptance speech. (I had not prepared it, because I didn't dare think it would happen.) I wrote the speech "To Fulfill the Dream," calling upon the United States of America to fulfill the dream of the people of every nation of the world who came here for greater freedom and opportunity. I proposed "A Choiceful Future," a time when we could invite all peoples to join together to meet basic needs on earth, to restore the environment, educate all people to realize their potential, and to explore the further reaches of outer space and the human spirit. I advocated the Peace Room in the White House.

Early the next morning we received a call from the Democratic National Committee that my speech had been moved forward by two hours. I felt the Committee had done this so that I would not be on prime time television.

I was sitting in Palo Alto in my bathing suit. We had less than two hours to get the speech xeroxed, dress and drive to San Francisco.

William Brault of Oregon drove Faye and me, breaking the speed limit as we prayed to make it. Finally we arrived at the gigantic Moscone Convention Center, and headed toward the enormous podium. A guard blocked me.

"I've been nominated for the vice presidency." I said.

"No you haven't," he declared belligerently, sure that I was some crazy lady.

"Yes I have; go check it," I ordered him. He came back sheepishly in a few moments and let Faye and me in. We climbed the back stairs, passing Sen. Kennedy and Sen. Cranston. I waved at them. They looked surprised. I felt like an extraterrestrial candidate dropped invisibly on earth to perform some task that would have meaning in the future.

They put on my makeup and ushered me upward toward the podium. "Don't worry if no one listens," a nice attendant said to me. "They never do."

Dick Celsi placed my name in nomination. I stepped in front of the microphone to make the speech that we had visualized for months in church basements and living rooms across the country.

I looked out upon the sea of indifference and spoke to the universe, feeling as though my words were somehow planted in the ethers, ready as seeds to be sprouted when the time was right.

At the end I turned my delegates over to Geraldine Ferraro, as I had promised. The effect of this campaign, however, was not on the current political reality, but on those of us who did it. We know that a small group can literally perform political miracles if they align on a vision and give it their all.

Mabel King, the black gospel singer, tried to get me to Jesse Jackson. She was convinced he should select me as his running mate. She had a dream that a black man and a Jewish woman would run together as a team.

As I had said at Operation P.U.S.H., the twenty percent oppressed and excluded combined with the twenty percent "inner-directeds," plus environmentalists and social justice advocates would make a powerful coalition to activate the Politics of the Whole.

Of course, my campaign took place before the massive public awareness of the environmental crisis occurred in 1988, when our planet was on the cover of Time magazine, as the "planet" of the year, as well as on National Geographic's cover and on countless news specials. It was an issue the media could understand... and it had no political labels. The greenhouse effect was neither Republican nor Democrat, liberal nor conservative. A well-organized campaign in the 90's would have a far greater effect.

In any case, Carole Hoskins, Carole Love and I drove back to San Francisco about 11:00 p.m., on the chance we could meet Jesse Jackson. We were totally worn out.

Mabel, who is big, took us to a jam-packed rally for Jesse. There was no room to enter, much less make our way to the stage to meet him. Mabel acted as a battering ram, dragging the two Carols and myself in her wake. I felt embarrassed. Surely there must be a more dignified way to meet Jesse.

In any case, Mabel got us to the stage. We were the only whites in the room. Suddenly Jesse began to speak, surrounded by scores of black men and women, packed in around him like sardines. Sweat glistened from his brow, as he shouted out his message that the poor, the excluded, and the oppressed would have their day in the sun. His power was electrifying. I knew that if he ever could understand our power, the power of the future-oriented innovators, we could restore this earth and build new worlds together. I longed to reach him... but it was not to be.

Nine

A New Relationship

So the campaign was over. What to do next was the question. A whole group of us met at Jeanne McNamara's beautiful "Omega House" in Mendocino. There was tremendous enthusiasm. David Harris and Bob Love were to manage a "meta-project" that would continue the work of the campaign. We would build our own Peace Room or strategic hub, and continue the process of building core groups. We discussed a radio outreach.

But shortly after this event, our non-organization began to fall apart. Without the driving momentum of the campaign, we did not have the focus. Bob and David really did not want to manage this enormous project. The Positive Futures Center, with no further political goal, began to disintegrate. I tried to rally them to continue but I, too, had lost focus. I was left with a $100,000 debt. Although we had raised a quarter of a million dollars, it was not enough.

I spent hours walking the headlands along the Mendocino Coast. I felt confused and defeated. Was I merely a crazy lady whose sense of mission was ridiculous or was there some immanent purpose in all of this that would soon be revealed? Should I be an ordinary political candidate and run for an office I could win, or was there another way?

With these questions I checked in at Mt. Calvary Monastery, where four years before I had experienced the most important spiritual event of my life, the day I experienced the joy of union with Christ and his partnership in our planetary awakening. Sitting in the exquisite garden, the humming birds hovering among the flowers, the beautiful gold and iron cross surrounded with blossoms, the air pure sweetness, I felt refreshed and renewed. Hot coffee sat steaming by my side. I had just taken communion. I wrote:

"Dear Journal: You have always been my thread of sanity when the forces of confusion surround me. Through you I have found my way through the maze of life to the threshold of the Most High. Now I stand before the next step, encumbered by a

thousand questions. Projects, debts, people, ideas are swirling through my mind, with no home, no office, no secretary, with six weeks of mail and phone messages. I ask now for guidance to awaken to my next step with clarity...."

The stream of ideas flowed effortlessly. I was here for the next step in my journey. I had done everything in my power to act in the world with a God-centered consciousness, yet I kept losing sight of this awareness when I moved into action in the world. My stay at the monastery put me once again in a state of clarity and purpose. I developed an "inner sound studio" that enabled me to hear the inner voice clearly, no matter what the distraction from outside.

Then a surprising new tangent occurred in my life. Directly after the campaign, Rama Vernon, director of The Center for Soviet-American Dialogue came to see me to persuade me to go to the Soviet Union with her. A gorgeous, dark-haired yoga teacher in her early forties, she had five children and had been motivated to take up to a thousand people such as myself to the Soviet Union. This trip, scheduled for May, 1985, was to be her first major effort.

I did not want to go, but when she said mysteriously, "Barbara, I know you will find a new vocation in the Soviet Union," I was persuaded. I said yes, despite my conscious desire not to travel at that time.

Rama had made friends with the Soviet Peace Committee officials and persuaded them to allow small group discussions and informal visits between Soviets and Americans. She brought her new-born baby, Mira to the preparatory meetings, calmly nursing the child during formal meetings. Her colleague, Linda Johnson, reported that once Rama became so engrossed in the discussion, the blanket dropped away, leaving Rama fully exposed and unaware. Linda named this "breast diplomacy!" Whatever we call it, it worked miracles. By the time we got there, doors were opened to us. We never experienced the dead formality. It had already changed.

Our group included actors Dennis Weaver and Mike Farrell, Swami Satchidananda, Patch Adams, a doctor who dressed like a clown, and a wide variety of transformational people who were committed to growth in both their inner and outer lives. The Soviet experience was a revelation for me.

One of the most exciting meetings was my first encounter with Joseph Goldin, a Soviet citizen who has subsequently become famous in the citizen diplomacy movement, largely for his development of space-bridges, which he believes create a living nervous system for humanity. We met in a tiny apartment. He was stolidly-built, short, with his gaze always fixed ahead. He wore a wool cap on his head and with his woolen sweater frayed at the edges, and his sheaf of precious xeroxed papers and books tucked under his arm, he looked like a true revolutionary.

He astonished me by taking out a dog-eared copy of my book *The Evolutionary Journey*, a written version of "The Theatre for the Future," published in 1982. He turned directly to the pages which described the planetary smile and told me that was what he was working on! The cosmic birth experience was his goal too. He had a project called "Mirror of Humanity," in which we would see ourselves throughout the globe on large screens, live space-bridges.

"Joseph," I said in amazement, almost as strongly moved as when I met Jonas twenty years before, "This is amazing." He was a Soviet, who seemed as close to me in motivation as anyone I had ever met.

He began to discuss Buckminster Fuller's ideas with me. He was as obsessed as I with how to create the planetary experience of oneness, before human error triggered a nuclear war. He had been ostracized by official Soviets. He was a non-person, and could not be invited to the Peace Committee.

As I discussed philosophy with him, a remarkable perception dawned on me. The Soviet Union is based on a philosophy which says that a quantum jump in the world is inevitable. It would be a classless, stateless society, "from each according to his ability, to each according to his need." It is to come through a synthesis of opposing forces: thesis, antithesis, synthesis. As I probed with him as to the nature of the synthesis, it was clear to me that it was not incrementally better socialism. It was radically new. It was like the Omega experience predicted by Teilhard, a society of radical freedom through union.

"Joseph," I asked. "Is it possible that what you call the 'dialectic,' the inevitable pattern in history leading to a higher order, is what we call the process aspect of God: the implicate order, the blueprint or pattern of evolution?"

"Of course it is," he said, shrugging his shoulders, and going on rapidly discussing his projects, as if further philosophical discussion was useless. They had too much of it already.

"But Joseph, if this is true, then those who believe in the quantum jump to Communism, in the Soviet Union, and those of us in the U.S. who believe in a similar jump to a global/cooperative society are natural allies. We are potential partners. We are not enemies. We are co-creators. Particularly if it is true that you will renounce the class struggle and the use of force and if we will too."

"Of course we are co-creators," he said. (On my next trip I was given buttons that said "Co-creator" in English and Russian, with a diagram of the evolutionary spiral.) Joseph subsequently was placed in one of the infamous psychiatric wards and forced to take drugs. He told me he used the time there to educate the nurses and doctors about humanity's potential.

I felt as though I was on a treasure hunt to find a very important jewel: a shared vision between the United States and the Soviet Union of the next stage of social evolution. What would attract us, the two great polar opposites on earth, to work together for a transcendent possibility that would fuse our differences into a new, holistic synthesis.

It began to dawn on me that transformationalists in the U.S. who are attracted to the new paradigm, and Soviets who believe in the reality of a social quantum jump beyond the horrible dictatorship and bureaucracy of Soviet socialism, are attracted to the same vision, which is the next natural step of evolution. If this is so, we have the opportunity, not simply for co-existence and cooperation, but for genuine co-creation.

I was amazed and delighted when on December 7, 1988 Gorbachev addressed the General Assembly of the United Nations, calling for "the kind of cooperation that could more accurately be termed co-creation and co-development." Robert Müller, former Assistant General of the United Nations called me up and said, "Barbara, you are the person in this world who sounds most like Gorbachev."

Another incident stands out vividly from that first trip. Rama had arranged for us to attend a service at a communist Baptist Church in Moscow. Swami Satchidananda was to give the sermon, which he delivered in his flowing orange robe, his white beard and deep loving brown eyes glowing radiantly. All eighty of us were to sing a One World Anthem from the balcony. After Swami's beautiful sermon on the oneness of humanity, we arose and sang our song in Russian.

Hundreds of Soviets, mainly women, were in the congregation below, wearing the familiar "babushkas." They looked up at us, trying to understand our words. When they caught on that we were singing of peace, they spontaneously took out white handkerchiefs and scarves and began to wave to us as we sang. Soon we pulled off hats and scarves and began to wave at them. It was their turn. They were singing about Christ, "Christos." I asked a Soviet the meaning of their words. "Christ is risen," she said. We echoed the words back to them, and something powerful began to happen. We sang in unison, tears streaming down our faces, waving in rhythm, "Christ is Risen, Christ is Risen." I felt the binding force spread through us, drawing us together just as at the SYNCONs where former adversaries had been attracted to one another, it now joined us all.

As we were finally led downstairs, the "babushkas" literally enfolded us, embracing us, one on one. It was a scene of powerful spontaneous love. One old woman, her wrinkled face glowing with an angelic, toothless smile, came up to me and put her arms around me. She wiped away my tears with her handkerchief and said in broken English, "Don't cry. Christ is risen." I sobbed as though some great dam within me had broken. The waters of joy poured forth as I held her. The pain of generations of wars, cruelty and injustice was released. An irresistible force of attraction joined us, more powerful because of our supposed separation.

We went directly from the church to the American embassy for a briefing. The tone was cool, sophisticated, and harsh. An attaché with a cigarette and coffee mug came out and told us there was no point in trying to get close to Soviets as it wasn't possible. When we shared our experiences he smiled as though we were naive fools.

What I discovered on that first trip is what so many Americans had found. There is a deep, passionate attraction between Soviet and American people that is spontaneous and irrepressible. The great irony of history is that the peoples of the two superpowers whose weapons are pointed at one another for the destruction of the world, *love each other.*

Perhaps the reason these two great nations have found themselves on the stage of history with nuclear arsenals poised for Armageddon is that we are the two peoples on earth with the most powerful visions of world transformation: "All men are created equal," and, "from each according to his ability, to each according to his need." We both seek to build a "new order of the ages," and are infected with the arrogance of that passion.

The horror of the Soviet system sprang from the absolutism and terrorism that began with the Bolsheviks. No matter how good the goal, the means were murder, assassination, and intimidation. Even during the time of Lenin, the opposition was killed. Stalin built on this pattern the most tyrannical bureaucracy ever designed, crushing his own people. Brezhnev consolidated the bureaucracy into a stagnant force of oppression. It was violent, premature, coerced holism. They were forcing an evolutionary goal. The tsars did not leave a tradition of human rights or government by law not men. And it was this system they tried to impose by force, subversion and propaganda, world-wide. There was a good reason for our fear of Communism, in the form that it has existed. But, now that the Soviets themselves are trying to restructure and democratize their society an unexpected possibility has emerged. When they turn toward the *vision* of communism in the spirit of democratization, glasnost and perestroika, we may find the Soviets to be in alliance with our own highest spiritual vision for a world in which all people have the opportunity to fulfill their creative potential.

Our visions have motivated both of our countries to try, in a perverse and diabolical way, to be the one to transform the world. Both were ready to sacrifice humanity in a nuclear holocaust in the name of their version of the vision of the future world. What a surprise it would be to discover that it is a similar vision. It comes out of the same Judeo-Christian, evolutionary tradition of a new heaven and a new earth, a time of radical freedom and equality in a world of abundance in which there is no state, no classes, and the freedom to create according to our abilities and pursue happiness according to our intentions in alignment with the will of God or the dialectic of history.

Beneath the apparent atheism of Communism I saw a deep faith in the inevitable rise of a new synthesis that is to come about through the innate tendencies of nature, human nature, and nature's deeper design or implicate order.

What a surprise it would be to discover that at the transcendent, growing edge of the vision of a spiritual democracy and a free, non-coerced communism is the same magnet, the next stage of evolution, which is pulling us forward from the future to fulfill our innate potential as a young species. Our collective fear would turn to collective love as it does now on a personal scale when we meet one on one, American to Soviet, human to human.

I thought of Gorbachev as a political Sputnik. When Khrushchev put up Sputnik, he surprised us, and we responded with Apollo. If we recognized that the Soviet Union need not be our enemy, but could be our co-creative partner in restoring the environment, freeing people's creativity and expanding outer space peacefully, what would happen over here? What would be our political Apollo? The Soviet Union is restricted by the fact that it is, in all respects but military and space, a developing country. They have an immense struggle ahead to make their economic and social system work, to bring democratization to their people. We have handled those basic problems of production and free institutions. At least we know how to do it. When we no longer put our vast resources: physical, intellectual and psychological into a rapidly obsolescing arms race, when we see that real security can only be had through mutual security and mutually assured development and environmental restoration, what would happen?

It could usher in the greatest age of cooperation and co-creation on a global scale that has ever been seen on earth. I felt that this is what we are preparing for now.

I felt that in some amazing way, Rama had been right when she said I would "find a new vocation in the Soviet Union." What I found is a key to the political, economic, social, and spiritual shift in this world. It was in the joining as co-creators of the Soviet and American people, in cooperation with all other people. Since we two superpowers have been the biggest problem, with our nuclear arsenals poised to destroy the world, therefore our shift in relationship could contribute most to the solution.

We made plans to return to the Soviet Union for the first world healing meditation on December 31, 1986. Joseph was to arrange some spectacular for us on Arbat Square. There was to be a live Moscow-New York radio dialogue. I returned to the States, committed to the proposition that in our lifetime we would see a new relationship between Soviets and Americans which would precipitate the "shift from weaponry to livingry," as Bucky said.

My life seems like a future history to me. What's already happened on the inner plane is about to happen in the outer world. Herein lies the drama, the mystery unfolding.

On Saturday, December 28, 1986, Rama, Linda, me, and approximately sixty people left for Moscow via Copenhagen. We were to spend a day of orientation at a beautiful hotel in Elsinore, the setting for Hamlet's famous "to be or not to be" speech. That night Morris Massey, the successful lecturer to business, pulled me aside in the bar of the hotel. His wife Judy said, "Morris is seething with an idea, you've got to hear it, Barbara."

Morris, in his famous staccato style, said, "Barbara, we've got to make this into a news event on December 31. We should use the talented people in this group to call hundreds of thousands of Soviets to Arbat Square on the television so that the media begins to cover it as a news event." In other words, we were to get on television live and invite people to come to the Square right then and there!

As he spoke I was flooded with memories of the original cosmic birth experience, in which people gathered in the squares and malls of the world. This particular strategy never happened but the idea was right.

We carried ten thousand candles to give to our Soviet counterparts in the celebration planned for Arbat Square on December 31st. As it turned out, on the 31st itself, we did not have the big event in the square. It was postponed until January 3rd. On December 31st, at Noon Greenwich Time, Rama, I, and some other members of our group were in a gigantic radio studio ready for the simultaneous five hour live broadcast between Moscow and New York. In the studio was a concert orchestra and a youth choir. Joe Adamoff, the Soviet commentator, was the Soviet host. He was nervous and upset because there was no time for rehearsal. Alfred Webre and Mary Houston were anchoring in New York City. It was a historic first.

I had urged that we begin with a moment of silence, which, of course, wasn't possible, for a live radio show.

Rama and I sat near the microphone, holding hands as the clock hands approached Noon Greenwich Time, which was 3:00 p.m. in Moscow. I felt the awesome sense of connection with millions of souls around the world, all now aligning in one thought, in one instant of time.

The hands of the big clock reached 3:00 p.m. Silence! There was a technological breakdown. We sat there in meditation for several minutes. Our Soviet hosts were not aware of the significance of those moments.

I tuned every fibre of my consciousness into the planetary event. I felt a subtle experience of deep kinship. No matter what the uncertainties of our personal lives, we were cells in the planetary body that was now linking up as one living organism, approaching, closer every moment to the actual experience of our oneness.

Three nights later we had our celebration in Arbat Square. Ron Kaufman was producing the event with Joseph Goldin. Ron, a student of Bucky Fuller's, believed that celebrational events are a vital art form to stimulate people's growth and commitment to taking action in the world.

The scene was something out of a surrealistic movie. The large screen at Arbat Square flashed comic and tragic news flashes, pictures of famous people, scenes of the destruction of war. A platform festooned and decorated was brilliantly lit beneath the screen. A large throng of Soviets: mothers, fathers, children, and infants stood numbly behind a thin rope, waiting patiently for the event. No where on earth is the desire for peace and the hatred of war more palpable than in the Soviet Union.

It was 30 degrees below zero!

We Americans standing on the sidelines threw off our coats, rushed up on the stage and sang "Peace and Friendship" in Russian with musicians Michael Elly and Allan Rosenthal. Then, as the pièce de resistance of the evening, we flung frisbees to the Soviets who were willing to stand in the freezing cold for hours waiting to catch them. Several of our group had frostbitten fingers or noses.

After we sang, we leapt down from the stage and danced around a smoldering effigy of a nuclear bomb which was wheeled in front of the large stage. As loud, rhythmic music blared in the air, Soviets and Americans danced, circling the bomb, shouting, singing, and demanding peace.

I danced with Gennadi Alferenko, a ballet dancer, as well as journalist and social inventor. His thin body twirling, his hair flying, his face glaring, he swept me up in a dance that lifted me from all consciousness of separation. At that moment, Soviets and Americans were one people.

Then we Americans reached for our candles to light them to give to the Soviets on the other side of the rope. We had to take off our gloves. Our hands began to freeze almost immediately. A sub zero wind blew out the flames as we lit the candles. Finally, I managed to light a candle and reached out to give it to a Soviet. Immediately the crowd around me became a tight knot of people, many hands reaching toward the flame; their faces glowing in the flickering light, smiling, lifting their red-cheek babies to see. Like a Rembrandt painting, this scene is indelibly printed upon my memory.

I remember sitting in the Cosmos Hotel on that very day with Gennadi Alferenko, who was the founder of the Foundation for Social Inventions in the Soviet Union, and Rustem Khairov, who was working with Yevgeny Velikhov, the special science advisor to Gorbachev. We were planning the next major symposium, to be held in March, 1987, in Moscow entitled "A New Way of Thinking in the Nuclear Age — Social Inventions for the Third Millennium."

The event was designed to allow for synergy among separate task forces in health, education, entrepreneurship, psychology, communications, global politics. I drew from my SYNCON experience and shared with Rustem and Gennadi the power of formerly opposing forces joining to create projects by personal interest and attraction. They understood it deeply. It is their philosophy! Thesis. Antithesis. Synthesis.

Suddenly Rustem reached out and embraced me in the dim twilight that descended upon our hotel room. He whispered in my ear, "You know what we are working for, Barbara... it's *Omega*." (He was an admirer of the works of Teilhard de Chardin, too.)

Omega! The cosmic birth experience flashed before my eyes. There it was again, the same vision of coming together as one planetary body motivating a Soviet management specialist and an American future-oriented woman.

"Rustem," I said. "We are siblings united in the same purpose."

I embraced him, feeling as I had when Bucky Fuller, the cosmic engineer, had held me in his arms and told me there was only God. The synthesis between science and spirit, between Soviets and Americans, was happening in us, through us, by us even though current social forms and institutions did not yet reflect the living experience of millions of people such as ourselves.

It seemed to me that Gorbachev's call for openness and reorganization was acting like a spark of fire in a highly compressed and inflammable solution. The Soviet people had been cruelly repressed by their own state, as well as decimated by the second World War. Yet underneath the pain there was still alive a vibrant vision of a new society. Furthermore, the Russian soul, the heart of Mother Russia, was spiritual, passionate, idealistic, and cosmic.

I felt that when the spirit of hope, creativity and globalism hit the suppressed vision and soul of millions of Soviets, it would produce a psychochemical combination. Perhaps a new social substance would emerge, a fusion of the new spirit of freedom with the collective, holistic passion of a people who have been disciplined to surrender to the larger whole. A new kind of cooperative individualism may emerge out of the destructuring totalitarian state.

The hunger of Eve was deeply nourished by this experience of union between citizens of the two great superpowers. I felt that some new social/political synthesis was about to erupt at the growing edge of Soviet and American cultures.

Ten

Manifestation Begins

While going back and forth to the Soviet Union, I was uncertain about how I should live. The fact that I had no stable home base was beginning to dawn on me. I felt like a displaced person. I wanted to stay with the campaign team. They had become my family. In the fall of 1984, Carol Hoskins and I had found a pleasant little house in Irvine, California. I felt as though I were camping out, renting by the month, waiting to see what my next step should be. Later, Carol and Bob Love had joined us.

I attempted to understand the organic unfolding of planetary evolution, to help guide our actions. I saw that we could view 1945 as the signal of our birth as Gaia, the living planetary system. In that year, with the dropping of the atomic bomb, it became clear that continued misuse of power to control one another would lead to global suicide. The 1960's could be seen as our physical birth, when we first left the womb of earth alive and saw ourselves from space as one body. The 1970's felt like the trauma after birth, a sort of "post-natal torpor," where we coped with the confusion and pain of having to manage a planetary system, handle our own wastes, stop overpopulating, stop depleting our mother, and learn to care for ourselves as a whole for the first time in human history.

In this birth analogy, I saw the 1980's as the time when the nervous system of the body politic began to link us up in consciousness as one living system. Though still on the trigger edge of possible nuclear destruction, our planetary nervous system was joining us in people-initiated, non-governmental, non-political acts of love, celebration and compassion for ourselves as one body, one human family. While on the political front a conservative reaction had begun in the United States and elsewhere, on the global communication front, mass union was occurring.

It started in the 1984 Olympics when the great ceremonies, particularly the "Reach out and Touch" event, where the spectators and the athletes from all nations sang together, were broadcast to billions of viewers world-wide. It felt as though the emotion of union was longing to burst out of the stadium into the streets, the homes, the offices to transform the world in a single instant of love. It had the same feeling as our singing in the church in Moscow. But it stopped. Not enough people felt their union with each other for it to spread to everyone. Critical mass had not yet been reached.

Throughout history, millions of individuals from all cultures and religions have had experiences of the unity of all life. But these experiences always occurred separately, never at the same moment. I believed that if enough of the people of the world attempted to connect in the spirit of love it would start a chain reaction of joining, until the whole world would experience itself as one. This is the counterpart of a nuclear chain reaction, which could destroy the world as a whole. The theory is that either could happen in the "twinkling of an eye," a change of mind or a nuclear explosion.

It was world hunger that awoke the planetary body out of its torpor. Live Aid, initiated by rock star Bob Geldof in 1985, produced by Hal Uplinger and Mike Mitchell was an eighteen hour live musical television broadcast on behalf of the world's hungry. "We are the Children, We are the World" was its theme song written by Michael Jackson and Lionel Ritchie. Rock stars of the world united in an extraordinary event of compassion.

Given the birth model, it is no accident that the world's first citizen-engendered link up of the mass nervous system was stimulated by hunger. Just after a baby is born, it does not nurse until it feels its first collective hunger pangs. In the womb, it is nourished by the mother, with no conscious effort on its part. Directly after birth, the experience of hunger triggers the baby's nervous system. It is forced to awaken as a whole organism and coordinate itself to seek nourishment. Very shortly after that, the baby usually opens its eyes, sees its mother and smiles.

So world hunger was the issue that awoke the planetary body for its first sustained citizen initiated broadcast. Our planetary nervous system was linked up for eighteen hours. Millions of dollars were raised. But most important, as Hal Uplinger, the producer, said to me, "the global brain was turned on." It was not merely an eighteen hour television show. It was hundreds of millions of people aligned to one thought of caring for the hungry of our body, our world. Our consciousness would never be the same again. Once the global brain is turned on, and the planetary nervous system linked up, could the planetary smile be long in coming?

John Randolph Price had said in his book *The Planetary Commis-*

sion, that if one percent of the human race, fifty million people, linked their minds in one thought of peace and good will simultaneously, it would shift the consciousness of everyone. A massive self-organizing act called the World Healing Meditation, had begun. Countless individuals, groups, churches and families joined together in prayer and celebration at Noon Greenwich Time, December 31, 1986. Rama and I had been in Moscow, on the radio, as our part of this event.

Concurrently with the World Healing Meditation, David Gershon and his wife Gail Straub had launched the first Earth Run. David was a marathon runner, a radiant being, motivated from within toward global action. He was the only person I have ever met who has the same intensity of drive as I do to undertake "meta-acts" that might catalyze global experiences of unity and social creativity. The moment I heard of the Earth Run I knew David and Gail were kindred spirits motivated by the same inner magnet that continually activated me. The Earth Run carried a torch, a flame of light, around the world, hand to hand, people to people, linking the whole world in a spirit of cooperation. They worked for many years on this splendid event. It reached millions of people in forty-five countries, welcomed by presidents, kings and the Pope. It received excellent publicity in most countries, except in the United States where other than for periodic reports on Good Morning America, the mass media scarcely noticed it.

When I realized that the World Healing Meditation and the Earth Run were happening the same year, my hunger was aroused to a profound degree. Despite the obsolete separatism of our nation states and military establishments, the *people* of the world were uniting. I thought of Bucky's phrase, "The world will be saved by individuals of integrity freely joining."

Our little group in Irvine, California, was working in support of these global events. Soon Jan St. John joined us. We created a radio series entitled: "The New News - Live From the Peace Room," and a manual describing the Rings of Empowerment learned during the campaign. It is called "Manual for Co-Creators of the Quantum Leap." We developed it as a team. I was invited to speak at many places. Everywhere, I rallied people for the world events, invited them to join the Soviet trips and asked them to form core groups to stabilize their own consciousness in the whole-centered state. We practiced the Rings and created a powerful field of resonance.

Cores sprang up all over the country, giving me once again, the opportunity to experience deep communion, even "fusion," especially during the "higher self dialogues" which happened spontaneously in the field of resonance.

> *People are experiencing fusion in their core groups. They join so deeply that they experience oneness, a merging of genius beyond separate personalities and physical bodies at the aspect of our natures which is one with God and nature. When we are at one with that within ourselves, our oneness with anyone else in that state is instantaneous, beyond ordinary time/space. For it is the same One in each of us. And in that Oneness lies the blueprint of growth, the creative design of action for each person and group who are tuned in to it. I remember John Yardley's drawing after the SYNCONs. The small groups of five, fusing for a transcendent purpose and picking up signals from higher intelligence within themselves.*
>
> *As the global events link us as one body, core groups provide sustainable units of social synergy, harmony and oneness. As we are becoming whole as individuals, and gradually as we are uniting as a world, so we are concurrently creating models of how to live and work holistically in small groups, core groups of all kinds. For after all, we do not live en masse. Everything we actually do, is done in small groups, even within large bureaucracies. Clearly the group is the unit wherein we can transform our daily lives: in our families, our businesses, our projects, our organizations, the work we do becomes the arena for personal and social growth.*

In 1985, while I was going back and forth to the Soviet Union and living in Irvine, I began the next surge of the effort to create a media outreach. Hazel Henderson and I had met again at Larry Wilson's Ranch in Santa Fe: a lush mecca for business conferences and transformational gatherings built by the ebullient Larry, founder of Wilson Learning Systems.

Hazel and I had discovered our "metaphysical differences," and consciously decided to remain linked: two dear friends whose pictures of the world were complementary but different.

While we were at Larry's, we planned an "Eagles Reunion" composed of one hundred successful, transformational, and entrepreneurial innovators. Hazel and I made a surprising commitment: to join together to do the "New News." We realized that the current interpretation of news as violence, accident, dissension and breakdown, was destructive to the collective public awareness. People had no idea of their options for positive futures. We felt we should put aside our personal teaching, writing and speaking for a time, to dedicate ourselves to creating a vehicle for a movement of positive change: a voice for Gaia on the media.

I also realized that my life in Irvine was unsustainable and incomplete. The same problems I have always had plagued me. I was attracting more and more people who wanted to give their lives to the work, but we did not have the entrepreneurial drive to earn enough money to support ourselves. The Irvine group was sinking into debt again, while I was still laboriously paying off the campaign debt out of my speaking fees and personal income.

So in another fateful move, with real inner sadness, once again I prepared to close the office at Irvine, and move to Gainesville, Florida, to stay with Hazel and Carter Henderson. In my inner life, I felt like I was "mutating," evolving into a new stage of being. The ordinary life of intellectual challenges, competition, and dissonance in relationship felt not only painful but downright abnormal. I was in an awkward stage: like a butterfly with wet wings, I could neither return to the safety of my life as a caterpillar, nor to the security of the cocoon. I was out in the world, but I could not yet fly. John Randolph Price called this stage "no man's land." I prayed to go the "whole way," and began to get the next stage of guidance as to how to become a fully stabilized co-creator: my potential self.

The Gainesville period was one of deep learning and creativity. We had come together to do something new.

First of all was the challenge of two speakers, presenters, "leaders," turning toward one another rather than to audiences.

For the first several weeks I was unconsciously and repetitively telling the story to Hazel; and she was presenting to me her economic models and theories.

Finally Hazel had the courage to say to me, "Barbara, I know the story. You're hosing me with it!"

Suddenly I realized this was true, and that I actually knew of no other way of being. I was either meditating or telling the vision! Tears came into my eyes as I apologized. And then I admitted to Hazel that I could not stand to hear one more time of the "seven globalizations" or the economic pie.

We laughed together, realizing that one of the real challenges of co-creation was joining with our peers, rather than our supporters.

co-creation was joining with our peers, rather than our supporters. It's not so easy. Perhaps this was especially true for women, who have less experience than men in working in teams, such as sports, business, or war.

I went through a depressing period when I couldn't think of anything to say to Hazel or anyone. I felt irritated, de-energized. It was an ego-death. I lost my identity. I probed within myself to find who I was, deeper than my beloved vocation of speaking and communicating, and I couldn't find it. I had been a big fish in a little pond. Now I was a little fish in a vast ocean, with no pool or eddy that seemed to be my own.

Greystone was gone. I had no home base. The excitement of the campaign and the Soviet Union were memories. I could feel every element of self-importance dissolve. I admired and loved Hazel with all my heart, but she seemed superior to me in every way. I kept ruminating over my past "failed" opportunities to create an on-going way to outreach into the world. *The Center Letter*, The Committee for the Future, the SYNCONs, the Theatre of the Future, the campaign, the Resonating Core Network, the New Testament writings... None had manifested in enduring form in the world. I felt deep pain.

Work rallied me somewhat. Our stated purpose was to create the "New News": an on-going media outreach for the stories, breakthroughs, innovations and insights needed by our world at this time of transformation.

Hazel and I spent hours at her kitchen table, identifying names of emerging leaders we knew in every field. We made an interconnecting spider web, connecting everyone with everyone else. Through our combined networks we realized we could reach anyone in the world and could discover the pattern or design of the emerging future.

Then we began a most enriching process. We met every morning early, either in Hazel's bedroom or in the garden, for what we called our "meditative dialogue." We sat in silence listening to the ever-singing birds and allowed our deeper mind to share whatever thoughts or insights arose, particularly in relationship to our common goal of the new media. We experienced ourselves as expressions of "Mother Gaia," as Hazel called the planet. I learned from Hazel the deep love of nature, plants, trees, squirrels, every living creature. As I turned toward the stars and Christ, she experienced earth, nature, and the All. We blended our ways of seeing, each expanding to include the other, overcoming all resistance to each other's metaphysical preferences. During these sessions the seed idea formed which we now call "Planet Live." We spoke for hours some days, letting ideas and images guide us, until the new pattern emerged.

At that time, we called it "Win Win World." Hazel, Carter, Sharon Glassman, a brilliant real-estate developer and founder of Friends of the United Nations, and I met intensively and developed the "template" or pattern for a new television media system which we believed could make a critical difference in the world. It consisted of three main elements.

One: A Global Intelligence System and a Global Collegium of innovators, thinkers and activists world-wide whose work and life successfully manifested the new value system. It would become an interactive global mind. It would be one of the sources that might reveal to us the design of how a planet works at this new stage of our evolution.

Two: An on-going television program that would take place in a live and real situation room that is actually tracking the "situation" on earth. On this show would come the people, ideas, and action needed by the world now. The program would be an on-going planetary story of humanity's magnificent effort to survive and grow.

Three: An 800 number to call that would get the audience involved in the projects on the show, and a "Making the World Work Catalogue." The Catalogue would represent the "best of the best" of other existing catalogues, and would list names of organizations to join, products to buy, guidelines for action. There were to be Win Win World Clubs to draw people together and build community.

The whole idea was another version of the Peace Room proposal for the vice presidential campaign. In fact, Hazel said that, "Win Win World is doing politics a new way."

Then began the laborious, painstaking effort to develop a business plan for Win Win World. It was to be "militantly profitable." Hazel, Carter, and I often had breakfast at Jerry's in Gainesville, coming up with such ideas as staging a "buycott" rather than a boycott. If Martin Luther King could launch the civil rights movement with a bus boycott, when Mrs. Rosa Parks refused to sit at the back of a bus, perhaps we could launch the positive futures movement by using our consumer system: buying products of those companies that met the "good-planet-keeping" seal of approval.

Hazel took on the main load with the advice of Larry Greene, a television direct response expert, and Carter, who spent endless hours "crunching numbers." He did all that he could to help us

Carter was so kind to me. Every night as we three went out to dinner, he would tell me stories of the news of the day. However, it soon became apparent that Hazel felt burdened with a task that she didn't enjoy doing. This work did not draw on her highest skill. I was totally out of my element, and we were not able to persuade a major publisher to join with us as our vital partner.

We saw the importance of the new system... yet, we did not seem to be the ones to actually do it at this moment in time.

Hazel and I recognized that we had joined to create something, which in fact had been conceived as Win Win World. Its actual gestation and birth was yet to come. We loved each other deeply. But we had different ways of working.

One day she said to me: "Barbara, you are the product. You embody the message. You are not to be packaging others. You need to be packaged."

We knew that our work together was changing to its next phase. Our relationship seemed to us to have a deep, almost mysterious significance. One time, when I was preparing to leave, Hazel came into my room and sat directly opposite me. She took my hands in hers and looked lovingly into my eyes. "Barbara," she said, "I am new worlds on earth, you are new worlds in space. I am an earth child. You are a star child. Together we can do it."

"I know, it's true, Hazel," I said. "We would not have stayed together this long if it were not so. You are an earth child. I am a space child. I am newer here on earth that you are. It has never seemed normal to me, the way people behave. The violence, the torture, the competitiveness feel unnatural to me. I know the future, but I have to study the present! Do you remember the panel we were on together at the World Future Society, 'The Reawakening of Eve?' I spoke of how Eve led Adam to the first tree, which began the human journey toward individuality and intellect, and that the second Eves will lead the second Adams to the second tree, the Tree of Life, the tree of the healing of the nations. If you and I, Hazel, can stay connected, we can do it. We are both attracted to the transformation of power, to humanity reuniting with each other and with nature as co-creators."

"Yes," she said, "It's true." We embraced and I gave thanks for my beloved friend. I felt that as more of us with differing metaphysical preferences form a human ecology that supports our diversity, as Hazel and I have learned to do, we shall all be strengthened together.

Hazel and I had breakfast alone early one morning at Jerry's.

"Barbara," Hazel asked. "What do you choose to do?"

I realized I could give up and try to be a normal person; or I could recommit to acting out the vision. "I choose to recommit," I said. I was obsessed by the image of the Peace Room, or the Strategic Hub. It felt to me to be an evolutionary necessity.

I took out my pen and signed the place mat at Jerry's. "I, Barbara Hubbard, commit to co-creating the Peace Room, the Strategic Hub." I signed my name, and placed the paper place mat in my files.

I vowed not to be so hard on myself. For if I felt a failure, there was nothing I could do. I simply paralyzed myself. I wanted to regain my self-confidence.

In the period that followed I happened to be in New York City at the apartment of a friend. It was a steamy hot summer day that I will never forget. My eldest daughter Suzanne was with me.

Alexandra, my third daughter, had married Robin Morton, a Canadian cinematographer. They lived together with Jarret, their four year old son, in Echo Bay, British Columbia, doing filming and interspecies communication research with the Orca, the killer whales. At 5:00 a.m. September 18, 1986 Alexandra called me. "Mom, Robin died. He was skin diving. He didn't come up. I went down and brought him up to the surface. Jarret helped me pull him into the boat. He was dead."

"Oh, God, Alex, this is terrible! Sweetheart, I'll be right there."

I fell into Suzanne's arms and we wept. It was too cruel. They had struggled so. They were 24-hour-a-day partners. I could not bear to think of her and Jarret alone. I immediately booked a flight to Pt. Hardy, British Colombia.

When I first saw Alex in the airport she was still in the clothes she wore when she dove in to rescue Robin. The salt water had stiffened her braided hair. She clasped my hand and told me the horrible story of his death.

Robin had just received a contract from the Canadian Broadcasting Company to do a film. National Geographic magazine was scheduled to come the next week to do their life story. Their life's work was finally succeeding. He was out taking last minute pictures. He dove in one final time, and that was it. His rebreather had failed, suffocating him. Alexandra remembers seeing a large grandmother whale approaching Robin at the time of his death and then turning, suddenly, and fleeing.

Alex felt that Robin's spirit was in the grandmother whale that had approached him and then fled to the sea.

That Sunday, hundreds of people met in Victoria to pay tribute to Robin. Alexandra has an extraordinary beauty of being and purity of purpose. Her long black hair cascades around her pioneer Madonna-type face. A Mona Lisa smile flickers mysteriously about her lips, her large dark eyes looking just beyond you, her slim, strong body standing erect, her child Jarret always held by the hand.

She returned to Echo Bay to sprinkle Robin's ashes in the sea and to begin the next phase of her work, which she sees as communication with the whales, entering their world, to be as they are, to see as they see, to love one another, species to species. She told me, "As I watch these deep bonds between whales, I've found myself longing to be a member of their family."

She described the scene of herself, Jarret and the little urn filled with Robin's ashes, riding on the bus, going home. "There it was. The circle closed. It's so ruthless," she said.

"Mom," she said, "Do you think the accident has any meaning? I don't think I can stand it if it's meaningless." I questioned her deeply. She finally mentioned that Robin had said, only a few days before he had died, that all he wanted to do was be with the whales.

"Perhaps, darling, at some deep level, he chose to be free, to be with the whales, leaving his success and his work to you whom he loved so much." He also had told her that she would do better in the world without him. I thought it possible that both Robin's apparently accidental tragedy and John's fatal illness were both the result of an unconscious choice not to pass on to this next step.

I moved from Gainesville to Boulder, Colorado, where my faithful friend Carol Hoskins was looking for a house. I chose Boulder, for at that time there was a possibility that a new television network might be established there. Hal Uplinger and Bernard Lietaer, a brilliant Belgian economist were considering establishing a global television foundation there. I thought we might be able to establish the new news hub with them. Yet it did not work out. They chose to establish the foundation in Washington. Nothing seemed to jell in my life. I felt as though I were dying. Often I could hear a flickering inner voice saying seductively, "Would you like to die?" I felt the temptation: to sleep, not to have to struggle...but I quickly turned away. "No, I choose to live. I have not completed my mission," I would quickly say, knowing my power of choice.

I went through a period of confusion in Boulder, assembling a new and high-powered team to build a Strategic Hub, raising funds, then finding a lack of focus, money and organizational skills.

One possible explanation for this experience of the difficulty of stabilizing new forms was given by Yatri in his book, *Unknown Man*. He wrote, "When a new form occurs, be it a new pattern of behavior or a new man, a certain number of such mutants must appear before the new 'habit' sticks, before a field comes into being of sufficient strength to ensure that everyone's doing it or being it."

The new forms we were trying to create such as the television system, the Peace Room, the core groups, had not yet engendered enough attracted people to create a habit or a field in which they could be sustained.

In March of 1987 I returned to the Soviet Union with Rama and thirty Americans, for the highly successful symposium we had planned for a year on Social Inventions for the Third Millennium. At that time, one of the most amazing events of my life occurred. At lunch one day at the Peace Committee in Moscow I was seated next to a Soviet cosmonaut who spoke no English. I asked for a translator, and discussed with the cosmonaut the idea of a joint Soviet-American Citizen Space Flight. I asked whom I should speak to about this. To my surprise he said, the director of the Cosmonaut Federation. He promptly got up, made a call, returned to me and announced that I had an appointment the next day with the director.

The next day, Rama, Patricia, Marty Lopata, a California businessman and leader in the Science of Mind Church, and myself met with Gennadi, Rustem, Vassily, and the director of the Cosmonaut Federation, Nikolai Nikolaevich Rukovishrikov, who looked like John Glenn.

I sat directly opposite him. My heart was pounding. We were close to my mission on earth: telling the story during an earth-space link-up. I tried to be as sensible and "grounded" as possible.

I explained to him that we proposed that a Soviet and American citizen be selected for a "Citizens Space Flight for Peace." Social innovators from all around the world would speak of what we can do. Musicians from all countries would play. (In other words, the plan.) He had been nodding his head.

He interrupted me. "Of course, of course... no problem.... Let's do it. Why not?"

I was thrown off balance. It was too easy.

I ventured a next step. "I think this event might have remarkable psychological impact, sort of a planetary birth experience."

"Of course," said Vassily, leaning forward and speaking with animation. "It is a planetary birth." He began to quote to us from Teilhard de Chardin. I was amazed.

My excitement rose. "Who do you think should go into space?"

"Why not you and Rama," Vassily said.

Rama then became very excited. She wanted to do yoga in space and had always dreamed of this (which I never knew, since we had never discussed it.).

The energy of synergy began to heat up! The whole group became alive. Nicholai, the Soviet cosmonaut, asked us to write a letter proposing the Citizens Space Flight for Peace.

Later that day I met with Vassily in Rama's suite. He added a remarkable paragraph to the letter. He said Raisa Gorbachev is interested in culture. He proposed we take on this mission videotapes of the highest cultural expressions of the world: our music, architecture, art and poetry to create a Library of Culture in the space station which we would beam out into space to let the extraterrestrials know we were ready for contact!

The cup of Eve runneth over. In the Soviet Union, the evolutionary vision seemed to be in phase with the consciousness of the Soviet leaders. I was stunned. We wrote the letter and I sent it to the director.

That night Rama, Linda Johnson, Patricia, Marcelle Kardush and I slipped away from the group to dine alone at the National Hotel in Moscow. We had been lifted up into an ecstatic state. What had seemed revelatory or "incredible" had entered the realm of manifestation. In fact, we stopped saying, "that's incredible," and said instead, "that's credible, believable and normal!"

In the golden light of the dining room, toasting with our glasses of champagne, we began to envision the whole scenario as real. Tears flowed down my cheeks as we held hands and visualized the apparently incredible plan which I had received over twenty years ago, unfolding before our eyes. During my cosmic birth experience I had seen a flash of light in outer space which helped us all to pay attention at once. I knew that someone or something had to be in space for the earth-space link-up to occur.

We proposed that at the time of the space flight, there be a presidential team in the U.S. with full cabinet, ready to speak of what we can do.

We felt their words would be understood, because for that time, the consciousness of millions would be joined. This team would transform the American presidency. It would be an extension of what could be established through a global network of social inventors.

We pledged ourselves to the fulfillment of this plan.

Shortly after our return to the United States, Rama said she felt we should move to Washington D.C. in preparation for the first Soviet-American Citizens' Summit. "A New Way of Thinking - Social Inventions for the Third Millennium," was to be held in November, 1987 (later moved to February, 1988). It would be the beginning of a "Citizens' Embassy," a Peace Room, the presidential team and the space flight which we scheduled in our minds for 1992. I was caught up in a wave of evolutionary initiatives. It felt normal and natural.

As the vision of the new relationship between Soviets and Americans grounded itself in reality, I was overjoyed to find that the campaign team and new colleagues were re-assembling. Carolyn Anderson and Jeff Daly of Palo Alto, who had joined as a couple, Carolyn's twin sister Marion Culhane, who had run the Denver Positive Future Center, Tim Michael Clauss who had been administrator for the campaign, along with Marian Head, Tom Foster and Michael Lach, publishers of the catalogue *Choices and Connections*, and myself met in Boulder, Colorado to form "Global Family." It was to be a new network to help support the linking and nurturing of core groups world-wide. Our stated purpose was to further the collective shift in consciousness from fear and separation to unity and love. We selected the name Global Family to signify the awareness that each of us is already a member of one human family. We were waking up to this reality in our lifetime.

Global Family was not conceived as an organization, but rather as a state of consciousness that we are all brothers and sisters. Every morning we would meet. Our first act would be to center our awareness in our hearts and focus on the essence of our life passion, our life purpose. Then we would consciously connect with each other, heart to heart, until we felt a resonance among ourselves and the formation of a nucleus which contained the combined genius of each person. It felt like the core of a social cell.

Then, in order to sustain and nourish the collective genius, we would practice unconditional love, non-judgment and forgiveness of one another in every aspect of our relationship. For we found that if we criticized each other, the resonance stopped and our social cell fell apart, scattering the potential group genius. Whereas when we supported each other, our field of resonance was strong and we experienced greater access to our individual and collective intuition.

Sometimes we enhanced our morning meetings with ceremonies

and rituals to remember the sacredness of our relationship and activities. We learned to coach each other, to assist one another in being our best. Rather than criticize another behind their back, we would speak directly to the person using discernment, but not judgement. This practice freed our energies to be far more creative and productive. Instead of being occupied with fault finding, we were free to create.

In this environment, our deeper vocations were aroused. Our hidden genius came forth, and we committed to working together for a shared purpose that could actualize all of us fully.

We began the process of "synergistic decision-making." This meant that the one who knew most about a particular area, lead in that area, and followed when someone else knew best in another area.

This process worked wonderfully. The final grounding of it was to become entrepreneurial so that our work together would be self-sustaining, thereby allowing us to continue to engage in this nourishing way of life. We committed to the full practice of the core group process as our way of being and acting in the world. The next stage of manifesting had begun. The Campaign for a Positive Future was reborn through this process.

One of the Global Family's first activities was to act as a communications hub for José Argüelles' Harmonic Convergence, a grassroots effort to harmonize with the earth as a sacred being, sending out his information and eventually receiving thousands of letters from all over the world. We did a live Harmonic Convergence radio show. People called in live from sacred sites around the world. José wept as the event which he had fathered and freely communicated to be designed by those who chose to do it, became the most publicized event of its kind ever to happen on earth.

The mass media covered it as a wierd and inexplicable rite, focusing on a few eccentrics rather than the large number of ordinary people who participated. A Voice of America woman called to interview me. "Don't you think it's wierd that people would rise at 6:00 a.m. all over the world to go to mountain tops to harmonize with nature?" she asked.

"No," I responded. "What I think is wierd is that people get up every morning to make bombs to destroy the world."

"Mm... I never thought of it that way," she said.

I immersed myself in intense preparations for the first Soviet-American Citizens Summit to be held in Alexandria, Virginia. Once again, I was fully focused.

The Center for Soviet-American Dialogue rented a small office from Paul von Ward, a Soviet-American expert, down near the Capital. Rama's team moved from Seattle to Washington, D.C. I was program chair. My task was to get American innovators as counterparts to the one hundred leading Soviets to be brought over by the Peace Committee, with whom Rama was in continual communications. She had done a heroic job in getting this level of Soviet participation. Rama was becoming a master diplomat. They were sending us their very best: cosmonauts, editors of Ogonyak, Pravda, Tass, members of the Central Committee, actors, writers; it was their first team. Our job was to match it with Americans of equal stature.

I did my best to attract so-called conservatives. One powerful Washington D.C. insider looked over our list of Americans and said he would never come, this was "too far left."

"It's not left at all," I said, really incensed. "You can't call people like Willis Harman, Virginia Satir, Amory Lovins and Hazel Henderson left! They're aiming at something new, something whole, cooperative, pragmatic, beyond right or left."

I went to see people from the Heritage Foundation, the bastion of conservative think tanks, which has been an intellectual guide to the Reagan administration. They refused to send anyone for fear of being "used to give credibility to the event."

Rama and I were called naive by State Department officials. The Soviet Peace Committee had a bad reputation (which was undoubtedly based on truth: it was used as a propaganda arm of official Soviet policy, but that policy had changed).

I asked what was meant by naive.

"It means you don't know enough to be afraid," said the State Department official.

We were well aware of the former dangers of the Soviet state. We also recognized that change had just begun in the Soviet Union. It could be reversed. Obviously a seventy year history could not be altered overnight. We were not advocating blind trust. We were taking an initiative along with countless other American "citizen diplomats" to develop a new relationship which could change our attitudes and help with the reversal of the arms race and the building of a positive future for the human race. When we tried to explain "Social Inventions for the Third Millennium" we met with raised eyebrows and smirks. "What in God's name does that mean?" a State Department official asked.

I spoke with one sympathetic official in the Arms Control Agency, who refused to come to the Summit because of his position. We were discussing Gorbachev's proposals for nuclear disarmament. "Barbara," he said, "our task is impossible. We are told to protect the United States against any possible threat which the Soviets, as an implacable foe, may plan to perpetrate. It's so complicated that it's impossible, given the assumption that their purpose is to destroy us. You trust-builders better get stronger. It's the only way. We can't rely on you yet, but eventually, we'll have to." By some strange quirk of history, American officialdom had taken on the mantle of the famous Russian "Nyet," while the Soviets' current buzz words were "No problem!"

While we struggled to get well-known establishment Americans to come to the Summit (we did get a few), the spiritual, futurist, globally-minded Americans were accepting in droves.

To pay for the Summit we had to have over three hundred "delegates" each contributing $900 to support their participation and the cost of the Soviets. (When we go to their country, they host us.) One hundred American invited participants, actual counterparts of the Soviets, were to be paid for by the Center, along with the Soviets for whom we were also responsible.

To invite delegates I spoke to thousands of people in churches across the country asking them to see the necessity of their own role in shifting the tide of history in the world. After each talk scores of folks would vow to take their vacation pay, their retirement funds, their extra savings and come to Washington to change the world. It was so moving to see how thrilled they were to make a contribution to an essentially political process that had for so long seemed the prerogative of government alone.

We ended up at the Summit with a hundred leading Soviets, over a hundred American innovative leaders, plus leaders of the Soviet-American citizen exchanges and projects, and an "army of angels" as the delegates.

It was a superb mix!

I will never forget the first evening at the Mark Raddisson hotel in Alexandria, Virginia. The Soviet delegation and some Americans had just arrived from a wildly excited party at the Soviet embassy where our camera people were let in without passes, and the doors were opened to unidentified Americans, all semblance of security waived by the Soviets in their desire to create a new relationship. Over four hundred Americans were waiting for the Soviets. I recognized countless faces of friends I had met from all over.

Paul Temple, president of Energy Capital and chairman of the board of the Institute of Noetic Sciences was the master of ceremonies. He asked the Soviets to stand up to be welcomed.

They stood, these sophisticated Communists: Henry Borovich, head of the Peace Committee, General Mikhail Milstein, Henry Trofimenko of the Institute for U.S. and Canada Studies, cosmonaut Gregory Grechko and many other veterans, well-educated men and women who have lived through the horrors of the Stalin years and the Brezhnev period, now representing perestroika and glasnost. Something surprising happened. The clapping became louder and louder, cheers began and suddenly the Americans were standing applauding thunderously, roaring in a crescendo of enthusiasm. I thought of the Moscow Baptist church. There it was again. Beyond politics, ideology, history, beyond all fear, the Americans were saying: "We care for you as human beings. We refuse to hate. We commit to create with you now."

It went on for what seemed like an eternity, maybe ten or fifteen minutes. The Soviets were standing and clapping, too, as is their custom. Yet, I could see they were astonished at this extraordinary outpouring. Paul stood there smiling. I felt the welling up of the tears of ages finally being released as people joined, transcending the barriers imposed by nation states, armies and religions.

I stood upon the podium, and welcomed people saying, "Can you imagine a process broad enough to allow every American and every Soviet citizen that would like to work together to do so? Well, my friends, that is the process we are initiating here and now." Roars of approval came from the audience.

I described the process of the Summit. It was very much the same as in the March Symposium in Moscow. People were to meet in task forces based on their personal interests, to find counterparts to accomplish joint projects of their choice. Teams of Soviets and Americans who committed to action were invited to speak at each morning's plenary session to gain further support for their projects from the larger group.

This time we had designed and created an actual "Convergence Center" or Peace Room or Strategic Hub. Finally, I was doing it! Marian Head and other members of Global Family, in a superb gesture of support for the Summit, had come to Washington to help. Marian translated my vision of this Convergence Center into an actual process. We had a room full of computers, a data base of existing projects, maps to be filled in by new projects. Tom Foster of Global Family and Noel McInnis served as American editors, with Anatoly Belyevev, editor of *20th Century and Peace*, as the Soviet editor of the *Daily Summit*.

Marian with Michaela Belding of The Center for Soviet American Dialogue created a core team to administer and coordinate the event. It was like the experience at the Democratic National Convention. We had practiced love, forgiveness, alignment and co-coaching throughout our preparation for the Summit. Our own harmony could be felt by the hundred volunteers and participants. Anselm Rothschild, who had worked on Live Aid, came to help as a contribution from Mike Mitchell, his current employer. We actually produced the event together. It was like being one inch ahead of an enormous wave. I loved it. The challenge was dynamic enough to call forth all my resources and capabilities. I felt profoundly enlivened. I did not want it to be over, ever, for it was an event expansive enough to allow me to feel totally myself. At one of the most interesting panels of the Summit, John Wallach, who had organized the State Department-supported Chautauqua events with high-level Soviet and American officials, invited several American conservatives to discuss the theme, "What would it take for American and Soviet conservatives to trust one another?" The Soviets brought their top leadership: Borovick, Henry Trofimenko, Gen. Milstein and several others. It looked like pictures of the Politburo, except the Soviets were smiling, while the Americans frowned. The Americans sat on the other end of the table, with Henry moderating.

The room was jammed. Dan Ellsberg was there, on a nine day fast of protest. The Soviets said, in sum, that nuclear disarmament was necessary. The Americans said it was impossible. Next door, Global Family USA and USSR had arranged a party. They were singing loudly: "Let there be peace on earth and let it begin with me," in Russian and English.

As the Americans were speaking of the impossibility of nuclear disarmament, the audience in our room caught the words and began to laugh. Finally one of the American panelists burst out in exasperation. "Don't you realize, singing won't help! Smiling won't help! I want peace as much as you do. I work eighteen hours a day for it... you don't know how hard it is from the inside." My heart went out to him.

During the question and answer period that followed, an American asked a most interesting question: "How is it," he asked, "that the Americans, who used to be the optimistic, hopeful, can-do people, are saying we can't solve this problem, while the Soviets, who have always said no, it's impossible, are now leading the way?"

One of the Americans answered thoughtfully, "It might be a theological matter," he said. "The Soviets expect heaven on earth, while we don't. We expect Armageddon and heaven in another realm, after this life."

Suddenly, I saw it: the new right, conservative Americans who were in political leadership in our country now, were being unconsciously motivated to fulfill their faith in the biblical prophesy in Revelation. Such leaders as Pat Robertson of the 700 Club, when he ran for president in 1988, said that he believed conflict between us and the "godless empire" was inevitable. Barbara Honneger, a former White House aide under Reagan, had sent me materials indicating that Reagan also believed the prophesy of Armageddon.

I flashed back to my memory of the alternative to Armageddon being a World Instant of Cooperation, a Planetary Pentecost. How could we substitute a *new* thought of a peaceful transformation for the old thought of the inevitability of conflict? The Communist "religion" had prophesied an inevitable conflict with capitalism before the "heaven" of synthesis would come. The conservative Christians still believed in the inevitability of Armageddon before the Kingdom of Heaven could be established. The Soviets were changing their dogma. We were not yet changing ours.

At the final plenary session, a long line of Soviet-American teams stood ready to announce their joint projects. A live satellite radio broadcast to the nation had been organized by Tami Simon of Sounds True, in Boulder, Colorado, a dynamic young woman entrepreneur in her twenties, who like all the women organizers of this event, had a life-changing passion for "the work." Project after project was put forward: peace parks, global economic conferences, educational projects, films, youth exchanges, war veteran exchanges.

It was overwhelming. Henry Borovik told the group that, "Finally, Soviets and Americans are on the same side of the net, while the problems are on the other side. Instead of trying to destroy each other, we're solving our common problems together. We were able to make decisions here in a few minutes that would have taken years to do officially."

Robert Müller, former Assistant Secretary General of the United Nations said it was the finest conference he had ever been to, because people did not have a chance to make speeches about their opinions, but about the actions they personally committed to accomplish. He suggested a Citizens' Summit for Non-Governmental Organizations at the United Nations.

At one point in the event we asked for financial support, since the Center, it turned out, was facing a serious deficit. I spoke before the large audience.

"The Center for Soviet American Dialogue needs help," I said. "This event has been far larger and more expensive than we expected. The Center has six board members that have been responsible for this event, and do you know how many members our counterpart, the Soviet Peace Committee has? Over ninety million! Each contributes a small amount each month. How can our citizens' groups gain comparable strength over here?" I asked.

Scores of Americans rose up and pledged a thousand dollars. But the financial burden was only slightly alleviated. We still have no supporting organization to empower this kind of action with the needed funds, while billions of our resources are spent on preparation for war. It truly seemed an insane situation.

We completed the Summit in a blaze of creativity. Ted Turner gave a rousing speech. John Denver called in live. Alexander Gratsky, their magnificent popular singer and composer, and David Pomeranz sang, "It's In Every One of Us" as a duet. The audience, Soviets and Americans, rose, locked arms, and swayed to the music, making the two singers repeat the refrain over and over again.

"It's in every one of us, to be wise,
Find your heart, open up both your eyes;
We can all know everything,
Without ever knowing why,
It's in every one of us, by and by."

© Pomeranz

I changed the words to, "It's in every one of us here and now."

The Summit was over, the first event of its kind ever held. It was a small taste of what is possible when we move from bureaucratic official dialogue to non-official, personal initiatives of individuals free to interact one on one in a process that enhances synergy and co-creation. We had discovered a social formula that works.

It has become so clear to me that if the U.S. and U.S.S.R. remained enemies in the nuclear age, it is indeed impossible to get rid of nuclear weapons, as Kissinger and McNamara had said on the panel after The Day After. The only hope is a changed relationship and a new set of goals. The odd thing is that these brilliant strategists never seem to see the obvious. They accept the enmity as a given, eternal condition of life, rather than being the very area in which change is possible, desirable, and sought after by the Soviets, as well as the majority of the American people, and all people on earth.

Our government is spending billions on maintaining the old relationship through force, and practically nothing on changing it. There seems to be a vested interest in the status quo and the arms race. People's jobs and expertise depend on the continuation of the Cold War. But deeper than any rational explanation can account for, the majority of Americans seem to be mysteriously paralysed, trapped by a soul-numbing idea, allowing the arms race juggernaut to continue using their precious resources to build nuclear bombs and other weapons while children starve and the environment is destroyed.

We took the Soviets to New York City following the Summit. At St. John the Divine's Cathedral in New York, under the guidance of the very Rev. James Morton, Father Luis Dolan had organized a magnificent celebration. There was singing, dancing, and an American choir sang Russian folk songs in honor of the guests. Cosmonaut Georgy Grechko, standing next to me in the enormous cathedral, said to me, "If I died today, I would be happy. This is the best day of my life." He had tears in his eyes.

We seemed to be living in two worlds simultaneously: the world of the Cold War, where both sides are pacing each other and can truly point out the danger each poses to the other, and the world of human relationships where both sides are opening up to and supporting each other and can point out the endless possibilities inherent in creating together.

While the Soviets sent a video crew to cover the whole event, we could not get any national television media to cover it. I was outraged when the president of one of the major networks said to me condescendingly, "Maybe if you get a group of Russkies together in Russian hats with some pretty girls near a monument, and if you can get a celebrity, then maybe we'll send a camera."

Even at CNN they told me it was not news. In the Soviet Union, however, they played their documentary many times, to audiences of several hundred million each time!

Rama returned to Seattle with a huge burden of the debt, to set up a process to follow-up and support the hundreds of new-born projects. Americans did not realize how difficult communications between our two countries still is. And the Center had to struggle for needed funds to set up a Communications Hub for joint projects.

Meanwhile, I realized that the Convergence Center at the Summit was the first time I had actually experienced an aspect of the "Peace Room" in real-time action. Marian Head and Global Family had done a superb job in working with the volunteers and Center staff in setting it up. But how were we to continue? There were no funds, organizational structure or staff.

As after the SYNCONs, and the campaign, I felt stranded, unsure what to do next.

I thought perhaps I could set up a Washington Convergence Center. Patricia Remele, a business woman in real estate who had contributed financially to the Summit, and I set about to explore the possibility. But we did not have the "field" around us. There were not enough of us to activate the project. I moved in with her, while my office remained in Boulder. I vowed to gain some clarity and stability rather than to continue this series of magnificent events that have no organizational continuity.

One of the things that gave me comfort was my children. Each of them had discovered their own vocation. My relationship with them was a continuity throughout all the changes in my life. Our relationship had endured and flowered amidst my total commitment to pursuing my life's vocation. I had not lost my children. I had, in fact, deepened my relationship with them, and for this, I am deeply grateful. Yet, I still find it hard to be separated from those I love.

Often people asked me somewhat skeptically, "What effect has your life had on your children?" The answer is that every one of them is passionately dedicated to their vocations, living on the growing edge of their own creativity. In 1980 they gave me a fiftieth birthday party. I asked them what they felt was the best thing I had done as a mother... and the worst. The best, they said, was that I did what I believed in. I followed my passion, and that encouraged them to follow theirs. The worst thing was not be firm enough with people. They felt I did not give strong enough direction. I allowed everyone to do what they wanted too much of the time... including them! However, it has all turned out well.

Lloyd, my youngest, found his life's purpose through flying. Before his first lesson, he was depressed, overweight, doing badly at a college he hated. Immediately afterward, he was directed. I have never seen such a rapid transformation. He took his Pilot Training at Vance Air Force Base in Enid, Oklahoma, and in October, 1986 graduated first in his class, receiving the Commanders' Cup, the Flying Training award, and a Distinguished Graduate award. When I asked him what motivated him, he answered, "Challenge. I decided to do the very best I could at everything I did." He is now an officer at Fairchild Air Force base in Spokane, living with his wife Laura, whom he has loved since they were both seventeen. I feel that he and other young men and women like him, will be prepared, when the political shift comes to guide the military in its next step of defense and protecting the planet, and all life on it.

Wade has devotedly pursued his love of music. He went through rough times in Los Angeles, struggling to survive in a cold and harsh world. He has had one record album released called *Foreign Shores*, and is now working for a music company, while writing his own music and developing his own band. He and Gale Whipple have a beautiful daughter, Danielle who has been living with me, while Gale has brought order to my life, as my assistant and colleague.

Alexandra has partially recovered from the terrible tragedy of Robin's death. Although she continues to grieve, and feels she will never get over the loss, she is becoming a true legend. She lives in Echo Bay, a tiny jewel of a community in British Columbia in her own Float House with Jarret, whom she rows by boat every morning to a one room school.

Over the last ten years Alex has recorded wild killer whales for hundreds of hours. Now she is entering all those sounds into a computer. John Galse has written a special program for her. When this immense task is complete, she will ask the computer to tell her the relationship between what they are saying and what they are doing. This will be a first step toward understanding their communication and their intelligence.

She is handling the media, film-makers, and television crews coming to record her story, and to utilize Robin's film, which has been called the best of its kind in the world. She earns her living crewing for fishing boats, writing articles and making beautiful whale cards for the benefit of her foundation: Lore Quest, to fund her personal research to understand and communicate with the Orca whale.

Suzanne has a become a fine weaver, creating splendid tapestries for clients throughout the country. She, her son Peter and husband Sandy live in Washington, D.C. She is a first-rate tri-athelon athlete, ranking eleventh in the country in her class. She says that "weaving is a way of life." She brings beauty to everything she does.

Stephanie, who changed her name to Woodleigh lives in New York City. She is an artist, fashion consultant, budding entrepreneur and above all a beloved coach and spiritual support for all who come across her path. No matter where I am, if I have a problem, I call Woodleigh. "Now, Mom. What is it?" she will ask, not letting me get away with the slightest unclarity. She has surmounted every obstacle to her own development in a truly inspiring way.

My children are with me always in spirit. In fact... I have a child in almost every port!

Earl has remarried a writer. They live an elegant life in Washington, D.C. He is continuing with his writing and painting. I see him at weddings and always hope the very best for him, as he does for me.

I know we discovered the formula for the Convergence Center at the Summit, but now, as after the SYNCONs and the campaign, I am faced with the eternal question, "How can I stabilize it?" This is a question I have not answered.

Hazel and I had heard from Linda Hope, Larry Wilson's former chief aide, that she had gone to work with J.J. Ebaugh, who worked for Ted Turner, head of Turner Broadcasting and president of Cable News Network. Hazel and I headed for Atlanta. Linda met us at the airport and drove us out to Ted's fishing lodge.

Linda expressed the problem they are facing at Turner Broadcasting. Hundreds of proposals to support good projects come to them. There is no way they can support them.

Hazel came up with the answer.

"Put the people with projects on television and have the viewers send in money to support the projects they like."

Linda was enthusiastic. We arrived at the lodge and met J.J., a beautiful thirty-one year old blonde, with piercing blue eyes. She was Ted's former pilot, and had a passion to use television to activate consciousness.

J.J. had issued an invitation to the most creative people she and Ted knew in television to come up with a new formula: a television show that could awaken people to action to save the earth! A meeting had been called in June 1988 to develop a "blueprint."

The four of us sat comfortably on the fishing dock, in the gentle Alabama heat, before Ted arrived. During the rambling conversation, J.J. asked us a pointed question, "What is the one television show that could change consciousness?" she asked.

"Well," I said, without much animation, pulling the ever-ready idea out of my mind, "it would be in three parts, A Global Intelligence System to gather innovations that work, a television show that takes place in a live situation room (Peace Room, Convergence Center, Strategic Hub), with stories of what people can actually do now, and a 900 number for viewers to call in to support and get involved in the projects they see."

J.J. sat bolt upright and said, "That's it!"

Linda, Hazel, J.J. and I became excited and began to strategize how Turner Broadcasting might actually do it. Years of efforts came flooding before my mind: the SYNCONs, Futures Network, Potentials, the campaign, the Summit. I knew the reality of this new evolutionary system with such intensity that I sometimes felt I must have experienced it somewhere before. It represented the awakening of the global community of humanity as one people, one planet, taking responsibility for our world.

Soon Ted came roaring up the driveway, changed clothes, and ambled toward us in his fishing clothes. He exudes masculine power and charm, with an edge of harshness.

As he approached the dock, he said teasingly, "Now, you ladies are *not* going to take over television. Why aren't you all playing bridge somewhere." He reminded me of my father, who liked to taunt in a way that could hurt or anger.

J.J. said, "Barbara, tell him the idea."

I felt like Barbara, the vice presidential candidate, who had thirty seconds to make a speech to someone who didn't want to hear it.

So I sat up and told him in about that length of time.

"Not bad," he said, and abruptly left to go fishing.

"Wasn't that great! He was so enthusiastic," said J.J.

"Enthusiastic?" I said, "he didn't sound all that interested."

"You should hear him when he doesn't like something," she said.

Hazel and I, who had come together and co-conceived the "New News," allowed ourselves to become excited. We had, after the incompletion of Win Win World, dampened down the fires of our enthusiasm. But the flame still burned. We knew that this television system was one of the most important evolutionary patterns which we had conceived. So "Planet Live: A Television Campaign for the Earth" was instigated in Alabama. J.J. Ebaugh became our CEO and our goal was to be on Superstation TBS in September, 1989.

Meanwhile, Global Family was ministering to a global network of core groups world wide including in the Soviet Union where millions of people have seen Carolyn Anderson on national television and consider Global Family-USSR to be their organization. We are just learning how to provide manuals and training in this new form of social life.

We held a "Global Family Reunion" in Colorado in the summer of 1988. It was heaven, literally. I experienced the manifestation of the vision which had motivated me all these years. The experience of resonance and co-creation mounted for four days. True friends, brothers and sisters from years of work, joined together in the exquisite Shadow Cliff Lodge. We had bunk rooms and all ate together in the lodge like a real family.

Every morning we met in "resonating cores," of about twelve people each. I was in Carolyn Anderson's core. She is a master in the activation of a field of resonance and love.

She led us in a relaxing meditation and then asked us questions such as, "What is my next step?" to be responded to from within, out of the silence, where we all hear the "still, small voice."

People spoke from the very depth of their being. At one point each of us sat in the center of the circle and stated our intention for our lives. "I am now ready to express my life's purpose in the world." . . . "I am committing to heal my relationship with my wife." . . . "I am, I am, I am . . . ." As each person spoke, the whole group enfolded him or her in unconditional love.

I felt that any wound could be healed, any intention fulfilled if we could remain in that field of love. It was a normalized state of grace.

Then we met in a large group: about seventy "family" members. Each person stated their deeper vocation, their life's purpose, with the intention of clustering together in "vocational" core groups, with team members who shared the same purpose. We listened to one another as though our life depended on it... and it did! The need to find our vocational partners was as powerful as the drive to find a sexual mate.

The passion for self-expression, self-actualization through chosen work was awakened in that room. "Vocational arousal," that drive to join not genes but genius to co-create works, acts, gifts was palpable. It was drawing people together in a magnetic field.

People self-organized by attraction to action, as we had done at the Eagles' Reunion, and the Soviet-American Citizens' Summit. I could feel "cooperative democracy" in the making. The Global Family Reunion had an added dimension. There was an infrastructure to hold us together, whereas at the other events we had no on-going way of connecting. The network of cores is held together by Field Team Coordinators, a Global Family Newspaper and periodic Reunions in different cities.

I sat there for hours, absorbing the joy of the people as they found one another. No one was forcing them to do this. It was love moving them. As I watched individuals joining together with such passion, I realized that Mother Nature had invented something as powerful as sex: suprasex! We were being attracted to co-create with the same power that we had been drawn to pro-create. This was what the core group process was really about: suprasexual co-creation! I saw that what was drawing us together in core groups was a suprasexual drive, and that this same drive was awakening in masses of people the world over. That night I made one of my longest journal entries:

> *Due to the environmental crisis, a signal has gone forth throughout the world. Do not be fruitful and multiply! Have fewer babies. This is not simply a cultural change in attitude, but a shift of an evolutionary order. A limit to population growth is rapidly being reached. We cannot continue to populate at the current rate and survive.*
>
> *Millions and eventually billions of women will have one, two or no children. And concurrently, we will be living longer lives. Instead of living an average of fifty years, we are approaching an average life span of over seventy. This means a vast hormonal reserve, that once was triggered by birth and caring for large families, is ready to be called into action in a new way. The energy, the passion, the love that goes into reproducing the species is becoming available en masse for a new purpose.*
>
> *As a woman, I have felt that passion being transformed within me into the drive for vocation, the desire to express my unique creativity in service to the world. Within almost every woman I know, whether we remain in a more traditional role, or are in a job, or are explorers at the social frontier of change, there is a hunger to give ourselves more fully, not to maintain the world as it is, not only to be equal to men, but rather to create a better world in which all life can fulfill itself.*
>
> *As women experience the "vocational arousal," we become excited. The passion that conceives the child is activated to create the work. We activate ourselves to extend ourselves, to grow. We become more attractive because we are attracted to a*

higher purpose. As this purpose animates our lives, it attracts men to serve those purposes with us. We are aroused to find our teammates, those individuals whose unique creativity is expanded by our own. For we can rarely do our vocations alone. The core group is the next stage of family, the co-creative family.

I believe that a suprasexual revolution is about to sweep throughout the world. Awareness of the environmental crisis has just hit public consciousness. We are told we have only one generation to change our behavior, stop overpopulating and polluting, or we shall destroy life on this earth. This is an unprecedented signal. I feel it is activating us, not only on the mental level but, more deeply, it is triggering our genetic code. It is releasing a drive to create through chosen function, or vocation. It is unlocking the untapped human potential that has lain dormant except in a privileged few. As nature stimulated us to populate the world through sexual attraction, she is arousing us to evolve the world through suprasexual attraction. As we move beyond the patterns of our traditional lives, we discover that this action satisfies our hunger, actualizes our potential and brings us joy.

From this point of view, everyone's genius is needed for the evolution of the world, just as every cell's function is needed for the growth of a biological organism. In the past, we reproduced the species, lived short lives, and died young. Now, that unique genius of each of us is being called forth, because that is exactly what is needed to solve this extraordinarily complex crisis and move us forward to the next stage of social evolution. Nature does not need more bodies. She needs evolved beings! She needs our genius.

Therefore, women are becoming co-creators as well as pro-creators. We are extending the love of the unknown child into the world as the love of humanity, the love of this earth, the drive to create a sustainable future for all life.

As we evolve, so too are men liberated. No longer do they have to care for large families. They are being freed to discover and express their deeper vocations. Even though it sometimes feels like a loss to a man when a woman falls in love with her vocation, it can actually foster renewal and deepening of their relationship. For her love of her work is not rejection, but rather the natural result of her expanded capacity to love and create. Instead of separating us from men, co-creation reunites us as partners in nurturing the larger human family, as well as our own social one.

Each child becomes a chosen child. Every life is cherished. Every individual is needed to do and be their best. As we shift from pro-creation to co-creation, the emphasis changes from caring for babies and dying young, to evolving ourselves and healing the earth.

We have felt the fear of nuclear winter and environmental destruction. We have recognized the pain of social injustice, hunger, disease and violence. We have felt the stick, but we have not fully experienced the carrot. The carrot is the joy of suprasex! The carrot is ourselves fully actualized, the world renewed and the environment restored. If we respond to this call, we will enter an "age of co-creation" that has only been envisioned by the saints and seers of the human race. The ecstatic quality of joining together to create goes beyond gender, beyond age, class or background. It is an endless source of growth and adventure. It is the fulfillment of our lives.

As the small Global Family Reunion in Colorado drew to a close, I knew we were discovering a natural pattern of social evolution. Once again I thanked the hunger of Eve within me for motivating me not to settle for adaptation to social norms that felt unnatural, but rather to move to co-create new social forms that fulfill our deepest aspirations.

In August, 1988 I was invited to give the keynote speech at John Denver's famous Windstar Symposium in Aspen, Colorado. I had heard that John proposed to go into outer space on a Soviet Rocket (NASA had turned him down; since the Challenger accident they were not accepting citizen astronauts). I wanted to end my speech with a vision of a "Global Citizens Summit" and the planetary smile.

I spoke to John backstage just as I was about to go on. The music of the Olympics was playing as eighteen hundred people assembled in a big tent. There was an electric excitement in the air. The theme was "Ethics in Action." It was the 25th anniversary of Martin Luther King's "I have a dream" speech.

"John," I asked, "would you mind if I mentioned you in the vision of the space mission... I know it's still not confirmed." He hesitated. It was sensitive: how the media would cover it? How NASA would react, if he were to go? Would the public understand?

"Barbara, do what's in your heart," he said. "I trust you."

Stark King, an Aspen businessman gave me a beautiful introduction. He described how he was taking a morning run at sunrise. He asked, "Where does the sunrise get its beauty, its power?" The answer, said Stark, "was simply from being true to its own nature. From awakening and arising, day after day, year after year, eon after eon, no matter what. The sun rises and just is. It is not aggressive nor loud. It is passionate in its persistence. Extreme in softness and awesome in its power. And then it dawned on me," he continued, "Barbara Marx Hubbard is like that sunrise. She is soft. She is persistent, and her life comes from a centered place. She lives and works and plays right in that very, very small place where spirit becomes action."

I was deeply touched by this beautiful introduction and felt a buoyant joy and empathy with every person in the audience as I rose to speak.

"At this moment hundreds of thousands of people are gathering in Washington in memory of Martin Luther King," I said. "Let's send them a message from Windstar. 'We are overcoming now!'

"Let that message go to Washington and all around the world. Wherever people are gathered together...."

I dramatized the hope we can feel in our hearts as we recognize that a new state of consciousness, a new way of being and acting is here now.

"We have discovered the awesome creative power of nature to transform to ever higher systems with ever greater consciousness, freedom and order. This is an implicate pattern in nature.... We see ourselves poised here, as we enter the 1990's, with the power to co-create or co-destroy.... When John Denver used the word 'co-create' the first evening at Windstar, I realized *co-creation is our theme*. Ultimately it is a new relationship between humans and God, or humans and evolution, however you choose to say it.... The human mind is so designed, as Buckminster Fuller told us, to penetrate nature sufficiently to understand the processes of evolution.... What we have been doing in the last few hundred years since the Renaissance is honing in on nature's invisible technologies of creation. Our understanding of the atom, the gene, the brain has put into our hands the power to be co-evolutionary. We can build new life forms. We can build new worlds. We are inheriting the powers of creation itself. We are at the beginning of a global renaissance.

"From a theological standpoint we have always known we are created in the image of God and that we are destined to move from being children of God to being heirs of God. We have inherited the power through the natural evolution of our mind, and with it we have inherited the fatal human flaw, which is appearing now more than ever. The fatal human flaw is the illusion that we are separated from each other, from nature, and from the creative processes of nature herself.

"When and if humanity overcomes that illusion, we will discover that we already have the power of co-creators. In consciousness we know that as we think it, so it becomes. We learn to think choicefully, purposefully, creatively, compassionately. When we rise up to full oneness with the force of creation, the manifestation of our powers is quick. When two or three or fifty or eighteen hundred as in this room should agree on something, what do you think happens? It manifests!.... We are at the threshold of conscious co-creation. Add to this our technological, industrial and military genius. If that power were connected to our consciousness of oneness, to our sense of the sacredness of all life, and our alignment with the innate tendency of nature to form more comprehensive whole systems, can you imagine the collective power of the human race! Everything we ever dreamed of we can do. We can feed, house, clothe, restore, educate, emancipate, explore, empower. We've got it all now, if we make that shift in consciousness from fear and separation to unity and love. Isn't that dramatic? Isn't that exciting? That's where we are!" By this time the audience and I were moving and breathing as one.

I continued, "Every culture is coded with a vision of this shift through its religions. The way nature evolves is through synergy, bringing together separate elements in such a way that they make a more comprehensive whole. Another word for this is *love*."

I mentioned the concept that the 1960's was our birth period, the 1970's our confusion, the 1980's our pulsing toward global link-ups, all heading for a planetary experience of oneness. I spoke of critical acts now occurring.

Looking directly at Vladimir Posner, the Soviet news commentator who was in the audience, I said, "Let's place the change in relationship between the Soviets and Americans in the context of a planetary body that is integrating into a whole: our environments, our economics, our communication systems are interconnecting. The two superpowers have been holding this world at ransom, in their quest to create a new world in competition with each other, at the moment when the whole world, by the forces of nature itself, has become interdependent.

"Now, a shift has started with perestroika in the Soviet Union. From the evolutionary perspective, perestroika is not only the internal restructuring of the Soviet Union to give its people more democracy, more free enterprise. I think it is a repatterning based on that shift in nature itself, which is aiming at a new synthesis.

"The real question is, 'What will happen in the United States of America when we have no enemy?' My sister Patricia Ellsberg feels that the recognition that security no longer lies in the superior ability to threaten destruction, but in mutual reassurance is as revolutionary as the American, French and Russian Revolutions themselves.

"Imagine the implications of that shift of perception, not just between Soviets and Americans, but all other people as well. It will release us from collective fear to collective love. And what does collective love mean in the context of our collective power? It takes our collective intelligence to know that. No one person has enough vision to comprehend the joy of this possibility. It's too big for any one of us. It will take new social processes to empower us to see together the enormity of our capacity to create when we no longer fear but we love.

"As we wind down the Cold War, and develop a new perception of security to mean defensive defense, rather than offensive defense, as we free the resources and the genius of the human race now locked up in our collective fear, as we liberate our military/industrial complexes to join in the solving of problems, we will act collectively in love for a new social agenda initiated in the 1990's.

"Let's have a global vision quest." I turned to Dennis Becker of Ark International, who was working with John to inspire the audience to personal commitment in their lives. "Who takes responsibility for that?"

Dennis raised his hand and nodded.

Then I described "Planet Live", as an example of the evolution of the mass media, with its Peace Room or situation room, tracking the planetary story.

"Now this is our vision, we don't have this yet. But this is how we see it. It is not only a television show; it is a Campaign for the Earth. The television show will take place in a live situation room, comparable to NASA mission control during the Apollo program. It is comparable in sophistication, urgency, excitement and wonder to the live space program. The fact is, we don't know what's going to happen next on this earth. It is a real live drama. Messages are coming in from all over the world. Onto this show come the innovators, the creators, the heroes and heroines, who speak from their hearts, just as we are doing here. If we have a problem, Dennis Weaver (the actor who is working on feeding the hungry in Los Angeles) is cheering us on." Dennis waved from the audience.

"If we have disabling beliefs, David Gershon is telling us, 'wait a minute turn that one around!' We are coaching each other. We're not just accepting ourselves as we are. We're going to be Olympic champions. All of us. On this television show come people who communicate their ideas, their projects, their solutions, their life purposes. There is a 900 number for people to call in. This is our global family. Who wants to help John? Who wants to work with Susie? Who knows someone to introduce to Jane? Maybe the viewers want to help with money. Maybe they want to join the project. To plant trees. To help the homeless. 'Planet Live' will mobilize social creativity by providing what Dennis Becker calls a new structure of fulfillment. You see? We're not sure how to do this yet with everyone who wants to help. See David Gershon and me later, we are having a meeting for those who want to participate in 'Planet Live.'

"The Windstar Symposium and other conferences like this are 'Planet Live.' When the show is on the air, our cameras will be here. The highest moments of this event will be going out over global television. This is news! It's the news of who we really are. We are the news. We are reconceptualizing news so that those of us who are news, know it, and help others to become newsmakers. We make news by our very being. That's what co-creation means.

"Now I would like to conclude with my favorite topic, the Suprasexual Revolution. We've all heard about sex, but very few of us have heard about "supra sex." Here is what it is: When you feel within you a frustration, or what I call a "vocational arousal" your life purpose kicks up and hits you. Just as in puberty, you suddenly have to do something more and you don't know how. What you have to do is to find your teammates and join together to co-create in a way that your life purpose gets manifested.

"The advertising industry is playing to sexual frustration, but they're missing the boat. It's supra-sexual frustration we're feeling. It is greater meaning in our lives we are seeking. When we find the way to join together to create, in small groups, right where we are, in Soviet/American relations, in relations around the world, we have unloosed the mighty force of creation itself that is dammed up by all of these unnatural divisions. There is nothing to stop supra sex.

Everyone will want to do it! Nature invented sex to get us to reproduce the species. She is now inventing supra sex to get us to evolve the species. This is really a gathering of suprasexual revolutionaries!"

At the conclusion of the speech I spoke of the cosmic birth experience in 1966. "There was a flash of light in outer space and the whole of humanity jumped into shared attention. We forgot we were separated and the force of love swept through the planet. Five billion people smiled. It was a planetary smile. We collectively opened our eyes and saw we were the light. We are the light!

"As we enter the 1990's, let's have a space mission with Americans and Soviets that initiates a planetary celebration of human creativity and compassion. Visualize it! As the space craft orbits the planet, people are rising up in every region of the world, demonstrating what we can do now. We *can* feed, we *can* house, we *can* educate. We are performing miracles now. The world will catch a glimpse of its collective potential, an image of its creativity as a whole. Music will flood the planet as each culture gives its gifts to the whole human race.

"When I heard of the possibility of John Denver's space mission, I realized I want to tell John, that if that happens, I personally believe it will be a major moment of transformation for the human race." I turned to look at John, who sat upright in the front row, like a beautiful Greek warrior, with his shining golden hair and boyish yet stern face.

"John, we pledge to create a storm of creativity such as the world has never seen when you are in space.

"Let's visualize such a planetary experience in which the whole human race knows it is part of one earth. One world. The creativity in every man, woman, and child on this planet is touched with a spark of joy at knowing they are needed. Each of us has a purpose.

"As innovators and creative people from every region demonstrate what we can do, let's feel for a moment the whole human race smiling at once. Let's open our eyes and smile at one another with the feeling that we've come through. We've done it, folks. We have overcome, now."

John Denver arose. "To meet Barbara again, yesterday, not for the first time and to find out that something she had in her mind and heart since 1966, that in its present form has only been in my heart for about five and a half years, blew me away. I commit myself to you to living up to that vision she described...."

I went back up upon the stage and stood beside him. "John, I too, commit. We will have a planetary event which will bring ourselves together as one. Thank you. Thank you. Thank you."

Kathy Crum, a beautiful dancer was poised behind me, ready to perform a dance we had rehearsed the day before. In her movements, she represented a person afraid to step forward alone. She teetered, she drew back, and then she flung herself forward as into an abyss, falling, rising, then standing directly by my side. We moved together in a dance, extending our arms, two moving as one. Then I said "When you have the courage to take a stand for what you believe, you will never stand alone." We embraced each other.

The audience rose and cheered, waves of response lifted our hearts into one chorus: "We do believe deep in our hearts, we are overcoming now." People turned toward one another, embracing and smiling... *the planetary smile.*

(To be continued, of course.)

Some Meaningful Books

Ainsworth-Land, George T. *Grow or Die: The Unifying Principles Of Transformation.* New York: Wiley, 1986.

Aurobindo, Sri. *Sri Aurobindo or The Adventures of Consciousness.* Pondicherry, India: Sri Aurobindo Ashram Press, 1968.

Argüelles, José. *Earth Ascending.* Sante Fe: Bear and Co. 1988.
———. *The Mayan Factor.* Sante Fe. Bear and Co. 1987.

Bird, Christopher, and Tompkins, Peter. *The Secret Life of Plants.* New York: Harper and Row, Publishers, 1973.

Bronowski, J. and Mazlish, Bruce. *The Western Intellectual Tradition.* New York: Harper and Row, Publishers, The University Library, 1960.

Capra, Fritjov. *The Tao Of Physics.* New York: Bantem, 1977.

Carey, Ken. *Vision.* Kansas City: Uni-son, 1985.

A Course In Miracles. Tiburon: Foundation For Inner Peace, 1976.

de Chardin, Teilhard. *The Phenomenon of Man.* New York: Harper and Row, Publishers, 1959.
———. *The Future of Man.* Harper and Row, Publishers, 1969.
———. *Building the Earth.* New York: Avon, 1969.

Drexler, Eric. *The Engines of Creation.* New York: Doubleday, 1987.

Esfandiary, F.M. *Optimism One.* New York: W.W. Norton and Co., 1970.
———. *Up-wingers.* New York: John Day Co., 1973.

Ferguson, Marilyn. *The Aquarian Conspiracy.* Los Angeles: J.P. Tarcher, Inc., 1980.

Fuller, R. Buckminster. *The Critical Path.* St. Martin's Press, 1982.

Henderson, Hazel. *Politics of the Solar Age: Alternatives To Economics.* Knowledge Syst., Date Not Set.

Houston, Jean. *Lifeforce.* New York: Delacorte Press, 1980.

Hubbard, Barbara Marx. *The Evolutionary Journey: A Personal Guide to a Positive Future.* Evolutionary Press, 1982.

Jampolski, Gerald. *Love Is Letting Go Of Fear.* Berkeley: Celestial Arts Press, 1979.

Jantsch, Erich. *Design For Evolution.* New York: Braziller, 1976.

Kahn, Herman. *Thinking About the Unthinkable* In The Nineteen Eighties. New York: Simon & Schuster Inc., 1985.

Lovelock, James. *GAIA.* Oxford, 1977.

Maslow, Abraham. *Toward a Psychology of Being.* New York: Van Nostrand Reinhold Co., 1971.

O'Neill, Gerald K. *The High Frontier.* New York: Bantem, 1977.

Price, John Randolph. *The Planetary Commission.* 1984.

Raphael. *The Starseed Transmissions: An Extraterrestrial Report.* Kansas City: Uni-son, 1983.

Rosenfeld, Alfred. *The Second Genesis.* Pyramid Communications, 1972.

Russell, Peter. *The Global Brain: Speculations on the Evolutionary Leap to Planetary Consciousness.* Los Angeles: J.P. Tarcher, 1983.

Salk, Jonas. *The Survival of the Wisest.* Harper and Row, Publishers, 1973.
———. *Anatomy of Reality.* New York: Praeger, 1985.

Schumacher, E.F. *Small Is Beautiful: A Study of Economics As If People Mattered.* New York: Viking Penguin Inc. 1988.

Sheldrake, Rupert. *A New Science of Life.* Blond & Briggs, 1981.

Vajk, J. Peter. *Doomsday Has Been Canceled.* Peace Press, 1977.

Whyte, Lancelot Law. *The Next Development in Man.* New York: A Mentor Book, New American Library, 1948.

Yatri. *Unknown Man.* New York: Simon & Schuster Inc., 1988.

For further information about Barbara Marx Hubbard, please write or call:

ISLAND PACIFIC NW
P.O. Box 999
Eastsound, WA 98245
(206)-376-5005